Loremasters and Libraries in Fantasy and Science Fiction:
A Gedenkschrift for David D. Oberhelman

edited by

Jason Fisher and **Janet Brennan Croft**

Mythopoeic Press 2022

Altadena, California, USA

Published by Mythopoeic Press, Altadena, California, USA
www.mythsoc.org/press.htm

Mythopoeic Press is an imprint of the Mythopoeic Society. Orders may be placed through our website. For general inquiries, contact:
press@mythsoc.org
Editor, Mythopoeic Press
P.O. Box 6707, Altadena, CA 91003, USA

ISBN: 978-1-887726-14-6
LCCN: 2022931423

ACKNOWLEDGEMENTS

David D. Oberhelman's essay included in this collection was first published as described below. It is reprinted here with minor revisions and by permission from the publisher.

Oberhelman, David. "A Brief History of Libraries in Middle-earth: Manuscript and Book Repositories in Tolkien's Legendarium." *Truths Breathed Through Silver: The Inklings' Moral and Mythopoeic Legacy*, edited by Jonathan B. Himes, with Joe R. Christopher and Salwa Khoddam, Cambridge Scholars Publishing, 2008, pp. 81–92.

David Dean Oberhelman's Curriculum Vitae is included in this collection with the kind permission of his family.

Cover art, *The Archivist*, by Julie Dillon
Cover design by Megan Kornreich
Internal design and pre-press production by Leslie A. Donovan (Mythopoeic Press Editor), Alex Espinosa, Paul Irwin, and Megan Kornreich
Index compiled by Janet Brennan Croft

Contents

She closed the book and put her cheek against it. There was still an odor of a library on it, of dust, leather, binding glue, and old paper, one book carrying the smell of hundreds.

— Shannon Hale, *The Goose Girl*

Introduction

Janet Brennan Croft and Jason Fisher

> *Festschrift.* The term, borrowed from German, and literally meaning "celebration writing" (cognate with "feast-script"), might be translated as "celebration publication" or "celebratory (piece of) writing." An alternative Latin term is *liber amicorum* (literally: "book of friends"). A comparable book presented posthumously is sometimes called a *Gedenkschrift* (pronounced [ɡəˈdɛŋkʃrɪft], "memorial publication"), but this term is much rarer in English. (*Wikipedia*)

AVID DEAN OBERHELMAN WAS born in Lubbock, Texas in 1965 and earned his Bachelor's Degree from Rice University in Houston, Texas, MA and PhD degrees in English from the University of California at Irvine, and a Master's Degree in Library and Information Science from the University of Pittsburgh in Pennsylvania. Oberhelman was the W. P. Wood Professor of Library Service at the Edmon Low Library at Oklahoma State University from 1997 until his untimely death of complications from influenza in early 2018. His scholarly interests were wide-ranging, as indicated by the *curriculum vitae* reproduced at the end of this volume, and he was a gifted teacher and editor as well. Oberhelman's books and papers were acquired by the Oklahoma State University Archives Repository and consist of some 35 linear feet of printed materials, science fiction film and television DVDs and other media, artwork, calendars, souvenirs, and realia, only partially cataloged at this date. Phillip Fitzsimmons's report on the opening exhibit of this collection is included in this volume.

The editors of this volume knew David best from his long association with the Mythopoeic Society, particularly his service as the Mythopoeic Press Editor from 2006 to 2010, continuing after that as Advisory Board Member, and as Mythopoeic Society Awards Administrator from 2007 to 2018. He also served from 2010–2013 as a judge for the Alexei Kondratiev Award for best student paper presented at Mythcon, and was paper coordinator for Mythcon 45 in Norton, MA, in 2014.

Janet writes:

> I most likely met David Oberhelman at a state library meeting of some sort shortly after I began working at the University of Oklahoma Libraries in 2001; he had already been at Oklahoma State University Libraries for two years by that time, and the Oklahoma library world is small, friendly, and tightly knit. But I first got to know David well when I hosted Mythcon 37 in Norman, Oklahoma in 2006 and he served as registrar for the conference. He quickly became indispensable to the Society, serving in many

capacities over the years. He was also indispensable to me, as a colleague in multiple professional and scholarly areas, and as a friend. We were active together in the Southwest Popular and American Culture Association, where he chaired the Digital Humanities Area beginning in 2013, and after his death just days before SWPACA's annual conference in February 2018, I had the sad duty of sharing the news with his panelists and his fellow area chairs. Reading through his curriculum vitae, I deeply regret that many of his perceptive, quirky, and fascinating conference presentations in both literary criticism and library studies were never worked up into published articles. I miss his booming voice and laugh, his encouragement of new scholars, and his insightful comments tremendously every year at Mythcon and SWPACA; I keep expecting to turn a corner and see him there.

Jason writes:

I met David in the spring of 2006 at the annual conference of the C. S. Lewis and Inklings Society. It was the first conference in which I was presenting a paper of my own. David missed hearing my paper in person, but he introduced himself afterwards. As it happens, the essay David presented at this very conference is the one we have reprinted in this memorial volume.

We hit it off immediately. We shared similar interests, including J. R. R. Tolkien and mythopoeic literature. And while David was born in Texas and moved to Oklahoma, I had made the opposite migration; I was born in Oklahoma and had moved to Texas. In our first conversations, David mentioned the Mythopoeic Society and encouraged me to attend Mythcon later that year. I was already planning on it, and I was delighted to learn more about the Society, in which David was a longtime Steward (like my co-editor, Janet Brennan Croft; and as I would be myself before long). Mythcon that year was being chaired by Janet in Norman, Oklahoma, an easy drive from my home in Dallas at the time. It would turn out to be the first of many Mythcons, at which David was always a perennial figure, always in good spirits and always willing to lend a hand.

In addition to crossing paths at many other academic conferences over the years, we both contributed to Michael Drout's encyclopedia on Tolkien—each writing twelve entries—and we bounced drafts and ideas off of each other. For a few years, I read for the Mythopoeic Awards Committee, over which David presided at the time. During my tenure as the editor of *Mythprint*, he was always good for a book review when I was running short of content. David was very active in the fan community, participating in Reading Room discussions on TheOneRing.net and threads of all kinds on the Mythopoeic Society's email discussion list and on Facebook. He was always supportive and encouraging, particularly to new and less experienced scholars. In the early years of our friendship, he read many drafts of my essays and reviews and always offered thoughtful comments and suggestions.

The core concept of this collection developed from panel discussions led by David Oberhelman at several different venues: the Mythopoeic Society annual conference, the Southwest Popular and American Culture Association conference, and visits with the University of New Mexico Hobbit Society. For these panels David drew together a group of fantasy, science fiction, and comics scholars to discuss libraries and librarians, archives and archivists, research and researchers, writing, book arts, and related topics as depicted in these genres. This then led to conversations about research methods useful to our audience, who might be undergraduates, established scholars, or a mix, who were hungry for advice about finding, accessing, and managing resources in these genres and getting their research published. The papers by Croft and Larsen are direct results of these panels. Papers by Seikel and by Gaydosik and Conner were inspired by professional interactions with David in the Oklahoma library and academic world.

In this collection we were not aiming for strictly serious scholarly literary criticism, but for a range of approaches exploring some of the topics, sources, and themes that interested Oberhelman. Our contributors explore the enduring importance of the historical record in its many forms, the concept of writing as a creative gateway to other worlds, the otherworldly geometries of the interconnectedness of information represented as what Terry Pratchett called "L-space," and the "presentation of empowerment through scholarship," to borrow a phrase from one of our contributors (Fitzsimmons 72).

Two pieces on aspects of librarianship lead us off. We start with a report by Phillip Fitzsimmons on portions of David Oberhelman's own collection which were exhibited at the Edmon Low Library at Oklahoma State University. Oberhelman's donations to the OSU Archives primarily consist of artwork, books, and objects relating to J. R. R. Tolkien and film adaptations of his work, with additional material awaiting cataloging. Michele Seikel uses examples related to Inklings scholarship to provide an introduction to principles of cataloging used by professional librarians, and considers the place of creativity in a process that is as much art as science.

Each paper in the second group of essays surveys a particular theme across multiple sources. Victoria Gaydosik and her student Conner Kirk report on an assignment to collect and annotate a list of novels featuring libraries as key elements of the story; the resulting reading list broadens the initial assignment to include bookstores, private collections, and book-loving characters in fantasy, romance, mysteries, historical fiction, and even a few works of non-fiction. For the voracious reader, what could be more delightful than a list reminding one of old favorites and recommending new things to read?

Kristine Larsen examines libraries as preservers of culture and knowledge in fantasy and science fiction. Larsen notes that books can save your life or get you killed in an essay that ranges widely across the genre—from *Doctor Who* to *Game of Thones* to the often-maligned disaster film, *The Day After Tomorrow*, in which physical books are burned to generate warmth in subzero temperatures. In addition to books being able to save our lives—"through the transmission of knowledge" or even through "the transmission of thermal radiation"— we have a duty to save them from wanton acts of "libricide" as well.

Nicholas Birns explores a melancholy trope in fantasy and science fiction novels: the fugitive archive, the book that disappears once read, the lost library. We confront, in these works, the ephemeral nature of what would ideally be permanent. In a similar vein, Phillip Fitzsimmons examines books and media that exist not in the real world, but only within the world of another book: fictional or invented books that are, in these particular works, essential to their plot, character development, and setting.

Janet Brennan Croft considers how research methods are depicted in the works of J. R. R. Tolkien, Terry Pratchett, Neil Gaiman, and Joss Whedon. Croft observes that in fantasy literature, we seldom see the application of such real-world finding aids as catalogs and indexes, even by authors who know perfectly well how libraries and librarians really work. More often, in the service of dramatic effect, fantasy and science fiction stories rely on the prodigious memories of single authorities, as well as serendipity, good instincts, technology, and magic.

The next section of papers deals with J. R. R. Tolkien, a major focus of Oberhelman's scholarship and collecting. Cami Agan meditates on the unique way in which the elven character Míriel records history through weaving—and her own highly significant place in the history and laws of the Elves.

Jason Fisher examines the "found manuscript" trope Tolkien used (in surprisingly many of his works) to lend an air of verisimilitude, to distance himself as creator from his creation, and simply to add, in the tradition of authors like Edgar Allan Poe, Mary Shelley, Jules Verne, and H. Rider Haggard, a frisson of mystery to the tale.

David Oberhelman's own seminal paper on libraries and archives in Middle-earth is reproduced here; in addition to cataloging the many material collections alluded to in Tolkien's legendarium, it considers the progression from oral to written culture and the development of collections of written material in our own world.

Complementing Oberhleman's essay quite well, Nancy Martsch takes a broader view of education and the acquisition of literacy as represented in the practice of poetry recitation in both our own real world and in J. R. R. Tolkien's Middle-earth. Martsch shows how poetry recitation in England during Tolkien's own day may have influenced similar depictions of literacy in his fictive world.

Our final group of essays deals with other individual authors. Elise McKenna returns to Terry Pratchett, touched on earlier in Croft's paper, to further explore the concept of L-space: the interconnectedness of libraries, both fictionally and in our primary world.

David L. Emerson then discusses the interconnectedness of genres in Jasper Fforde's Thursday Next series, in which the fictive worlds inside books are in some sense actually "real" and can be entered into and explored. Moreover, these inner realities are all connected to each other in BookWorld, a kind of fictive meta-universe that Fforde's characters—and likewise his readers—can access directly.

From here, Susan Adams-Johnson and Anna Holloway introduce us to the fascinating thought-experiment of *1632*, in which Eric Flint, and subsequently other authors, ask what would happen if a piece of present-day West Virginia were transported intact through time and space to 17th-century Germany. Of more moment to the present collection, how important might 20th-century books, archives, and libraries become in an alternate history of the Thirty Years' War and the American Revolution?

And finally Liorah Golomb looks at information-seeking behavior as depicted over the course of the long-running television series *Supernatural*, a series that relies heavily on searching out and using esoteric information in order to protect humanity from the monsters lurking in the dark spaces of our world.

There is something recursively satisfying in books about books, research about research, writing about writing, the librarianship section in a library. We hope that you enjoy reading this collection as much as we enjoyed collecting the material in it!

A Partial Bibliography of Works Written or Edited by David D. Oberhelman: On Fantasy and Science Fiction Topics

"Angband," "Class in Tolkien's Work," "Hierarchy," "J. M. Barrie," "Justice/Injustice," "Marxist Readings of Tolkien," "Oral Tradition," "Philippa Boyens," "Possessiveness," "Textual History: Errors and Emendations," "Towers," and "Valinor." *J. R. R. Tolkien Encyclopedia: Scholarship and Critical Assessment*, edited by Michael D. C. Drout, Routledge, 2007.

"A Brief History of Libraries in Middle-earth: Manuscript and Book Repositories in Tolkien's Legendarium." *Loremasters and Libraries in Fantasy and Science Fiction: A Gedenkschrift for David Oberhelman*, edited by Jason Fisher and Janet Brennan Croft, Mythopoeic Press, 2022, pp. 155–65. Originally published in *Truths Breathed Through Silver: The Inklings' Moral and Mythopoeic Legacy*, edited by Jonathan B. Himes, with Joe R. Christopher and Salwa Khoddam, Cambridge Scholars, 2008, pp. 81–92.

"'Coming to America': Fantasy and Native America Explored, an Introduction." *The Intersection of Fantasy and Native America: From H. P. Lovecraft to Leslie Marmon Silko*, edited by David D. Oberhelman and Amy H. Sturgis, Mythopoeic Press, 2009, pp. iii–vii.

"From Iberian to Ibran and Catholic to Quintarian: Bujold's Alternate History of the Spanish Reconquest in the Chalion Series." *Lois McMaster Bujold: Essays on a Modern Master of Science Fiction and Fantasy*, edited by Janet Brennan Croft, McFarland, 2013, pp. 159–71.

"'Out of the Unknown Past into the Unknown Future': Information Technology and Degradation in H. G. Wells's *The Time Machine*." *Presentations of the 2010 Upstate Steampunk Extravaganza and Meetup*, edited by Gypsey Elaine Teague, Cambridge Scholars, 2011, pp. 33–44.

With Amy H. Sturgis, editors. *The Intersection of Fantasy and Native America: From H. P. Lovecraft to Leslie Marmon Silko*. Mythopoeic Press, 2009.

Part 1: Archives and Librarianship

The David Oberhelman Collection of Science Fiction, Fantasy, and Tolkieniana at Oklahoma State University

Phillip Fitzsimmons

IN SEPTEMBER 2020 I drove to the Oklahoma State University (OSU) Stillwater campus to see "The David Oberhelman J. R. R. Tolkien Collection" exhibit, on display on the Edmon Low Library's second floor mezzanine in the Lisa and Mark Snell Gallery.

Photograph and Facebook post by William Davis

Honoring the memory of David Oberhelman, my friend and colleague in the Mythopoeic Society, this exhibit introduces the viewer to the life and work of J. R. R. Tolkien and discusses the development of *The Hobbit* and *The Lord of the Rings*. It concludes with a demonstrable truth about Tolkien's legendarium and Middle-earth: posthumous works such as *The Silmarillion* and the volumes of *The History of Middle-earth* have continued to "further flesh out the world and its history."

Whitney Vitale, the Head of Access Services, noted that the exhibit was being promoted heavily on the library's social media and said the Facebook post on the previous page "sums up what is on display."

William Davis, Senior Communications Specialist, emailed me that the exhibit presents only part of the collection officially named the "David Dean Oberhelman Collection of Science Fiction, Fantasy, and Tolkienana Books" that resides in the OSU Archives.

Davis continued to describe the collection:

> There's a wide array of materials in the collection, including several editions of all of Tolkien's published work, I believe two items featuring hand-written notes and signatures from Tolkien, several statuettes and miniatures of the film adaptation's depictions of characters and locations, a tile from one of the sets of the film adaptations, Tolkien themed calendars featuring paintings of scenes from the books, a large print of a painting of Gandalf riding to Minas Tirith, other bits of memorabilia, as well as a plethora [of] other fantasy and sci-fi books and movies.

According to David Peters, Head of Archives, the exhibit would remain on display through March 2021 and perhaps longer. He writes that the collection "is housed in the Library Auxiliary Building which is not open to the public. The collection utilizes 35 shelf feet of space." Information about the collection may be accessed through archivesspace.library.okstate.edu/repositories/3/resources/1456.

Although it is not open for immediate walk-in viewing by the public, the collection is well worth a visit for fantasy scholars and enthusiasts. To view the materials with proper notice to the Archives department, requests can be made at archives.library.okstate.edu.

Cataloging Creatively

Michele Seikel

A PERSON WALKS INTO A library with a memory of having heard of a Tolkien prequel which wasn't published until long after *The Lord of the Rings*. But she has no idea what the title of the prequel is. So, on her first try she plugs the name "Tolkien" into the library's online catalog. If the person doesn't know the title, where will that keyword search take her? To a jumble of records, obviously. The well-known Tolkien works will come up, but also records for several lesser-known works, perhaps, and very possibly records for works about Tolkien literature and literary criticism. If the searcher looks carefully at each of those records, she might find information to tell her something about the plots. That's what might lead her to an informed choice of works to take home or download. But where do all those catalog records come from?

What is cataloging, and what does it do for the seeker of information?

What, really, is the purpose of cataloging? In the results of a Delphi study conducted with the editorial board of *Cataloging & Classification Quarterly* in 2010, the following concept emerged:

> **Cataloging:** an active process of resource description, the purpose of which is to facilitate resource discovery for information retrieval and collection management. The process involves rendering the details of a resource in a surrogate description, linkage of the description with authority files that identify the resource's creators, subjects and bibliographic relationships, its placement via classification within a curated collection, and maintenance of the entire apparatus, including external links to bibliographic databases and the semantic Web. (Smiraglia 649)

The definition emerging from the study certainly does not rule out the application of creativity to the cataloging process, which can be ongoing in the case of serials and has been a worldwide collaboration since the OCLC database enabled record-sharing activities within the library community in the 1970s. OCLC maintains the largest bibliographic database in human history, with over a billion records. It is deeply international, multi-linguistic, and collaborative by definition. Most records to be found in it were created by individual catalogers working with books in hand. However, there are also millions of catalog records describing electronic resources which were simply copied from the records for the original, printed titles, with descriptive elements added for the digital aspects. Many of these were machine-generated. That may continue to be the case for digitized electronic resources for the foreseeable future.

The types of data that modern bibliographic records can contain include such elements as summaries, content notes, established name headings, and elaborate sets of subject headings. These elements are brought together by the cataloger to enable the library user to more easily find, evaluate and access works both in library collections and on the Web.

In the case of the catalog record for *Truths Breathed Through Silver* (OCLC #191245039), it includes a reproduction of the complete table of contents and 24 subject headings covering numerous topics addressed in the chapters. The cataloger must have been very familiar with the book by the time this catalog record was completed. Shown below is how the record displays in a local catalog.

Truths breathed through silver: the Inklings' moral and mythopoeic legacy.

Contributor

Jonathan B. Himes editor.

Joe R Christopher

Salwa Khoddam

Subjects

Tolkien, J. R. R. (John Ronald Reuel), 1892–1973—Criticism and
    interpretation

Lewis, C. S. (Clive Staples), 1898–1963—Criticism and interpretation

MacDonald, George, 1824–1905—Criticism and interpretation

Williams, Charles, 1886–1945—Criticism and interpretation

Lewis, C. S. (Clive Staples), 1898–1963

MacDonald, George, 1824–1905

Tolkien, J. R. R. (John Ronald Reuel), 1892–1973

Williams, Charles, 1886–1945

Inklings (Group of writers)

English literature—20th century—History and criticism

Fantasy literature, English—History and criticism

Christianity and literature—Great Britain—History—20th century

Christianity and literature

English literature

Fantasy literature, English

Inklings (Group of writers)

Intellectual life

Inklings

Oxford (England)—Intellectual life—20th century

England—Oxford

Great Britain

1900–1999

Criticism, interpretation, etc

History

Description

C. S. Lewis's three paths to God : A keynote address for "C. S. Lewis for the twenty-first century" / Doors out and doors in : the genius of myth / From ruined city to edenic garden in C. S. Lewis's The magician's nephew / The allegory of lust : textual and sexual deviance in The dark tower / A Brief history of libraries in Middle-earth : manuscript and book repositories in Tolkien's Legendarium / Tolkien's fortunate fall and the third theme of Ilúvatar / Screwtape and the philological arm : Lewis on verbicide / The role of mathematics in the spiritual journey of George MacDonald / The sacrament of the stranger in C. S. Lewis, J. R. R. Tolkien, and George MacDonald / Lewis, Tolkien, and Williams as spiritual mentors /

Publisher

Newcastle, U.K. : Cambridge Scholars Pub.

Creation Date

2008

Format

xviii, 160 pages ; 22 cm.

Language

English

Identifier

ISBN : 9781847184443

ISBN : 1847184448

Some of those subjects are FAST headings which were added to the record later. FAST terminology is an enumerative, faceted subject heading schema derived from the Library of Congress Subject Headings (LCSH) ("FAST"). OCLC Research and the Library of Congress invented this schema in 1998. It's simple, easy to use, and modern, with 1.7 million individual headings for use. FAST is designed to produce better matches to the user's keyword searches. The record also has a URL for an online version of the table of contents. This bibliographic description of a work of literary criticism will bring readers interested in numerous issues related to the members of the famous Inklings group of British fantasy writers of the 20th century to it, as well as to help them decide if it contains data of specific interest to them.

The record for *Baptism of Fire: The Birth of the Modern British Fantastic in World War I* (OCLC #919098451) includes a summary note taken directly from the back cover of the volume as well as fourteen subject headings and a reproduced table of contents. The contents and summary notes are reproduced below.

"The purest response of fantastika to the world storm" / Janet Brennan Croft—Section 1 The Inklings—The shell-shocked hobbit: the First World War and Tolkien's trauma of the ring / Michael Livingston—Faramir and the heroic ideal of the twentieth century; or how Aragorn died at the Somme / S. Brett Carter—Wounded by war: men's bodies in the prose tradition of The Children of Húrin / Margaret Sinex—Sméagol and Déagol: secrecy, history, and ethical subjectivity in Tolkien's world / E. J. Christie—The preservation of national unity by [dis]remembering the past in Tolkien's The Hobbit and The Lord of the Rings / Nora Alfaiz—"Now often forgotten": Gollum, the Great War, and the last alliance / Peter Grybauskas—Beyond the circles of this world: the Great War, time, history, and eternity in the fantasy of J. R. R. Tolkien and C. S. Lewis / Shandi Stevenson—Silent wounds / Andrew Krokstrom—The Great War and Narnia: C. S. Lewis as soldier and creator / Brian Melton—Horses, horoscopes, and human consciousness: Owen Barfield on making meaning in his post-WWI writings / Tiffany Brooke Martin—Section 2 Outside the Inklings—The door we never opened, British alternative history writing in the aftermath of World War I / Nick Milne—"A deplorable misfit": the symbolism of desire in G. K. Chesterton's The Crimes of England / Philip Irving Mitchell—Lord Dunsany and the Great War: Don Rodriguez and the rebirth of romance / David J. Carlson—From Lolly Willowes to Kingdoms of Elfin: the poetics of socio-political commentary in Sylvia Townsend Warner's fantasy narratives / Meyrav Koren-Kuik—The conqueror Worm: Eddison, modernism, and the war to end all wars / Jon Garrad—E. R. Eddison and the age of catastrophe / Joe Young—T. H. White and the lasting influence of World War I: King Arthur at war / Ashley Pfeiffer—Contributors—Index.

"World War I has been called "the poets' war," as it was characterized by a massive outpouring of works of literature during and after the war. Much of this literary harvest, as Paul Fussell brilliantly demonstrated in The Great War and Modern Memory, hinged on an ironic response to the deadly absurdities of World War I. Yet, Fussell also acknowledges that fantasy could be a legitimate literary response to the war, a way of transforming the horrible experiences of the war into something more bearable, applicable, and relevant; into myth and "Escape" in the sense that Tolkien used the term in "On Fairy-stories." This present volume sprang from a desire to examine selected examples of the fantastic response to World War I among British authors. The contents comprise a mix of five classic articles from the pages of *Mythlore* and twelve new essays. The first half of the book considers the Inklings, the Oxford literary group centered on J. R. R. Tolkien and C. S. Lewis, while the second half deals with other authors" —Back cover.

All of the words in these notes are fully indexed. Catalogers can choose to provide these detailed descriptive elements within a catalog record—they are not required by bibliographic standards. Does their inclusion in the catalog record produce what could called "a work about a work?"

What are some of the tools/systems librarians use?

Over a billion bibliographic records have been created and contributed to the world's largest bibliographic database, OCLC WorldCat, which is located in Ohio. Each of these records contains information about a work, usually published, and the record is designed to help a library user find it in a database or catalog. These records are shared with local libraries all over the world via subscription. Within the OCLC WorldCat database are records of works from all over the world, but the majority remain English language records written to describe and record English-language works. These records are of varying length and quality. Many older records contain little more than title, author, and publication information. But more recently written records can be far more detailed and contain a great deal of information about the works they describe. The OCLC database also contains tens of thousands of records for established (standardized) author and editor names, names of corporate bodies of all kinds, and the Library of Congress subject headings, which are designed to help users search for specific names and topics.

When creating and adding to catalog records, the goal of catalogers is to support the library users' tasks: to find, identify, select, and obtain information resources. We must use judgement to determine which elements of a work will make that work easier to find and evaluate. Writing about cataloging in 1991, Bolin said, "There are a number of arguments against quantity standards. One is that cataloging is so item-specific—each piece is unique and must be given individualized attention—that it is not possible to impose a production line mentality on the process" (359).

However, these elements Bolin mentions are not in bibliographic records by accident. In 1990 the IFLA (International Federation of Library Associations and Institutions) called for a study which produced a document entitled "Terms of Reference for a Study of the Functional Requirements for Bibliographic Records." The study group recommended in its report that the basic national bibliographic record should assist the user to do the following:

o Find all manifestations embodying:
  ▪ The works for which a given person or corporate body is
    responsible
  ▪ The various expressions of a given work
  ▪ Works on a given subject
  ▪ Works in a given series
o Find a particular manifestation:
  ▪ When the name(s) of the person(s) and/or corporate bodies(ies)
    responsible for work(s) embodied in the manifestation is (are)
    known
  ▪ When the title of the manifestation is known
  ▪ When the manifestation identifier is known
o Identify a work
o Identify an expression of a work
o Select a work
o Select an expression
o Select a manifestation
o Obtain a manifestation (Madison 157)

By focusing on bringing together these bibliographic elements to help the user find, identify, select, and obtain information sources, the study group's report was the beginning of a definition of exactly what information a user might expect to find in a bibliographic record and how that information might be used by a broad spectrum of users. During the following twenty years, the world cataloging community developed new standards based on the ideas set out in the report, and modern catalog records began to reflect these user-centered ideas.

The newest bibliographic conceptual model is the Library Reference Model, approved by IFLA in 2017. The LRM includes a number of bibliographic entities that can be used to organize data about a work. Each of the entities in turn can be connected with others via relationships, as is common, for instance, in such metadata formats such as RDF (Resource Description Framework). These relationships help users find resources. Each of the entities has attributes and can have sub-entities. These entities are designed to be broad in scope, to describe human creative works of all kinds, published all over the world. For instance, a work could have several expressions, and each of those expressions might have multiple published manifestations (versions or editions). Some of the key entities included are:

Work—The intellectual or artistic content of a distinct creation

Expression—A distinct constellation of signs conveying intellectual or artistic content

Manifestation—A set of all carriers that are assumed to share the same characteristics as to intellectual or artistic content and aspects

Item—A physical object carrying signs resulting from a production process and intended to convey intellectual or artistic content

Agent—An entity capable of deliberate actions, of being granted rights, and of being held accountable for its actions

Person—An individual human being

Collective agent—A gathering or organization of persons bearing a particular name and capable of acting as a unit

Nomen—An association between an entity and a designation that refers to it (Riva et al. 21–31)

The Library Reference Model is being used to create specific cataloging and metadata systems, and it will be modified or replaced as the cataloging community continues to discuss how to supply our users with resources. The advent of the Internet during the past twenty years has allowed some computer-specific means of adding to and changing catalog records. But it has not changed the nature of literature, which is that each work is unique, and requires a unique description.

Where does creativity come into the cataloging process?

The summary statement within the catalog record for *Perilous and Fair* (OCLC #903655969) is a particularly well-written example: "Includes seven classic articles as well as seven new examinations of women in Tolkien's works and life bringing together not only perspectives on Tolkien's most commonly discussed female characters—Éowyn, Galadriel, and Lúthien—but also less studies [sic] figures such as Nienna, Yavanna, Shelob, and Arwen." This brief statement was specifically placed within the record to help the library user determine if the book's content is of interest. It is not, however, original to the catalog record but is copied from part of the publisher's materials on the book's back cover. However, perhaps the choice to use those words within the catalog record can be considered a creative choice in the record's design, since it was abstracted from the cover and added for the purpose of helping a potential reader know what the contents of the book contains.

A record for *The Inklings Handbook* (OCLC #47142077), published by Chalice Press, includes an amazing twenty-nine subject headings, a mixture of Library of Congress and FAST headings, each of which is designed to provide access to one of various aspects of the subjects covered in the book, including each of the names of the Inklings members, the group itself, Oxford, England in the 20th century, English fantasy literature, and English authors. The subject headings for the cataloger's view of the record are shown below, with their MARC (machine-readable coding) intact. (The public OCLC WorldCat view has display labels for the headings that are designed to make them easier for users to understand.)

600 10 Lewis, C. S. ǂq (Clive Staples), ǂd 1898–1963 ǂv Handbooks, manuals, etc.

600 10 Tolkien, J. R. R. ǂq (John Ronald Reuel), ǂd 1892–1973 ǂv Handbooks, manuals, etc.

600 10 Williams, Charles, ǂd 1886–1945 ǂv Handbooks, manuals, etc.

600 10 Barfield, Owen, ǂd 1898–1997 ǂv Handbooks, manuals, etc.

600 17 Barfield, Owen, ǂd 1898–1997. ǂ2 fast ǂ0 (OCoLC)fst00040983

600 17 Lewis, C. S. ǂq (Clive Staples), ǂd 1898–1963. ǂ2 fast ǂ0 (OCoLC)fst00029827

600 17 Tolkien, J. R. R. ǂq (John Ronald Reuel), ǂd 1892–1973. ǂ2 fast ǂ0 (OCoLC)fst00030031

600 17 Williams, Charles, ǂd 1886–1945. ǂ2 fast ǂ0 (OCoLC)fst00033685

600 17 Lewis, Clive S. ǂ2 swd

600 17 Williams, Charles. ǂ2 swd

600 17 Tolkien, John R. R. ǂ2 swd

600 17 Barfield, Owen. ǂ2 swd

650 0 Inklings (Group of writers) ǂv Handbooks, manuals, etc.

651 0 Oxford (England) ǂx Intellectual life ǂy 20th century ǂv Handbooks, manuals, etc.

650 0 Authors, English ǂy 20th century ǂx Biography ǂv Handbooks, manuals, etc.

650 0 English literature ǂy 20th century ǂx History and criticism ǂv Handbooks, manuals, etc.

650 0 Fantasy literature, English ǂx History and criticism ǂv Handbooks, manuals, etc.

650 7 Authors, English ǂx Biography. ǂ2 fast ǂ0 (OCoLC)fst00821949

650 7 English literature. ǂ2 fast ǂ0 (OCoLC)fst00911989

650 7 Fantasy literature, English. ǂ2 fast ǂ0 (OCoLC)fst00920876

650 7 Inklings (Group of writers) ǂ2 fast ǂ0 (OCoLC)fst00973589

650 7 Intellectual life. ǂ2 fast ǂ0 (OCoLC)fst00975769

651 7 England ǂz Oxford. ǂ2 fast ǂ0 (OCoLC)fst01205511

650 7 The Inklings ǂ2 gnd ǂ0 (DE-588)4577711–6

648 7 1901–1999 ǂ2 fast

655 7 Criticism, interpretation, etc. ǂ2 fast ǂ0 (OCoLC)fst01411635

655 7 Handbooks and manuals. ǂ2 fast ǂ0 (OCoLC)fst01423877

655 7 Handbooks and manuals. ǂ2 lcgft

655 4 Biography.

The subject analysis for this single work is multi-leveled and carefully designed to make the book findable by anyone interested in virtually any aspect of it. The German National Library (Deutsche Bibliothek) has added one of its own name headings, "The Inklings" (DE–588) 4577711–6, and four name headings have also been added by the Swedish National Library. This is a good example of the way cooperative cataloging works. Once a record has been uploaded to WorldCat, it can be shared and edited by libraries all over the world.

In that database of over a billion bibliographic records created and shared by the world's libraries, are there elements that could be labeled creative? Theimer replies, "Creating quality records, and records that may be able to migrate and crosswalk correctly, relies on consistency of data, which requires adherence to standards, both national and local. 'Creative cataloging' is often referred to in the same way as 'creative accounting', meaning something that is done by bending the rules in order to hide or make things look better to shareholders or in the case of libraries, patrons" (Theimer 897). But creative cataloging is not cheating. It is the judicious choice of descriptive elements from within a work to describe, or, to use a cataloger's phrase, to "bring out," certain elements in that work which constitutes a design.

Cataloging is a modular system, with some elements that are always placed in a record, and some chosen as the cataloger considers them to be appropriate for the description. Yes, we may record the number of pages; no, that's not creative. But we also can decide whether to record the table of contents in a contents note, so that each chapter or article is individually indexed (and even each author's name, as well). Or, we can create a summary note to give the reader a better overall impression of the book's "aboutness," which its title might not do. Cataloging is always about choices regarding how to describe a work.

This can be especially important in the case of fiction and works of literary criticism, and in this realm, genre headings can be especially helpful. Genre headings are subject headings used to index many works of the same type using the same term, such as "Fantasy fiction." The genre heading "fantasy fiction" will bring the reader to a list of titles. All the reader will need to do is search for the keyword "fantasy" in a typical library online catalog. Or a mystery reader can walk into any library and type in the keyword "mysteries." His search results will include every book in the library's collections that has the genre heading for "Mysteries (Stories, films, etc.)" in the record. The Library of Congress has compiled a comprehensive listing of possible genre terms of many types, including such terms as Animated films, Fantasy fiction, or Underground comics, which are designed to help readers find the type of material that is wanted. There are also numerous genre term lists from all kinds of fields, including the sciences and technology. A creative cataloger can add one or more of these terms to a record to give the library user another way to search for works in a favorite genre. These terms work well with keyword searches, which library users prefer.

Genre headings can also bring out search results for works that are about a genre itself. Miller stated that "[W]hile library users of all kinds may incidentally be interested in both *works about* or *examples of* a given form or genre, they rarely are so indiscriminately. That is, at any given time—in any given catalog search or research trip—one need or the other is likely to predominate, and it is part of good service to make the distinctions as clear as possible" (Miller 170, italics in original). Thus in the record for *Inklings Handbook,* some of the genre headings include "Criticism, interpretation, etc.," "Handbooks and manuals," and "Biography."

If a cataloger establishes a name heading for an author, that record can stand for many years as a single source of information about the author. It can be added to and updated several times as more becomes known about an author, so that it becomes a kind of mini-biography, enabling future catalogers to choose the right name to place in each bibliographic record for the author's works as they are published. The heading will distinguish one author with the name from another with exactly the same name, which becomes more and more important as the list of published authors grows ever longer. For instance, the established name heading for J. R. R. Tolkien contains his names, dates, place of birth, his professional fields, the universities where he taught, his name translated into various languages, and a short biographical paragraph. The record is shown below, its MARC coding intact.

Tolkien, J. R. R. ǂq (John Ronald Reuel), ǂd 1892–1973

370 Bloemfontein (South Africa) ǂb Bournemouth (England) ǂ2 naf

372 Philology ǂa Fiction—Authorship ǂa Novels ǂa Poetry ǂa Fantasy fiction—Authorship ǂ2 lcsh

373 University of Leeds ǂa University of Oxford ǂ2 naf

373 Exeter College (University of Oxford) ǂ2 naf ǂt 1919

374 Authors ǂa Novelists ǂa Poets ǂa College teachers ǂa Philologists ǂ2 lcsh

375 Males ǂ2 lcdgt

377 eng

378 ǂq John Ronald Reuel

400 1 ǂw nna ǂa Tolkien, John Ronald Reuel, ǂd 1892–1973

400 1 Tolkin, Dzh. R. R. ǂq (Dzhon Ronal'd Ruel), ǂd 1892–1973

400 1 Толкин, Дж. Р. Р. ǂq (Джон Рональд Руэл), ǂd 1892–1973

400 1 Tolkin, Dzhon Ronal'd Ruel, ǂd 1892–1973

400 1 Tolkin, Dzshey. R. R., ǂd 1892–1973

400 1 טולקין, ג׳.ר.ר

400 1 ר. ר. דשיי., ‏טאלקין‎ ‡d 1892–1973

400 1 톨킨, J. R. R, ‡d 1892–1973

400 1 Tʻolkʻin, Jon Ronald Ruel, ‡d 1892–1973

667 Machine-derived non-Latin script reference project.

667 Non-Latin script references not evaluated.

670 Prikliūcheniā Toma Bombadila i drugie istorii, 1994: ‡b t.p. (Dzhon Ronal'd Ruėl Tolkin)

670 Vlastelin koletŝ, 1992: ‡b t.p. (Dzhon Ronal'd Ruėl Tolkin) cover (Dzh.R.R. Tolkin)

670 Contemporary authors online, 8 March 2013 ‡b (J. R. R. Tolkien; Tolkien, John Ronald Reuel; born January 3, 1892, in Bloemfontein, South Africa; died of complications resulting from a bleeding gastric ulcer and a chest infection, September 2, 1973, in Bournemouth, England; Education: Exeter College, Oxford, B.A., 1915, M.A., 1919; author and scholar; professor at University of Leeds, Oxford University)

670 Di ḥavrusè fun dem fingerl, c2014: ‡b t.p. (‏טאלקין‎ ר. ר. דזשיי. = Dzshey. R. R. Ṭolḳin)

670 English Wikipedia website, viewed July 29, 2016: ‡b (John Ronald Reuel Tolkien CBE, FRSL (3 January 1891–2 September 1973), known by his pen name J. R. R. Tolkien, was an English writer, poet, philologist, and university professor who is best known as the author of the classic high-fantasy works The Hobbit, The Lord of the Rings, and The Silmarillion. He served as the Rawlinson and Bosworth Professor of Anglo-Saxon and Fellow of Pembroke College, Oxford, from 1925 to 1945 and Merton Professor of English Language and Literature and Fellow of Merton College, Oxford from 1945 to 1959. He was at one time a close friend of C. S. Lewis—they were both members of the informal literary discussion group known as the Inklings. Tolkien was appointed a Commander of the Order of the British Empire by Queen Elizabeth II on 28 March 1972. After Tolkien's death, his son Christopher published a series of works based on his father's extensive notes and unpublished manuscripts, including The Silmarillion. These, together with The Hobbit and The Lord of the Rings form a connected body of tales, poems, fictional histories, invented languages, and literary essays about a fantasy world called Arda, and Middle-earth within it. Between 1951 and 1955, Tolkien applied the term legendarium to the larger part of these writings)

The cataloger's work certainly is based on standards, but it is not rigidly rules-based. "The creative cataloger appreciates the needs of the patron and makes necessary local adjustments to accommodate the requirements or vagaries of the local database. In many cases library administrators need to be educated to understand that in cataloging one size does not fit all" (Baia et al. 314).

Copyright issues

These records do have value. They can and have been copyrighted. After catalogers contribute them to the WorldCat database, OCLC sells them to various interested entities, including libraries and library management systems.

It is also true that copyright statements concerning catalog records, not the works they describe, have begun to appear within some bibliographic records in the OCLC database. For instance, a statement that appears on the record OCLC #801683391 reads as follows: "This bibliographic record is available under the Creative Commons CCO 'No Rights Reserved' license. The University of Florida Libraries, as creator of this bibliographic record, has waived all rights to it worldwide under copyright law, including all related and neighboring rights, to the extent allowed by law."

Why would any sort of copyright statement be thought necessary for a bibliographic record unless it is thought of as a work in itself? On the other hand, the statement claims that the University of Florida Libraries was the record's creator, not the individual cataloger who wrote it. The University of Florida Libraries is a large institution which employs many people; calling it a creator seems to be a kind of legal fiction, and the copyright statement, therefore, can be seen as a clarification of ownership more than anything else. So, this copyright statement seems to be an argument against the idea that the bibliographic record in which it is embedded is a creative work.

Writing in 1990, Maria Luisa Cabral explained,

> Cooperation and enduring universal availability of data, are more important than the legal aspects involved. Issues of ownership of bibliographic records arose with the emergence of commercial utilities which became intermediaries, obtaining profits that producers of the records did not receive. In response, libraries producing records developed a self-interested and over protective attitude which resulted sometimes in policies contrary to their initial intentions. In relation to the availability of data, and the cost, what is really required is promotion of cooperation and communication between libraries making the fullest use of modern technology. (Cabral 42)

Cabral concluded that use of computers to share, increase, and control the uses of bibliographic records would reconcile the distinct interests of those who use bibliographic data, and so has it turned out in the ensuing nearly thirty years.

The Politics of Cataloging

Examining a work to determine what topics it includes and which are the predominant topics is what leads to the decisions about which subject headings a cataloger will add to the bibliographic record, and also the choice of classification number for the work. This is the "aboutness" which catalogers must decide on. The choice of subject headings can be tricky, particularly if the work which one is cataloging was published in the 19th or early 20th centuries, when racial, religious, and other kinds of inequality were much more overtly expressed in Western society. Some Library of Congress subject headings which were established in the early 20th century have since been changed to reflect changing societal values. For instance, many headings concerning African Americans were changed from the original "Negro" to "Black," and then to "African American" during the late 20th/early 21st century. There are some headings using the word "black" left, such as "Women, Black" and "Police, Black." But almost no headings now remain using the word "Negro." "Negro leagues" would be the single example. "The most important consideration for keyword searching of subject headings in African American studies is that LCSH [Library of Congress subject headings] uses both the terms "Blacks" and "African Americans" (Howard and Knowlton 84).

Forty years ago, there were far fewer headings containing the word "women." Terms such as "Fantasy fiction—Women authors" didn't exist until the late 20th century. Today, there are 4,100 Library of Congress subject headings for topics related to women. Many of these have been created in response to the explosion of documents published in the latter half of the 20th century concerning women. However, that there are separate subject headings for "Women rap musicians" and "Women rugby players" also reflects the fact that female is not considered the norm in our society and therefore must be differentiated from male.

Catalogers, being human beings, can succumb to personal biases when creating bibliographic descriptions. The choice of subject headings will bring readers to a work or may very well steer them away from it.

> In fact, some professionals providing access to specific titles might find themselves tasked with assigning access points to publications that are in direct opposition to their belief system. Is there room here for error or, perhaps, misjudgment and, ultimately, erroneous or misleading subject headings?
>
> Many a cataloging acquaintance has joked that access and the allure of certain books can be controlled by the access points and descriptive language used by catalogers. You don't want an anti-romance reader to label romance fiction as "smutty" for an access

point, but a fan of romance also can't provide a list of subject headings that dilute the function of these headings. (Tarulli 173)

Many catalogers are required to provide bibliographic descriptions for works on subjects about which they know little or nothing. With experience, we learn to use tables of contents, abstracts, and sometimes even bibliographies to determine the "aboutness" of a work. Occasionally, we also find ourselves cataloging materials about which we may have a pronounced opinion different from the author's. Part of the cataloger's mandate is to maintain the same kind of objective view about the material we describe as that espoused by journalists, and for the same reason: to offer readers a clear description of the materials so that they can find and choose according to their needs.

Conclusion

What has been described above doesn't conform to the definition of "creativity" that most people would recognize. Cataloging is not an art form, in that no one will read the resulting records for pleasure. Yet, as in accounting or coding, the techniques can be used to create new things. The goal of making these new things is to bring millions of works on every subject known to the attention of the world. It is a collective enterprise in which individuals from many different countries with different languages and cultures participate. Perhaps what can be concluded is that the work of bibliographic description offers some opportunities for creative placement of descriptive elements in the design of each record. The choice of that placement of possible descriptive elements results in records for each information resource that are unique, as are the resources. Regardless of what system or model a cataloger uses, the bedrock intention of catalogers will continue to be to share knowledge of books and other resources with our users, so that they can find, identify, select and obtain materials that they need.

Works Cited

Baia, Wendy, et al. "Creativity in Serials Cataloging: Heresy or Necessity?" *The Serials Librarian*, vol. 34, no. 1–4, May 1998, pp. 313–21, doi.org/10.1300/J123v34n03_10.

Bolin, Mary K. "Make a Quick Decision in (Almost) All Cases: Our Perennial Crisis in Cataloging." *Journal of Academic Librarianship*, vol. 16, no. 6, Jan. 1991, pp. 357–61.

Cabral, Maria Luisa. "Copyright on Bibliographic Records." *IFLA Journal*, vol. 16, no. 1, Mar. 1990, pp. 41–43. Sage Publications, doi.org/10.1177/034003529001600110.

"FAST (Faceted Application of Subject Terminology)." OCLC Research, 2020, www.oclc.org/research/themes/data-science/fast.html.

Howard, Sara A., and Knowlton, Steven A. "Browsing through Bias: The Library of Congress Classification and Subject Headings for African American Studies and LGBTQIA Studies." *Library Trends*, vol. 67, no. 1, June 2018, pp. 74–88, doi.org/10.1353/lib.2018.0026.

Madison, Olivia. "The IFLA Functional Requirements for Bibliographic Records: International Standards for Universal Bibliographic Control." *Library Resources and Technical Services*, vol. 44, no. 3, July 2000, pp. 153–59, doi.org/10.5860/lrts.44n3.153.

Miller, David P. "Out From Under: Form/Genre Access in LCSH." *Cataloging & Classification Quarterly*, vol. 29, no. 1–2, June 2000, pp. 169–88, doi.org/10.1300/J104v29n01_12.

Riva, Pat, et al. *IFLA Library Reference Model: A Conceptual Model for Bibliographic Information.* International Federation of Library Associations, 2017, pp. 21–31, www.ifla.org/publications/node/11412.

Smiraglia, Richard P. "A Research Agenda for Cataloging: The CCQ Editorial Board Responds to the Year of Cataloging Research." *Cataloging & Classification Quarterly*, vol. 48, no. 8, Sept. 2010, pp. 645–51, doi.org/10.1080/01639374.2010.508998.

Tarulli, Laurel. "Bias in Readers' Advisory Services." *Reference & User Services Quarterly*, vol. 57, no. 3, Mar. 2018, pp. 172–75.

Theimer, Sarah. "A Cataloger's Resolution to Become More Creative: How and Why." *Cataloging & Classification Quarterly*, vol. 50, no. 8, Nov. 2012, pp. 894–902, doi.org/10.1080/01639374.2012.711440.

Part 2: Surveys and Multiple Sources

The Novel in the Library and the Library in the Novel: At the Intersection of Literature and Library Science

Conner Kirk and Victoria Gaydosik

The Course of Study as Proposed: The Instructor Sets a Task

IN THE FALL OF 2018, my advisee Conner Kirk discovered that he had already completed every literature course that my small Language and Literature Department at Southwestern Oklahoma State University had on offer; however, he needed the senior-level course entitled The Novel, which would not be on the teaching schedule again until after he had already completed his BA degree. In order to allow him to graduate on time, I offered him an independent study course. Since the content of The Novel can vary from term to term, and since I knew Conner was headed for a graduate program in Library Science at the University of Oklahoma, I combined these areas and assigned him the task of finding all the novels in our library that featured libraries as key story elements. A little bit of mission creep also allowed in bookstores and private book collections, and mere book-loving characters tagged along. One or two nonfiction works masqueraded so effectively as novels that they could not be kept out.

I remembered an article that a colleague had sent me upon the passing the previous late winter of a librarian at Oklahoma State University who was also a long-time member of the Mythopoeic Society, David Oberhelman. In "A Brief History of Libraries in Middle-earth: Manuscript and Book Repositories in Tolkien's *Legendarium*" (reprinted on pp. 155–65), Oberhelman considered the role of Tolkien's fictional libraries throughout the imagined world of Middle-earth. I sent the article to Conner as a point of departure for his own inventory of the intersection where novels meet libraries. Since our university library also serves the needs of the Elementary Education program at SWOSU and of public schools in western Oklahoma, Connor was able to locate titles of interest to all ages, not just adult readers. And although he began with a focus on fantasy literature, following Oberhelman's example, his charge was to find all the novels he could that featured libraries in significant ways, and so romance novels, mystery and detective fiction, historical fiction, and works of serious literature were all included.

While he undertook the research to identify, cite, and annotate selected texts from this list of unknown dimensions, we began reading a series of novels that featured libraries, bookstores, or private book collections used in significant ways: *The Name of the Rose,* by Umberto Eco; *Codex,* by Lev Grossman; *The Shadow of the Wind,* by Carlos Ruiz Zafon (trans. Lucia Graves); *Unseen Academicals,* by Terry Pratchett; and *Midnight at the Bright Ideas Bookstore,* by Matthew Sullivan. The additional titles for the course would be selected as a result of Conner's search for the novels in our library that had libraries in them. He ultimately chose to add five novels to our reading list: *Possession,* by A. S. Byatt; *The Eyre Affair,* by Jasper Fforde; *Beautiful Creatures,* by Kami Garcia and Margaret Stohl; *Carry On,* by Rainbow Rowell; and *Mr. Penumbra's 24-Hour Bookstore,* by Robin Sloan.

As we began reading *The Name of the Rose* as a study text for identifying the formal features of the novel, we could see that a library, although it is technically a setting, can function very much like a character. Libraries can influence other characters and steer plot developments; they can even, in circumstances of sufficient mysteriousness, appear to defend their secrets, threaten intruders, or kill the unpermitted seeker of knowledge. If libraries contain multitudes, then the book containing a fictional library brings those multitudes with it by implication. The library in the novel can greatly exceed the mere locational function of a setting: it is the repository of the rational, the garden of the imagination, and the storehouse of a cultural heritage. The novel in the library opens a door into authors' creativity; the library in the novel makes an additional world inside authors' stories.

The Report as Concluded:
The Researcher Discovers the Many Libraries in Novels

This term while reading for an independent study course called "The Novel in the Library," I found my work—and my future career plans—greatly influenced by the late David Oberhelman, a brilliant scholar in the literary and library world. I had first heard of Oberhelman through the Oklahoma Library Association (OLA) during the 2018 Annual Conference in Tulsa, Oklahoma: there, I learned of his passing, of his incredible character and scholarship, and of his accomplishments in the library world. I heard more of Oberhelman's contributions to the Mythopoeic Society when I joined that group and attended a local meeting. Finally, I used some of his scholarship during my Novel in the Library class at Southwestern Oklahoma State University. My professor, Dr. Victoria Gaydosik, sent me a link to Oberhelman's article, and from that study I saw the importance of libraries in Tolkien's work. This information opened a new doorway through which I could look at the presence of libraries in other works—especially in works of fantasy. Oberhelman's research directly benefited my project from its very beginning.

I've learned that libraries figure significantly in a surprising number of fictional works in general and in works of fantasy in particular, as Oberhelman noted in his article. A novel may contain a library through a tiny reference: despite there not being a major setting in a library for the most important novel developed in Tolkien's fantasy world, *The Lord of the Rings*, there is one brief moment when Gandalf mentions that he located the history of the Ring—the information that fuels the plot for the entire series—in the archives of Gondor. The plot might not have ever begun or at least might not have turned out the same way if Gandalf had not gone to the library (or archives) and made this discovery. Tolkien based the libraries of Middle-earth on the libraries of reality. In his article, Oberhelman writes, "The history of libraries in ancient and early modern civilization provides the template Tolkien used in forming his own history of writing from the First through the Fourth Ages of his subcreated universe" (156). Oberhelman is saying that the libraries of our world directly influenced the work of Tolkien in his creation of Middle-earth's libraries: real libraries are the source and exemplar of fictional, fantastical, and mythic libraries, and there are many novels through which to enjoy imagined libraries.

Whether it is the Hogwarts Library from the *Harry Potter* series or the Lunae Libri from the *Caster Chronicles* series, libraries hold great importance in works of fantasy, serving both as settings and as devices to drive plots and develop characters. This use of a familiar location—the library—with the force of a character is found in works of fantasy and in other genres, including the detective genre. This technique is found in the quintessential novel concerning libraries: *The Name of the Rose*. Umberto Eco wrote this novel in the latter part of the twentieth century, and its popularity in the literary world seems to have greatly influenced several contemporary authors to set works in libraries. Although the novel is technically not fantasy, following instead the format of a work of mystery and detective fiction, the medieval setting seems to be somewhat fantastical in its nature, and the supernatural-seeming dark powers at work in the novel's library intensify the fantastic connection. The conflict point of finding a dead body in the library, as in *The Name of the Rose,* is also found in Matthew Sullivan's novel, *Midnight at the Bright Ideas Bookstore.* Notable authors like Lev Grossman even mention *The Name of the Rose*: his novel *Codex* refers to Eco's tale and has key passages set in unusual and highly specialized libraries and book collections. Portions of the novel *Mr. Penumbra's 24-Hour Bookstore,* by Robin Sloan, also have similarities to Eco's novel. *The Name of the Rose* is a lasting, powerful, and influential text that will surely be enjoyed by bibliophiles for generations.

In delineating the boundaries of this study, certain novels came into question for inclusion on my list but did not meet my qualifications for a listing in this bibliography. One such novel is *Call Me by Your Name,* by Andre Aciman, and this title is not listed since the main plotline uses a library almost incidentally—merely as an identifiable place. The two main characters both spend time in the library, and their romance might have blossomed because of the time they spend in the library; however, the novels on this list are primarily set in a library, bookstore, or private collection, or the plot is driven by events that occurred in the library, or the characters depend in some way on the world of books. Another item that could have possibly been included in the bibliography is *Game of Thrones,* but as of now my bibliography is limited to works of writing. The book version of *Game of Thrones* does not have a major plot line set in a library; the library location occurs only in the case of the television series, which features a new storyline that takes place in a library. If I were ever to expand this project to include television and film, then *Game of Thrones* (HBO) would be one of the entries.

Oberhelman's work inspires me to keep on my path while working toward developing my career as a librarian. As an institution, the library has repeatedly proven to be a valuable reservoir of information and knowledge. When scholars or citizens meet there, books and ideas come to life in lively conversations or on the pages of manuscripts and books. Libraries are often only thought of as the place where history is chronicled and kept; however, scholarly activities and other discussions based on library collections or services often lead to ideas that either influence the future or illuminate the past. Because of the tremendous role that libraries have played in our society, they have, of course, migrated into literature, which is the handbook of life, as I learned from Dr. Gaydosik. There are lessons to be learned from libraries themselves, and these lessons are right there on the shelves of these magnificent places, waiting to be checked out.

Selected Annotated Bibliography

Austin, Lynn. *Wonderland Creek.* **Bethany House, 2011.**
Writer Lynn Austin creates Christian fiction and has earned eight Christy Awards for her novels, probably best categorized as Christian romances. In *Wonderland Creek*, a young librarian loses her boyfriend, her job, and her hometown; she travels to a remote Appalachian village to deliver a book donation and finds herself stranded there only to discover more happiness than she had imagined would ever come to her.

Brooks, Geraldine. *People of the Book.* **Viking Penguin, 2008.**
This story relates a fictionalized history of the Sarajevo Haggadah, a real-world illuminated manuscript dating to the mid-1300s in Spain, where it was created by Sephardic Jews. The story of this manuscript's travels rehearses much of the history of the Jews in late Medieval to modern Europe. The protagonist, Hanna Heath, is a book conservator charged with the restoration of the Haggadah; the structure of the novel alternates chapters about Hanna's examination of and discoveries about the manuscript with those relating the journey of the Haggadah from medieval Barcelona to modern Sarajevo. In this novel, readers can see the risky existence of a book without a library to call home.

Byatt, A. S. *Possession.* **Random House, 1990.**
This dazzling novel is the story of two literary sleuths as they grow closer among the secluding shelves of an academic library. Maud and Roland are two young academics who specialize in the Victorian poets Christabel LaMotte and Randolf Henry Ash, respectively. They begin investigating long lost letters and journals trying to learn more about the relationship that Ash and LaMotte might have had. Byatt shows how two great minds can be brought together by curiosity, all while in the library, and has created a double love story with Maud and Roland falling in love as they research the previously unknown love between Christabel and Randolf.

Christie, Agatha. *The Body in the Library.* **Dodd, Mead, 1942.**
Miss Marple leads the search for the killer of an unknown young woman found strangled in the private library at Gossington Hall.

Christopher, Nicholas. *The Bestiary.* **Penguin Random House, 2008.**
The narrator of this adventure is Xeno Atlas, who from childhood is fascinated by his grandmother's stories of chimerical animals, and who eventually learns of the "Caravan Bestiary." This ancient text is said to enumerate the animals, now considered mythical, that Noah prohibited

from joining the survivors on his ark: manticores, hippogriffs, and other creatures found today only in fantasy stories. He becomes obsessed with the search for this long-lost book, following clues to many parts of the earth; along the way, he draws on the resources of many libraries rather than relying on just one. At one point, he even becomes a small-scale Noah in the rescue of some African animals. His story of personal development intertwines with his search for the missing bestiary and concludes in an unexpected discovery.

Clarke, Susanna. *Jonathan Strange & Mr Norrell.*
Bloomsbury USA, 2004.
In this charming fantasy-and-alternate-history novel, the private library of magic that Mr. Norrell is amassing during the Napoleonic era becomes the means by which he monopolizes magic and deprives other parties of access to the books that would help them develop their powers—at least, until the magically gifted Jonathan Strange manages to educate himself without the resources he needs. He comes to study with Mr. Norrell, who continues to stingily hoard his books, doling out only the least useful to his student until the tension between them splits their partnership. But the decay of magic is so severe that they are not even certain what enemies they may have aroused in the mysterious lands of faerie once ruled by the Raven King, from which a powerful fairy is taking possession of humans to serve as the exhausted and unwilling companions of his endless balls and revelries. Once this thistle-haired gentleman takes possession of Mrs. Strange, however, they can no longer afford to remain ignorant. The book features detailed passages of historical fiction wonderfully transformed by Jonathan Strange's imaginative and peculiar contributions to the war against Napoleon. Footnotes covering selected imagined magical texts from Mr. Norrell's library aid the reader in understanding the nature and history of magic in this alternative England.

Clifford, Eth. *HELP! I'm a Prisoner in the Library!*
Houghton Mifflin, 1979.
This young-adult title (recommended to grade 8) is the first in a series of five books chronicling the adventures of sisters Mary Rose and Jo-Beth. In this story, they find themselves locked overnight in the public library while a blizzard rages outside and assures that no one will be available to help them as soon as they would like. It was originally published with illustrations by George Hughes.

Cogman, Genevieve. *The Invisible Library*. **Pan Macmillan, 2015.**
Five books constitute the *Invisible Library* series: *The Invisible Library* (2015), *The Masked City* (2015), *The Burning Page* (2016), *The Lost Plot* (2017), and *The Mortal Word* (2018); a sixth volume, *The Secret Chapter*, is scheduled for publication in January of 2020. The wellspring for the series is the eponymous library of the initial volume, which exists outside of normal time and space. Librarian/collectors are dispatched from there to every quadrant of space and time to acquire texts in need of preservation in the Invisible Library; London is a favored destination. This time—and space—traveling device might make the books sound like a science fiction series, but individual volumes include settings replete with genre formulations from fantasy (magic, dragons) and mystery and detective fiction (murders and the search for the culprit).

Dahl, Roald. *Matilda*. **Jonathan Cape, 1988.**
In this award-winning classic children's book, Matilda reads omnivorously at Mrs. Phelps's library at the age of only four years and three months. Her negligent parents and cruel headmistress at school make life miserable, but when Matilda discovers that she has telekinetic powers, she devises a plan to set the world to rights and restore the stolen inheritance of her sympathetic teacher, Miss Honey. The original edition included illustrations by Quentin Blake.

Dean, Pamela. *Tam Lin*. **Tor Books, 1991.**
In 1992, *Tam Lin* was a finalist for the Mythopoeic Society Award for adult fantasy fiction. The story draws inspiration from a Scottish border ballad of the same name with supernatural elements. The novel is set at a midwestern private college, Blackstock, and follows the development of a young woman enrolled there, Janet Carter. The cast of characters includes the ghost of a past (and passed) student, and two Classics majors turn out to have an unexpected supernatural secret.

Dominguez, Carlos Maria. *The House of Paper*. **Alfaguara, 2004;**
English translation, Harcourt, 2005.
Everyone who loves books eventually comes to the realization that every shelf of every bookcase in every room of the house is full. In this Argentinian novel, an elusive protagonist builds himself a house of books and disappears from a world still interested in knowing him.

Eco, Umberto. *The Name of the Rose.* **Fabbri-Bompiani Snzogno, Etas, Gruppo Editoriale, 1980; English translation, Harcourt Brace Jovanovich, 1983.**

This novel is an excellent work of historical and detective fiction. The novel follows a monastic inspector and his apprentice as they investigate a series of murders in an Italian abbey at the height of the Medieval period. The murders all center on one place, the library at the top of the Aedificium. In this abbey, the library is private to only the librarian and his assistant, but there are rumors swirling amongst the Franciscan monks that the library is haunted. Those who enter are plagued with confusion and hallucinations, and everybody is vying to get into the library. The investigators sneak into the library at night to search for clues, but they are continually afflicted with visions and confusion since this library is a poisoned maze in its layout. Here, the library takes on a vexing and enigmatic persona, and Eco brings the library to life as a character, not just a setting. The library, a place that houses information for all, becomes the one which hides the manuscripts and books from its potential patrons until the truth of the mysterious murders can be resolved.

Enright, Elizabeth. *Thimble Summer.* **Square Fish, 1938.**

This 1939 winner of the Newbery Medal relates the adventures of a Wisconsin farm girl growing up in hard times. In one of her adventures, she and her best friend, quietly and voraciously reading of much bigger adventures, are locked in the town library until the grown-ups finally locate them, frightened and hungry, at midnight. Readers aged 8 to 12 will enjoy this realistic view of life in earlier days.

Fforde, Jasper. *Thursday Next Series.* **Penguin, 2001–2012.[1]**

This fantasy series revolves around books in a highly creative manner, even though the Great Library doesn't appear until the third volume of the series. Fforde has created a seemingly parallel universe in this novel, and in this world, there is a second plane of existence specifically for literary characters, as if the entire world were a library in which the books come to life—literally! People are able to cross back and forth from the mortal world to the world of the characters in novels. There is even a specific police force that investigates literary crimes (Jurisfiction), and the protagonist, Thursday Next, is an agent in this department. In the initial volume, she and her partner are attempting to stop a heinous villain, Acheron Hades, from murdering a 19th century character from

[1] See also the essay by David Emerson in this volume. –Eds.

the novel *Jane Eyre*, because if the murder happens there the character will disappear from all other copies of the novel, effectively killing the narrative. Loaded with witty humor, clever wordplay, book talk, and even time travel, this fantasy novel is a treat for any bibliophile.

The series consists of seven books to date, exploring and elaborating upon the overarching concept of a world of living books that unites these stories: *The Eyre Affair* (2001), *Lost in a Good Book* (2002), *The Well of Lost Plots* (2003), *Something Rotten* (2004), *First Among Sequels* (2007), *One of Our Thursdays is Missing* (2011), and *The Woman Who Died a Lot* (2012).

Flint, Eric. *Ring of Fire Series*. Baen Books, 2001.[2]
In the opening novel of this series, *1632*, realism, alternate history, and science fiction mingle, making classification of the novel difficult. At a realistic wedding in small-town West Virginia, a sudden blinding light completely alters the setting in which the characters will henceforth live: some unknown force has instantly transferred a six-mile chunk of West Virginia through time and space to Baroque Germany in the midst of the Thirty Years' War. The American town retains its population, buildings, vehicles (until the fuel runs out), power plant, weapons, and institutions—including the library, with its precious records of history, technology, and general how-to instructions. The resourceful townspeople decide that this new world is a good moment to initiate a new American Revolution to secure their safety and well-being.

The series continues, in a reading order recommended by Eric Flint (regardless of the order of composition), with the anthology *Ring of Fire* (2003, by various hands, including fan-fiction authors), *1633* (2002, written with David Weber), *1634: The Baltic War* (2007, also with Weber), *1634: The Ram Rebellion* (2006, with Virginia DeMarce), *1634: The Galileo Affair* (2005, with Andrew Dennis), *1634: The Bavarian Crisis* (2007, also with DeMarce), *1635: A Parcel of Rogues* (2016, with Dennis), *Ring of Fire II* (2008), *1635: The Cannon Law* (2006, with Dennis), *1635: The Dreeson Incident* (2008, with DeMarce), *1635: The Papal Stakes* (2012, with Charles E. Gannon), *1635: The Eastern Front* (2010), *1636: The Saxon Uprising* (2011), *Ring of Fire III* (2011), *1636: The Kremlin Games* (2012, with Gorg Huff and Paula Goodlett), *1637: The Volga Rules* (2018, also with Goodlett and Huff), *1636: Commander Cantrell in the West Indies* (2014, with Gannon), *1636: The Cardinal Virtues* (2015, with Walter H. Hunt), *1636: The Vatican Sanction* (2017, with Gannon), *1636: The Devil's*

[2] See also the essay by Susan Adams-Johnson and Anna Holloway in this volume. –Eds.

Opera (2013, with David Carrico), *1636: The Viennese Waltz* (2014, with Huff and Goodlett), *Ring of Fire IV* (2016), *1636: The Ottoman Onslaught* (2017), *1637: The Polish Maelstrom* (2019), *1636: Mission to the Mughals* (2017, with Griffin Barber), *1636: The China Venture* (2019, with Iver P. Cooper), and other titles entirely written by various of Flint's co-writers. Additional titles are forthcoming.

Funke, Cornelia. *Inkheart Trilogy*. Dressler, 2001–2007; English translation, Scholastic, 2001–2007.

Translated from German, this trilogy consists of *Inkheart* (2003), *Inkspell* (2005), and *Inkdeath* (2007). Rather than focusing on a library specifically, the story follows the daughter, Meggie, of a bookbinder named Mo who has the Silvertongue power of reading fictional characters into actual existence in the reader's world, sometimes to disastrous effects. Meggie turns out to have the same power; however, reading characters back *into* the books where they belong is not as easily accomplished. Fantasy characters in the real world have complex adventures, but they long to return to the familiar world of their origin stories.

Garcia, Kami and Margaret Stohl. *The Caster Chronicles Series*. Little, Brown, 2001–2012.

Initiated in 2009 in the volume *Beautiful Creatures*, this series of fantasy romance books is set in the modern world of the Deep South—specifically, South Carolina. This novel follows a mortal, Ethan Wate, and his love interest, Lena Duchannes, as they prepare for Lena's sixteenth birthday when she, being a "caster," or witch, will claim herself for the dark or the light by the power of the moon. While attempting to break the curse on her family, who wish Lena to choose the dark, she and Ethan turn to their small-town librarian, Marian Ashcroft. Marian is the Gatlin librarian, but she is also the Keeper of the Lunae Libri, a magical library below the streets that exists for casters alone. Mortals are not physically able to read the books there or touch them. The statues and carvings in the pillars of the library move and slither about in the presence of a caster. Garcia and Stohl have personified this mystical library since the library chooses to allow only a select few to access its most precious and powerful volume, *The Book of Moons*. Lena's final decision in the first book is made after reading this text, and the course of the novel is changed by that decision. In the following novels, Lena and Ethan continue to visit the Lunae Libri whenever they are in search of answers. The library also does not allow mortals, like Ethan, even to touch the collection, so the library itself conceals its items instead of a librarian hoarding them away. The series continues with *Beautiful Darkness* (2010), *Beautiful Chaos* (2011), and *Beautiful Redemption* (2012).

Grabbenstein, Chris. *Escape from Mr. Lemoncello's Library*. Random House, 2013.
This novel for readers aged 8 to 12 depicts the ultimate escape room adventure when renowned board game designer Luigi Lemoncello creates a library and invites a select group, including the protagonist, Kyle, to spend opening night enjoying the library's surprising features. But in the morning, when no doors open, the library patrons must solve a multitude of puzzles to work their way back out of the structure. The sequels to this novel include *Mr. Lemoncello's Library Olympics* (2016), *Mr. Lemoncello's Great Library Race* (2017), and *Mr. Lemoncello's All-Star Breakout Game* (2019).

Grey, Melissa. *The Girl at Midnight Series*. Delacorte Press, 2015.
In the titular first novel of this young adult series, the protagonist is teenaged orphan Echo, thief and book lover who takes refuge when she can in the New York Public Library. She is free to visit the under-street world of the Avicen, feathered bipeds, where she learns magic and lives by her wits. When she is captured by the Drakharin, dragonish ancient enemies of the Avicen, she must seek the firebird in the hope of bringing peace. Additional titles in this series include *The Shadow Hour* (2017), and *The Savage Dawn* (2017).

Grossman, Lev. *Codex*. Houghton Mifflin Harcourt, 2004.
Grossman sets his novel in the stacks of a private collection of ancient books and manuscripts. This library includes novels, manuscripts, and codices from all across Europe dating from the Medieval period up until the time it is packed up for travel across the Atlantic just before World War II. The wealthy family that owns the collection sends it across the ocean before the air raids that devastated Britain began, and the crates that contain the books have remained untouched until Edward Wozny is hired by the Wents—the Duke and Duchess of Bowmry—to unpack and catalog them. Edward, the protagonist, is specifically tasked with finding a codex by a medieval scholar, Gervase of Langford. While researching this writer, Edward—and through him, the reader—is introduced to a further special type of library. This is an exclusive private library where members have to pay a fee to borrow books, and the books that are kept there are extremely rare. Here, Edward meets Margaret Napier, a grad student who is writing her dissertation on Gervase of Langford. Thus begins the storyline that

follows the trail of Edward and Margaret in their search for the Gervase manuscript. Their quest leads them from the private collection to the private library and all the way to a remote annex for still other works. This place is a massive warehouse filled with rare editions that have fallen out of popularity at the private library. A subplot follows Edward's adventures in a computer game named Momus that seems to evoke Edward's main task of finding the Gervase manuscript. Edward and Margaret come to the brink of love before each is severely tested.

Hamilton, Masha. *The Camel Bookmobile: A Novel.* **Orion Books, 2007.**
In northeastern Kenya, the mobile library comes to its patrons, but only if they always return the books they have checked out. The ideas inspired by the innovation of the camel bookmobile, however, set off an intense dispute between modern ways and traditional customs.

Hammer, Joshua. *The Bad-Ass Librarians of Timbuktu: And Their Race To Save the World's Most Precious Manuscripts.*
Allen and Unwin, 2018.
Sometimes, historical testimony and journalistic reporting are as riveting as the best thrillers and spy novels, and this nonfiction book is one of those examples. Archivist Abdel Kader Haidara races to save thousands of Arabic written texts from jihadists wishing to eradicate a past that doesn't conform to their dictates.

Hanff, Helene. *84, Charing Cross Road.* **Viking Press, 1970.**
The relationship between letter-writing and novel structure is an intimate and ancient one, dating to those 18th-century epistolary English novels that founded a literary tradition. In this work of nonfiction that reads like a novel, a voracious New York book lover finds herself corresponding with a proper English bookseller established at the titular address of the book. Their book-centric commercial relationship quickly develops into something much deeper.

Harkness, Deborah. *All Souls Series.* **Viking Penguin, 2011–2014.**
In the first volume of this gothic adventure-romance series, *A Discovery of Witches* (2011), a Yale scholar (and secret witch from a long line of witches) discovers a manuscript in the Bodleian Library that may contain the secret to immortality. Awareness of the document's existence provokes a panoply of supernatural creatures to reveal themselves, and the protagonist acquires a collaborator who is an ancient vampire (and eventual love interest). A war among the many newly-revealed sentient species threatens, calling the protagonist into

action. The subsequent volumes in the series include *Shadow of Night* (2012) and *The Book of Life* (2014).

Hawkins, Scott. *The Library at Mount Char.* **US Crown, 2016.**
In this fantasy thriller, a pyramidal library containing the sum of all knowledge becomes the home of twelve orphans and the figure—"Father"—who has adopted them. He teaches them in such a way that each sibling must master a separate realm of knowledge and never dabble in the studies of the other siblings: dire punishments are imposed on those violating this rule. But a mysterious disaster forces the siblings out of the library and severs them from Father with no way to know his circumstances. The sibling who had studied all known languages, Carolyn, emerges as a leader of the siblings and manipulator of this situation, eventually solving the mystery of Father's fate at a terrible price.

Hines, Jim C. *The Magic Ex Libris Series.* **Ebury, 2011–2016.**
Those rare individuals who are able to extract material objects from books are known as Libriomancers, and they are invited into a secret society founded by the still-living Johannes Gutenberg. But in addition to the willed extraction of objects from books, there is also the mysterious sublimation of bookish evils, such as vampires, into the real world. The protagonist here, Isaac Vainio, is drawn into the struggle to contain this transmission after Gutenberg is kidnapped and vampires begin attacking the world's magicians. Additional books in the series include *Codex Born* (2013) and *Unbound* (2015).

Kostova, Elizabeth. *The Historian.* **Little, Brown, 2005.**
A modern novel based on Bram Stoker's *Dracula*, this story combines history and Gothic fiction to explore vampire tales and the real and imagined life of Vlad Tepes.

Lovett, Charlie. *First Impressions: A Novel of Old Books, Unexpected Love, and Jane Austen.* **Viking, 2014.**
In a book-lover's love story, a clerk in an antiquarian bookshop, Sophie Collingwood, is drawn into the search for information that may radically affect our knowledge of *Pride and Prejudice*. As her investigation unfolds and the risks she faces increase, two suitors vie for her affections while evidence accumulates that calls Jane Austen's authorship into question.

——. *The Bookman's Tale: A Novel of Obsession*. **Penguin, 2013.**
If libraries and bookstores are important cultural features that can figure significantly in fiction, then there must be a correspondingly significant role for librarians and booksellers—the people who keep the institutions functioning. In *The Bookman's Tale*, readers follow a recently widowed bookseller, Peter Byerly, to his new shop in the Cotswolds. He finds a painting that appears to be a portrait of his beloved deceased wife, and his growing obsession with it leads him into Victorian and eventually Elizabethan explorations.

Makkai, Rebecca. *The Borrower: A Novel*. **Windmill Books, 2012.**
A librarian finds a ten-year-old patron—and compulsive reader well known to her—hiding out in the library after hours with a knapsack stocked for the long trip he plans for her to take him on in order to escape his parents' plan to "cure" him of being gay. The after-hours library visit turns into a road trip for the pair.

Morgenstern, Erin. *The Starless Sea*. **Penguin Random House, 2019.**
An unexpected biographical tale appears in a book hidden in a normal university library; however, the tale relates a story from the childhood of a graduate student who has never shared this part of his life with a biographer. His search to discover how his life came to be chronicled leads to an even more fantastical underground library and to a world where mysterious powers struggle to preserve or destroy the hidden library.

Morley, Christopher. *The Haunted Bookshop*. **J. B. Lippincott, 1919.**
This sequel to *Parnassus on Wheels* (listed below) shifts the setting to Brooklyn at the close of World War I and continues the adventures of Roger Mifflin.

——. *Parnassus on Wheels*. **J. B. Lippincott, 1917.**
Instead of a library on wheels, Roger Mifflin manages a bookstore on wheels, traveling wherever he wishes through the New England countryside and encountering adventures and colorful characters along the way. But when he meets Helen McGill, both of their lives take new directions.

Morris, Carla D., Ill. Brad Sneed. *The Boy Who Was Raised by Librarians*. **Peachtree, 2007.**
This illustrated children's book follows Melvin as he scours his local library, with the help of the all-knowing librarians, for knowledge about all the things his curiosity turns to.

Murakami, Haruki. *The Strange Library.* **Vintage Digital, 2017.**
This novella relates the story of a group of unusual characters trying to escape from a library that is the opposite of the typical inviting locus of devoted book lovers.

Niffenegger, Audrey. *The Night Bookmobile.* **Harry N. Abrams, 2010.**
This graphic novella illustrates how the protagonist, Alexandra, encounters a mysterious night bookmobile stocked with every book she has ever read.

——. *The Time-Traveler's Wife.* **MacAdam/Cage, 2003.**
Proving that librarians may have adventures outside the confines of a library, this novel follows Henry, a librarian and the first person known to suffer from "Chrono-Displacement Disorder." He marries Clare, but since he periodically comes unhinged in time, their relationship and their desire for the achievements of normal married life face unusual challenges.

Nix, Garth. *Lirael. Old Kingdom Series* **Book 2. HarperCollins, 2001.**
In the fantasy realm of this series, the Clayr have the special powers of the Sight—all except Lirael, who buries herself in her job as the third assistant librarian, unaware of the future that lies in store for her and her loyal Disreputable Dog. Volume 1 of this series is *Sabriel* (1995); volume 3 is *Abhorsen* (2003); volume 4 is *Clariel* (2014—a prequel); and volume 5 is *Goldenhand* (2016).

Peck, Richard. *Here Lies the Librarian.* **Scholastic, 2007.**
This comic young adult novel relates the impact new librarian Irene Ridpath has upon arriving at her new home in a small town in Indiana.

Pratchett, Terry. *Unseen Academicals.* **Harper, 2009.**[3]
Unseen Academicals, while a stand-alone novel, is a book that is part of the Discworld collection. This fantasy realm has one major university, the Unseen University, which serves as the setting for this comedic novel. This university has an extremely intriguing library containing all of the books already written as well as the books that are waiting to be written. Pratchett is bringing every bibliophile's dream to life by creating his fantastic library this way. Pratchett's powerful skill in world building is clearly shown here since the librarian of Unseen University is an orangutan; he is the only being that knows enough to navigate this mystical library, but his capabilities of speech are extremely limited.

---

[3] See also the essays by Janet Brennan Croft and Elise McKenna in this volume. –Eds.

Rothfuss, Patrick. *The Kingkiller Chronicles Series*. Orion, 2001–2014.
In *The Name of the Wind* (2007), the Archives of the great university of
Temerant contain vast and deep reaches of knowledge on all topics—
presumably including the secrets of the evil Chandrian who were
responsible for the deaths of both of the parents of Kvothe, the novel's
protagonist. His adventures before being orphaned and his search for
justice afterward are unraveled in a detailed fantasy plot. The sequel
to this novel is *The Wise Man's Fear* (2011); *The Slow Regard of Silent
Things* (2014) constitutes book two-and-a-half.

Rowell, Rainbow. *Carry On*. Macmillan Children's Books, 2015.
This fantasy novel about a young magician and his friends combatting
a mysterious magical terrorist eventually has its plot driven by
discoveries in the library. This library is a private family collection
assembled by one of the oldest magical families in this universe, and
Baz, a character who is half-vampire and half-magician, is part of this
family and also the roommate of the protagonist, Simon Snow, who is
searching for information on the unknown malevolent force at work.
While in the library, they find the information they seek, and Simon
and Baz find each other as love interests while conducting their
research. The library, once again, is used in literature as a tool to bring
characters together and advance the plot.

Rowling, J. K. *The Harry Potter Series*. Bloomsbury, 1991–2007.
No fantasy adventure series set in a boarding school for training
wizards and witches can escape having some role for the library to
play, and J. K. Rowling's phenomenal sprawling narrative does not
disappoint. The magical world of Harry Potter is filled with the
importance of books, beginning with the purchase of each new term's
textbooks at Flourish and Blotts, in Diagon Alley, and continuing to
the one place that bibliophile Hermione insists on visiting for any
questions that need to be solved: the Hogwarts Library. Filled with
floating books, the library draws the trio of Harry, Ron, and Hermione
to make several trips to the library in the series, and the plot is driven
or aided by these actions in several of the books. Without the library's
restricted section in *The Sorcerer's Stone*, the trio would have never
learned about the stone or Nicholas Flamel. In *The Chamber of Secrets*,
Hermione is petrified by the basilisk, but she ultimately finds the way
into the Chamber through this visit. During Buckbeak's trial in the
Prisoner of Azkaban, Harry and friends visit the library to research legal
texts to assist Hagrid with putting together a case for Buckbeak. In
preparation for the third trial of the Triwizard Tournament in the

Goblet of Fire, Harry does some reading in the Hogwarts library, and in *The Half Blood Prince,* Harry studies the Advanced Potion Making textbook in the library. Rowling makes a point to show that when her characters are stumped, all they need to do is visit the library.

Ruiz Zafón, Carlos. *The Cemetery of Forgotten Books Series.* Planeta, 2001–2017; English translation, Harper, 2001–2017.
The Shadow of the Wind introduces this series of books about books, writers, book sellers, and those who wish to preserve books. This initial novel is definitely part of the mystery and detective genre since most of the story is spent trying to get more information about a novel entitled *The Shadow of the Wind,* by the elusive Julian Carax. The plot does not spend much time in the library-like setting of the Cemetery of Forgotten Books, the place where Daniel, the protagonist, first discovers *The Shadow of the Wind.* This "cemetery" is the place maintained by antiquarian booksellers where books go to escape banishment in the seemingly mystical city of Barcelona. With Zafón's descriptions, 1940s Barcelona seems to take on a somewhat fantastical persona, as does the Cemetery of Forgotten Books. Daniel attempts to find all of the information about Carax since someone truly villainous is burning every last copy of his books, a heinous crime in the literary world. The sequels to this novel include *The Angel's Game* (2008—actually a prequel), *The Prisoner of Heaven* (2012, continuing Daniel's story), and *The Labyrinth of the Spirits* (2018, focused on exposing the crimes committed against authors and books, among others, in Franco's regime).

Sanderson, Brandon. *Alcatraz Versus the Evil Librarians Series.* Hachette Children's Group, 2001–2016.
Launched with the titular first book in the series, these comic young adult novels follow the adventures of Alcatraz Smedry and his grandfather and cousins, all named after various American prisons. And, shockingly, the villains are the Evil Librarians who rule the world in secrecy. The plot follows the adventures of Alcatraz and his band of freedom fighters, and continues into volume 2, *The Scrivener's Bones* (2008); volume 3, *The Knights of Crystallia* (2009); volume 4, *The Shattered Lens* (2010); and volume 5, *The Dark Talent* (2016).

Sansom, Ian. *The Mobile Library Mystery Series.* Harper, 2001–2010.
The initial book in this comic four-book series is *The Case of the Missing Books;* in it, the new driver of the mobile library for a town in Northern Ireland is young Israel Armstrong, who immediately wonders what has happened to the library's 15,000 volumes, since they are not in the

bookmobile. He embarks on an investigation to uncover the missing books, and continues finding missing things in the next book, *Mr. Dixon Disappears* (2007). The third book in the series is *The Book Stops Here* (2009); the fourth is *The Bad Book Affair* (2010).

Schwab, Victoria. *The Archived Series*. Hyperion, 2011–2018.
The library meets the cemetery in these Gothic-influenced young adult books. In the first book, *The Archived*, readers meet the protagonist, Mackenzie, a teenaged "Keeper" working in the otherworldly archives that contain the corpse-like Histories of everyone who ever lived—histories that can grow restless and attempt to return to the material world. Young men become significant and puzzling parts of her life while she also copes with the loss of family members and the risks of her special calling. The series continues with *Unbound* (2014); both books are available, with an additional short story, in *The Dark Vault* (2018).

Setterfield, Diane. *The Thirteenth Tale*. Atria Books, 2006.
How could libraries exist without authors? In this novel, an elderly renowned author who has previously fabricated a series of false life stories decides that she is ready to reveal the painful truths of her life. She chooses a young biographer as the amanuensis of her tale, and this young woman turns out to have an equally troubled past that she hides from by recounting the lives of others. The elder story-teller holds the young biographer mesmerized as they both face their pasts.

Sloan, Robin. *Mr. Penumbra's 24-Hour Bookstore*.
Farrar, Straus, and Giroux, 2012.
This book will also appeal to bibliophiles as it takes place not in a library, university library, or a private collection; instead, the majority of the plot is set in a bookstore in San Francisco. The store seems to be a normal bookstore at the beginning, but a secret there hides in plain sight. There are the usual normal books as in a modest version of a commercial bookstore, but these are primarily a façade. Looming on the towering, dim-lit shelves are the hundreds of books all written in a strange code. These are only to be checked out by a select clientele, each of them being oddities themselves. Eventually, the action of the plot transfers the characters to a private library owned by the secret society of the Unbroken Spine. The only books shelved in this library are those coded books called Codex Vitae. This society and its library are reminiscent of medieval monastic practices, and the influence of *The Name of the Rose* is apparent in the story's settings and developments. There is a prequel, *Ajax Penumbra 1969*, Atlantic, 2014.

Sullivan, Matthew. *Midnight at the Bright Ideas Bookstore.*
Scribner, 2017.
Following the trope of investigating in the library as Eco did, Sullivan brings readers to the bookstore world. When a troubled frequent patron of the Bright Ideas Bookstore is found dead at midnight among the shelves, Lydia, a clerk at the store, is bequeathed a few of the man's possessions. Upon reviewing this sad inheritance, she feels compelled to unravel the mystery of his death; doing so, however, continually brings back terrifying memories from her own past. Lydia searches and searches for the answers to Joey's death and what he was hiding until she is reliving a nightmarish incident from her own notorious past.

Swyler, Erika. *The Book of Speculation.* **Corvus, 2016.**
The protagonist of this novel, Simon Watson, is a librarian, but the book of the title comes to his doorstep from a bookseller seeking information on it instead of being tracked down in a library. The water-stained handwritten book contains his grandmother's name and tells of the mysterious deaths, by drowning, of circus mermaids such as Simon's own mother, whose death followed the pattern established in the book. The drownings all occur on July 24—the date his mother drowned—and Simon's sister may be the next victim unless he can find a way to break what he has come to believe is a family curse. The author also illustrated the initial publication of this novel.

Tolkien, J. R. R. *The Lord of the Rings.*
George Allen and Unwin, 1951–1955.[4]
Libraries do not figure prominently as settings where the action of this high fantasy quest unfolds. But the quest itself is set in motion only after Gandalf, a kind of wizard or sorcerer (revealed to be one of the Maiar in *The Silmarillion*), visits the archives of Gondor, the White City of men. There, he discovers the long-forgotten record of the origin of the evil One Ring, found by Bilbo Baggins in *The Hobbit*, and how it passed into the hands of an ancient king before disappearing from the historical record. Once Bilbo's ring is definitively proved to be the One Ring when its inscription becomes visible after the ring is heated in the fireplace, Gandalf knows that the ring must be destroyed if the creator and true owner of the ring, the evil Sauron, is to be prevented from eradicating all that is good in Middle-earth. The value of libraries in their endless amassing of manuscripts and books, and the preservation of those

---

[4] See also the essays by Janet Brennan Croft, Jason Fisher, and David Oberhelman in this volume. –Eds.

resources even after their worth has been forgotten, directly leads to the quest of the Fellowship of the Ring, setting the novel's plot in motion.

Trigiani, Adriana. *Big Stone Gap Series.* **Random House, 2001–2006.**
Book-lover and thirty-something self-proclaimed Italian-descended spinster Ave Maria Mulligan copes with life in a small Appalachian town in Virginia in this semi-autobiographical series of novels, with the help of best friend and bookmobile driver Iva Lou Wade. The series consists of *Big Stone Gap* (2000), *Big Cherry Holler* (2001), *Milk Glass Moon* (2002), and *Home to Big Stone Gap* (2006).

Turgeon, Carolyn. *Rain Village.* **Unbridled Books, 2006.**
The plot of this novel takes the protagonist, Tessa, from the shelter of the library where she works with Mary, a former trapeze artist who eventually drowns herself, to Tessa's own adventures in the circus world. There, Tessa escapes the sexual abuse she suffered at home and makes a new family in the circus, finding love and support, while she also seeks the truth of Mary's past life.

Walters, Louise. *Mrs. Sinclair's Suitcase.* **G. P. Putnam's Sons, 2015.**
A clerk at an English new-and-used bookstore, Roberta, finds a mysterious letter in her grandmother's suitcase hinting at a dark secret in the elderly woman's life; the novel develops a double narrative following the lives of Roberta in the contemporary world and her grandmother in World War II and its aftermath, as each seeks fulfillment in family and love.

Wharton, Thomas. *Salamander.* **Washington Square Press, 2001.**
Set in the 18th century and centered on the adventures of book printer Nicholas Flood, this novel follows its protagonist to the magical-seeming, puzzle-castle of a Slovakian count who hires Nicholas to create an infinite book of all knowledge. Nicholas's search for the materials is complicated by his forbidden love for the count's daughter. To create the endless story the count desires him to make, Nicholas travels the globe and collects characters, tales, and experiences from every quadrant of it.

Zusak, Markus. *The Book Thief.* **Alfred A. Knopf, 2005.**
Libraries are living repositories, but they can also die, and wars in particular may be fatal to book collections. In this novel set in 1939 Nazi Germany, the young protagonist, Leisel Meminger, can barely keep body and soul together, and she cannot resist books. When she encounters a book, she steals it and shares it with her neighbors and a Jewish refugee hiding in the basement, becoming a de facto one-person lending library.

"Books! Best Weapons in the World": How Libraries Save the World in Popular Culture

Kristine Larsen

I N "TOOTH AND CLAW," A 2006 episode of the long-running British science fiction series *Doctor Who*, the alien Timelord and his human companion Rose Tyler are holed up in the library of a Victorian era Scottish mansion trying to discover a way to vanquish a threatening werewolf. The house's owner bemoans the fact that they don't have any weapons, but the Doctor retorts "You want weapons? We're in a library. Books! Best weapons in the world. This room's the greatest arsenal we could have." As he tosses a book to Rose he urges "Arm yourself." Indeed, it is only by reading through some of the library's many books that our heroes find a way to stop the beast. As the old adage states, knowledge is power, and there is no greater source of knowledge than a library. Similarly, in George R. R. Martin's epic novel series *A Song of Ice and Fire*, ancient Maester Aemon's parting words to Jon Snow are an admonition to carefully read a marked passage in the *Jade Compendium* concerning the legendary sword Lightbringer. The wise Aemon advises that "Knowledge is a weapon, Jon. Arm yourself well before you ride forth to battle" (Martin, *Feast* 121).

It is therefore not surprising that many of the important seats of power in Martin's mythical continent of Westeros are said to house libraries. These include the Red Keep at King's Landing (the home of the infamous Iron Throne), and Horn Hill, the ancestral home of Jon Snow's right-hand man, the bookish Samwell Tarly. Less expected perhaps is the library at the Ten Towers lovingly maintained by Asha Greyjoy's uncle Lord Rodrik Harlaw. As Martin describes, unlike many members of his aggressive seafaring culture, Rodrik was "an ordinary man, distinguished only by his love of written words, which so many of the ironborn found unmanly and perverse" (Martin, *Feast* 231). Even Winterfell, the seat of House Stark that is best known for its precarious location dangerously close to the uncivilized wilds of the North, had rare parchments in its Library Tower (much to the intelligent and well-educated Tyrion Lannister's delight) (Martin, *Game* 87). What potentially lifesaving (or condemning) secrets were to be found within the rare volumes of the Winterfell family library? Alas, we may never know, as it was burned during the thwarted attempt on Bran Stark's life (to forever silence him about witnessing the incestuous twins Cersei and Jaime Lannister *in flagrante delicto*) (*Game* 131).

Castle Black, the headquarters of the Night's Watch, those who protect the gigantic wall of ice built to prevent the demonic White Walkers from taking over the known world, also has an exceptionally well-stocked library of thousands of works, including many old and rare scrolls. The scholarly Samwell Tarly understands well the great potential of these ancient works, and indeed learns much about the dreaded enemy through his readings, including a reference to something called "dragon steel," a blade made of which was used to kill White Walkers during their last attack upon Westeros many ages before (*Feast* 115). Since the audience reads the books in the series much faster than author George R. R. Martin writes them, we don't know for certain what this material is, although there are numerous hints (perhaps misleading) that it is Valyrian steel. But Sam Tarly, like the reader, needs more information in order to aid Jon Snow and the Night's Watch in the upcoming battle against the icy invaders. Sam is therefore sent to the Citadel, the headquarters of the scholarly Maesters, to begin his academic training. As Jon Snow notes in *A Dance with Dragons*, "There are so many books at the Citadel that no man can hope to read them all" (*Dance* 117). Of course Sam doesn't need to read them all—just the right one. But for that, Martin needs to finish writing two volumes of his own. Fortunately the HBO series based on the novels didn't have to wait for Martin's glacial writing pace to catch up, and viewers were treated to some remarkable CGI "book porn" as Sam lovingly undressed the myriad volumes of the Citadel's legendary library with his eyes in the ironically named Season 6 episode "The Winds of Winter" (the name of the long overdue sixth volume in Martin's series) (S. Davis). The Library ultimately yields to Sam a cure for Jorah Mormont's greyscale as well as the location of a huge stash of dragon glass—obsidian—that can be fashioned into weapons with which to fight the dreaded White Walkers' army of the undead.

Book knowledge can therefore come to your aid in the universe of Westeros, but it can also get you killed as well. After the poisoning of long-time friend and brother-in-law Jon Arryn, Eddard "Ned" Stark sought a mysterious book that had led to Arryn's demise. Written by Grand Maester Malleon, *The Lineages and Histories of the Great Houses of the Seven Kingdoms, With Descriptions of Many High Lords and Noble Ladies and Their Children*, made for "ponderous reading" (Martin, *Game* 274). But it turned out to have a rather important genetics lesson within its pages, that when the blonde Lannisters had previously married the dark haired Baratheons (as in the case of King Robert and Queen Cersei), the children were always dark haired. So why were Cersei's three children blonde like herself, and her incestuous twin brother Jaime? Obviously some heads were bound to roll to prevent this knowledge from coming out, in this case literally Ned's.

Whereas Ned Stark's ultimately fatal interest in this specific tome was sparked by Jon Arryn's death, it may seem surprising that Ned Stark's ancestral home Winterfell had a well-stocked library, including ancient and rare works. Now granted, there probably wasn't much to do in this far northern kingdom when the winds of winter approached (apparently faster than the long-promised book of the same name) except read and perhaps add progeny to the next generation, but the Starks openly valued literacy, going so far as to make sure that the (incorrectly) presumed bastard son Jon Snow was able to read. Literacy is generally highly valued by (most) of the Houses of Westeros. In the novels, the illiteracy of Ser Davos, the Onion Knight, is one of many reasons for his self-doubts in his ability to serve as the Hand of the King to Stannis Baratheon. *"I cannot read, I cannot write, the lords despise me. I know nothing of ruling, how can I be the King's Hand? I belong on the deck of a ship, not in a castle tower,"* he anguishes (Martin, *Storm* 730). When Davos admits his illiteracy to Maester Pylos, the scholar offers to teach Davos, as he is already tutoring the Onion Knight's son Devan.

It is notable that both sons and daughters are taught to read in Westeros, for example Shireen, the daughter of Stannis, as well as Ned's daughters Sansa and Arya Stark. In fact in the HBO series it is Shireen who not only teaches Davos to read, but also the Wildling woman Gilly (who, like her sisters, had been kept as an illiterate sexual slave by her father). It was later quite fortuitous that Gilly decided to amuse herself in Oldtown by perusing the awkwardly detailed diary of High Septon Maynard, who "even recorded his own bowel movements" ("Eastwatch"). She innocently inquires of Samwell if the annulment and secret remarriage of "a Prince 'Ragger'" in Dorne she read about in the journal was "a common thing in the South." This vital piece of exposition is nothing less than proof of perhaps the most famous fan theory in all of *GoT*-dom, that the "bastard" Jon Snow is actually Aegon, the legitimate son of Rhaegar Targaryen and Lyanna Stark (or, in the commonly used fan shorthand, R + L = J), giving Jon rights to the Iron Throne. As Samwell explains to Bran Stark in the final episode of Season 7, "It's what the High Septon wrote in his private diary. I don't know why he'd lie" ("The Dragon and the Wolf"). Although this particular piece of literary revelation did not lead to Aegon Stark-Targaryen's death or kingship in the television series, we see the vital importance of not only seemingly obscure and unimportant books but literacy in general in Martin's subcreation.

The same is certainly true of the wonderful wizarding world of Hogwarts. Indeed, the library of the wizard academy plays such a vital role as both a fount of knowledge and setting of important scenes that a case can be made for its being the "true hero" of the series (Bittiner). While books certainly play a vital role in discovering how to blind the Slytherin basilisk or surviving the long-promised winter in the world of Westeros, they can also apparently save your life in the event of a sudden Ice Age affecting New York City, at least according to the often panned 2004 disaster movie *The Day After Tomorrow*. Paleoclimatologist Dr. Jack Hall races to rescue his son Sam and friends who are holed up in the New York Public Library from the Arctic tundra that has become the Big Apple. Their most pressing issue, after raiding the junk food machines, is trying not to freeze to death. At Sam's urging (and despite the librarians' protests) the immediate decision becomes which books to burn in a large fireplace. Jeremy, one of the librarians, accompanies Elsa and Brian on their task to select sacrificial volumes, determined to make sure that they don't burn the *wrong* books. For example, he protests that they "cannot burn Friedrich Nietzsche. He was the most important thinker of the Nineteenth century." After an exasperated Elsa offers that "Nietzsche was a chauvinist pig who was in love with his sister" the standoff is solved for the moment when Brian notes "a whole section on tax law down here that we can burn."

While it is true that when faced with the imminent death of not only individuals, but perhaps human civilization itself, taxes seem irrelevant, consider what could be learned about said civilization by future archaeologists through these tax documents, not unlike the importance of tax records in understanding the history of Roman Empire and other ancient civilizations. When Jon Snow scoffs at the value of an old inventory listing "how much pickled cod they ate six hundred years ago" at the Wall, Sam corrects his friend, explaining that it could "tell you how many men were in the Night's Watch then, how they lived, what they ate" (Martin, *Clash* 95). Every book has its story, and each gives us some insight into not only the mind of the author but the time and place of its conception.

All books have their story, but some stories are more compelling than others. In a later scene in *The Day After Tomorrow*, while the library refugees are all trying to keep warm huddled around the book-fueled fireplace, Elsa notes that Jeremy is lovingly pouring over a large book cradled in his lap. It is the Rare Books Room's copy of the Gutenberg Bible, a work that Jeremy is determined to protect as it "represents the dawn of the Age of Reason. As far as I'm concerned, the written word is mankind's greatest achievement." Elsa initially scoffs at this seemingly futile effort, but changes her mind when Jeremy explains that "if Western Civilization is finished, I'm gonna save at least one little piece of it."

The initial horror expressed by the librarians Judith and Jeremy at Sam's intention to burn books was mirrored in reactions to a January 2010 report that Welsh pensioners who were unable to afford coal were instead burning bargain bin books purchased in secondhand stores (Erwin). Leo Hickman of *The Guardian* called this "an act of wanton barbarism" and offered four alternatives to "this outrage" — burning telephone directories, dried cow dung, discarded wooden pallets, and briquettes made from old newspapers. Likewise, more than one viewer of Emmerich's film has wondered why they didn't just burn the many chairs and other piece of wooden furniture in the New York Public Library before turning to the books ("Headscratchers"). Interestingly, Hickman's call for the intentional burning of old newspapers, although certainly not uncommon, is also the destruction of the written word. While newspapers are typically seen as far more ephemeral than books, it should be noted that the British Library has spent a significant amount of resources attempting to conserve and digitize three centuries worth of newspapers before they literally disintegrate from the ravages of time (N. Davis).

Finally, there is another very concrete way that one specific book saves a life in the film. When Sam's love interest, Laura, becomes gravely ill due to an infected leg wound, librarian Judith uses a medical reference book to diagnose the problem and suggest a plan of treatment. As Judith reminds them all, "Books can be good for things other than burning," a rather upside-down way of looking at the world.

Despite the less-than thoughtful nature of much of the film, including a great deal of its science (Naughten), the desire of characters to preserve particular books, and the insinuation that the burning of books is a regretful, albeit necessary, action, does afford us an opportunity to contemplate the following: why is it that book burning evokes such a visceral response from many people, even those who are not librarians? For example, Ariel Cook calls book burning "much more oppressive and insulting" than flag burning. In her words, "Through the process of book burning, it's an attempt to control what information people should be allowed to learn." This is not merely a modern perspective. John Milton argued in his *Areopagitica* that "as good almost kill a man as kill a good book: who kills a man kills a reasonable creature, God's image; but he who destroys a good book, kills reason itself, kills the image of God, as it were in the eye" (6). Haig Bosmajian reflects that the image of Nazis feeding "un-German" books to bonfires in 1933 "still conveys the atavism and horrors of the fiery public ritual of the destruction and obliteration of literary, political, and scientific works" (3).

Book burning as a means to destroy subversive or obscene works (the specific definitions of which are, of course, in the eye of the beholder) certainly did not begin or end with the Nazis. Qin Shi Huang, the first emperor of a united China, ordered a "burning of the books" in 213 BC, an event that has "often been cited as one of the earliest examples of censorship in history" (Chan 101). More recently, when a North Dakota school board burned copies of Kurt Vonnegut's *Slaughterhouse-Five*, the author opined that the nationwide outcry against this attempt at censorship should teach the valuable lesson that "books are sacred to free men for very good reasons, and that wars have been fought against nations which hate books and burn them." Rebecca Knuth found that the "ideologically driven, systematic destruction of books and libraries," or what she terms *libricide*, was repeatedly used in the 20th century by "extremist regimes" in order to maintain control over their specific society (13). A particularly extreme example is the burning of nearly two million volumes at Bosnia's National and University Library in 1992 in a fire started by Serbian incendiary grenades (Bosmajian 212). The loss of "thousands of rare Muslim and Jewish writings" in what is possibly the largest modern book burning certainly constitutes a cultural crime, if not a crime against humanity (Bosmajian 212). Certainly far less culturally damaging (but more widely reported) has been the burning of copies of J. K. Rowling's *Harry Potter* series of fantasy novels ("Harry Potter"). In large part due to its use of magic (which is conflated with a support for the occult or Satanic), the series has been named the "most challenged books" for 2001–2005 (Clark and Morales). The burning of Winterfell's library in the failed attempt to permanently silence Bran can also be seen as an example of burning books in an attempt to suppress dangerous knowledge that threatens the established order (or the desires of an invader or dictator). While Jaime Lannister's torching of the House Stark library certainly lacked the conscious intention of this Serbian war crime, comparisons with such real-world book burnings demonstrates how this callous act is one in a string of character flaws meant to set Jaime up as a less than sympathetic character in the first novel.

Thankfully, large-scale acts of libricide are mercifully rare, but far smaller acts of violence against books increasingly abound, namely the seemingly random destruction of books that are seen as no longer necessary (often to make room on overcrowded shelves). We've all seen it in our own public or university libraries, and many of us are guilty of retrieving volumes destined for the recycling bin and squirreling them away for some vague future use that often never comes to pass. When it was revealed in 2000 that the British Library, the repository of nearly every book published in Britain since 1662, had begun disposing of books in 1989 which, according to an article in *The Guardian*, "in its judgment, the world is least likely to miss," there was serious blowback from scholars and book aficionados (McKie). In response to the resulting negative publicity, David Bradbury, the Library's director general, explained that the 80,000 volumes that had been disposed of by that time were mainly older editions of now-updated reference volumes and that no British volumes had been destroyed (Milner). While Bradbury argued that there was no reason for the Library to hold on to its 1960-era "Russian government department of transport's vehicle engine emissions survey," some scholar, somewhere, would probably beg to differ (Milner).

Fast-forward to 2008 and the two-part *Doctor Who* serial, "Silence in the Library" and "Forest of the Dead." Here the Doctor and his human companion, Donna Noble, materialize in the 51st century, in the planet-sized complex called "The Library. So big it doesn't need a name. Just a great big *"The"* ("Silence in the Library"). It not only has electronic copies of every book ever written (stored in its index computer) but brand-new paper editions, specially printed for this purpose. However, instead of librarians it has "Courtesy nodes," robotic roving computer terminals with real human faces donated by library benefactors upon their deaths.

The villains in this story are the Vashta Nerada—"piranhas of the air"—who had, a century before, hatched from spores contained in all those books, as the paper had been pulped from the trees of their forest ("Silence in the Library"). The library's index computer had tried to teleport all 4,022 patrons to safety, but realizing that nowhere in the library was safe, the computer instead saved the patrons on its huge hard drive, their physical bodies stored as "an energy signature" ("Forest of the Dead"). Unfortunately the computer had insufficient memory to reconstitute the patrons in the flesh until the archaeologist

River Song sacrifices herself by creating a neural link with the computer. In a central plot twist, it is revealed that the computer, CAL (aka Charlotte Abigail Lux), is actually the consciousness of the youngest daughter of the Library's creator. He had built the facility and "put her living mind inside" after her body died at a tender age, connecting her with "all of human history to pass the time. Any era to live in, any book to read. She loved books more than anything, and he gave her them all" ("Forest of the Dead"). However, it is noted numerous times (and by several characters) that the virtual existence of CAL (and the uploaded patrons) within the computer is only "half a life" ("Forest of the Dead"). But half a life is better than none, at least in the Doctor's mind, as he uploads a digital copy of River's consciousness into CAL after she dies in the reconstruction of the patrons in their true physical form.

I argue that this arc is not only a commentary on the wholesale destruction of books that are no longer deemed necessary or relevant, but also on the current tension between not only paper and electronic books, but physical brick and mortar libraries versus digital libraries. Then there is the strange hybrid of the physical library that only houses electronic books, such as the BiblioTech of San Antonio, Texas, founded in 2013 and proudly billed as "the first all-digital public library in the United States" ("About Us"). In addition to its digital archive, this library loans out e-readers for its patrons who do not have their own electronics.

In a 2002 study Hong, Thong, Wong, and Tam argued that digital libraries (DL) should exert effort into "providing customized interfaces for different users to accommodate their different background knowledge of search domains" (118). Similarly, since Hariri and Norouzi found that navigation and search functionality are the two most highly used criteria in evaluating DL interfaces, it is no wonder that a "DL is only as good as the interface it provides to its users" (699). While this may be true, the courtesy nodes in The Library seem to be a tad extreme, in particular how the face of Mark Chambers was "actualized individually" for Donna Noble "from the many facial aspects saved to our extensive flesh banks. Please enjoy" ("Silence in the Library"). Similarly, one of the most horrific villains of The Walking Dead franchise are the psychotic Whisperers who blend in with zombie herds by wearing the skinned faces of the undead as masks. Arya Stark is visibly unsettled in George R. R. Martin's novel series when she first comes face to face (literally and figuratively) with the Faceless Men's gallery of thousands of skinned human faces. She forces herself to think of them as merely masks or "leather hoods" in order to steel herself as one is attached to her as a disguise (Dance 921). The viewer of Doctor Who is unambiguously meant to be creeped out by these electronic librarians with human faces as well as the notion of a virtual library housing a human mind.

In creating its bookless library, San Antonio was following in the footsteps of another Texas institution, the University of Texas at Austin, who in 2005 transferred nearly all of the 90,000 volumes from the undergraduate library to other collections in the system, focusing instead on "digital learning laboratories" and other spaces where students could work electronically (Blumenthal). But as student Jessica Zaharias opined about the change, "this is a library—it's supposed to have books in it" (Blumenthal). Recall the Doctor's explanation that even in the 51st century the greatest library in the universe has both digital and paper copies of each and every book ever written. Despite the technology of "holovids, direct to brain downloads, fiction mist" human beings still "need the smell, the smell of books" ("Silence in the Library"). While we are increasingly encouraged to "go paperless" in academia, many of us still cling to primitive yet highly portable paper copies of student assignments (and in some cases, even paper gradebooks). When electronic copies of journal articles are retrieved from a database or interlibrary loan they are often printed out, like the patrons of The Library transferred from the less desirable virtual form into a physical and tangible body. Despite the technological advances in e-readers, word processing programs, and electronic course management systems, in many situations it is still easier to highlight or notate texts and grade papers when they are literally on paper.

Studies suggest that the Doctor isn't wrong about our stubborn love for paper books. A 2016 Pew Research Center telephone survey of over 1,500 Americans found that while the percentage of adults who had read an e-book over the prior year had increased from 17% to 28% from 2011 to 2016, readership of print books had only declined slightly from 71% to 65% during the same period (Perrin). While the increasing availability of Open Educational Resources (OER) including e-textbooks undoubtedly saves college students a significant amount of hard-earned money, these same students report that they find it "easier to concentrate on print than on eBooks [sic]" (Baron 214). Similarly, Naomi Baron explains that e-books "generally discourage" important skills and techniques such as rereading, retention (due to a lack of making written annotations), "deep reading," and reading texts of significant length (213). In addition, she offers that e-books make it less likely that a reader will come upon a text unintentionally or develop a "strong emotional involvement" (213). It might not be the smell, but there is undeniably something about real, physical, tangible books that apparently makes them an integral part of many human lives.

In *A Dance with Dragons* the less than scholarly Dolorous Edd Tollett disparages Sam Tarly's bookish ways by opining that "books are dead men talking. Dead men should keep quiet, is what I say. No one wants to hear a dead man's yabber" (Martin 104). But one of the central lessons of the *Song of Ice and Fire* novel series (as well as the adventures of the Doctor) is that Dolorous Edd is dead wrong. Sometimes the wisdom of the departed is the very thing that will assure our survival, whether through the transmission of knowledge, or, as in the extreme case of *The Day After Tomorrow* and cold Welsh winters, the transmission of thermal radiation. It is clear that books and libraries (as well as flesh-and-blood librarians) make our lives richer, and it is only right that we work together to save these precious resources in return. Our culture, our sense of identity, and, in rare cases, our very lives depend on it.

Works Cited

"About Us." *Bexar County Digital Library.* bexarbibliotech.org/about-us.

Baron, Naomi S. *Words Onscreen*. Oxford UP, 2015.

Bittiner, Sally. "6 Reasons Why the Hogwarts Library is the True Hero of the Harry Potter Books." *Oxford University Press Blog,* 12 June 2016, blog.oup.com/2016/06/hogwarts-library-hero-harry-potter.

Blumenthal, Ralph. "College Libraries Set Aside Books in a Digital Age." *The New York Times*, 14 May 2005, www.nytimes.com/2005/05/14/education/college-libraries-set-aside-books-in-a-digital-age.html.

Bosmajian, Haig. *Burning Books*. McFarland, 2006.

Chan, Lois Mai. "The Burning of Books in China, 213 B.C." *The Journal of Library History*, vol. 7, no. 2, 1972, pp. 101–08.

Clark, Larra, and Macey Morales. "Harry Potter Tops List of Most Challenged Books of 21st Century." *American Library Association.* 21 Sept. 2006, ala.org/news/news/pressreleases2006/September2006/harrypottermostchallenge.

Cook, Ariel. "Why Book Burning is Worse Than Flag Burning." *Odyssey*, 18 Apr. 2016, www.theodysseyonline.com/why-book-burning-is-worse-than-flag-burning.

Davis, Nicola. "Not Fade Away… How Robots are Preserving Our Old Newspapers." *The Guardian*, 5 July 2015, theguardian.com/books/2015/jul/05/british-library-digitising-newspapers-boston-spa.

Davis, Sarah S. "My Body is Ready for the Citadel Library." *Book Riot*, 29 June 2016, bookriot.com/my-body-is-ready-for-the-citadel-library.

The Day After Tomorrow. Directed by Roland Emmerich, Twentieth Century Fox, 2004.

"The Dragon and the Wolf." *Game of Thrones*, created by David Benioff and D. B. Weiss, season 7, episode 7, HBO, 27 Aug. 2017.

"Eastwatch." *Game of Thrones*, created by David Benioff and D. B. Weiss, season 7, episode 5, HBO, 13 Aug. 2017.

Erwin, Miles. "Pensioners Burn Books for Warmth." *Metro News*, 5 Jan. 2010, metro.co.uk/2010/01/05/pensioners-burn-books-for-warmth-13123.

"Forest of the Dead." *Doctor Who*, season 4, episode 9, BBC America, 27 June 2008.

Hariri, Nadjla, and Yaghoub Norouzi. "Determining Evaluation Criteria for Digital Libraries' User Interface: A Review." *The Electronic Library*, vol. 29, no. 5, 2011, pp. 691–722, doi.org/10.1108/02640471111177116.

"Harry Potter Books Burned by Polish Priests Alarmed by Magic." *BBC*. 1 April 2019. www.bbc.com/news/world-europe-47771706.

"Headscratchers/*The Day After Tomorrow*." *TvTropes*. tvtropes.org/pmwiki/pmwiki.php/Headscratchers/TheDayAfterTomorrow.

Hickman, Leo. "Why Are They Burning Books in South Wales?" *The Guardian*, 5 Jan. 2010. theguardian.com/money/2010/jan/06/burning-books-wales.

Hong, Weiyin, James Y. L. Thong, Wai-man Wong, and Kar-yan Tam. "Determinants of User Acceptance of Digital Libraries." *Journal of Management Information Systems*, vol. 18, no. 3, 2002, pp. 91–124, doi.org/10.1080/07421222.2002.11045692.

Knuth, Rebecca. *Burning Books and Leveling Libraries*. Praeger, 2006.

Martin, George R. R. *A Clash of Kings*. Bantam Books, 2011.

——. *A Dance with Dragons*. Bantam Books, 2013.

——. *A Feast for Crows*. Bantam Books, 2011.

——. *A Game of Thrones*. Bantam Books, 2011.

——. *A Storm of Swords*. Bantam Books, 2011.

McKie, David. "Library Brought to Book." *The Guardian*, 14 Aug. 2000, theguardian.com/books/2000/aug/14/society.

Milner, Catherine. "British Library Chief Defends Book Purge." *The Telegraph*, 13 Aug. 2000, telegraph.co.uk/news/uknews/1352530/British-Library-chief-defends-book-purge.html.

Milton, John. *Areopagitica: And, Of Education*. Edited by George H. Sabine, Harlan Davidson, 1951.

Naughten, Kaitlin. "The Day After Tomorrow: A Scientific Critique." *ClimateSight*, 26 April 2012, climatesight.org/2012/04/26/the-day-after-tomorrow-a-scientific-critique.

Perrin, Andrew. "Book Reading 2016." *Pew Research Center*, 1 Sept. 2016. pewresearch.org/internet/2016/09/01/book-reading-2016.

"Silence in the Library." *Doctor Who*, season 4, episode 8, BBC America, 20 June 2008.

"Tooth and Claw." *Doctor Who*, season 2, episode 2, BBC America, 6 Oct. 2006.

Vonnegut, Kurt. "Books into Ashes." *New York Times*, 7 Feb. 1982, p. E19.

"The Winds of Winter." *Game of Thrones*, created by David Benioff and D. B. Weiss, season 6, episode 10, HBO, 26 June 2016.

When You Have Read It, It Will Be Destroyed: The Fugitive Archive in Fantasy and Science Fiction

Nicholas Birns

The Fugitive Archive in Fantasy

ARCHIVES ARE BUILT TO ENDURE, but they are also fragile and vulnerable. This essay will explore how a sampling of classic and contemporary fantasy and science fiction novels explore the potentially ephemeral nature of archives.

In *The Dark is Rising* (1973), the second book in Susan Cooper's five-volume fantasy sequence of that name, Will Stanton, an eleven-year-old boy, finds out that he is the youngest and last of the Old Ones, a society stretching across time that exists for the defense of good against evil. As part of his initiation, Will is pulled back in time, to the Middle Ages, to read the Book of Gramarye, a storehouse of all the lore and knowledge the Good has as its disposal in its perilous and desperate efforts. The book cannot be taken forward in time: it is medieval book, part of manuscript culture, and therefore Will, a 1970s product of late print culture, must go back to it. Will is taken back in time, although in the same space of the Buckinghamshire in which the book is set in its own present day. Will is to have only one encounter with the book, says Merriman Lyon, a senior figure among the Old Ones (in fact, as his name indicates, he is Merlin) and Will's chief mentor. Merriman tells Will that after he has read it, "it will be destroyed" (102). Will is destined to be the last of the Old Ones, so there will be no more use for the book afterwards.

Thus, Will's reading of the Book of Gramarye is at once one of ultimate meaning but also of urgent rapidity. It is an experience that pulls him out of ordinary time: "So much went into him from its pages that the reading might have taken a year; yet so totally did it absorb his mind that before he came to an end he felt it had only that moment begun" (104). Will is at a transition-point between the medieval and the modern, in both at once; he is also, in his own life, at a transition point between boy and man, child and adult. Though Will is young for this highly unusual rite of passage from boy to the ultimate responsibility of being an Old One, for the reader, part of the thrill of Will's time with the Book of Gramarye is an awareness of their own transition into adulthood. For Will, reading the book is a rite of passage; reading the book quickly and for one time only indicates how sudden and determinative such a rite of passage is. And, aptly enough, for Will the experience of reading the Book of Gramarye is one of exuberance—he knows all there is to know, all that he might know in the future or might have wanted to know in the past, but also the experience is melancholy. The exuberant high of one moment of reading is offset by melancholy in another: "Will closed the book, slowly, and sat staring at nothing. He felt as though he had lived for a hundred years. To know so much now, to be able to do so many things; it should have excited him, but he felt weighed down [...]" (108). The key here is that it is not the sheer amount of knowledge only, or the responsibility that knowledge entails, but the rapidity with which Will has had to gain it, a rapidity which has the force of revelation, but also the urgency of pressure.

Indeed, the book is destroyed in an apocalyptic way by the spell which Merriman has woven, destroyed not just because Will no longer needs it, but because otherwise Hawkin, the human from medieval England Merriman has used in an inevitably exploitative manner for the purpose of Good, will betray it to Evil. And yet, beside this apocalyptic note, there is also the simple melancholy of reading, of having used a text up and gleaned its knowledge. The text of the Book of Gramarye, as Will reads it, ends with this quatrain:

> I have plundered the fern
> Through all secrets I spie;
> Old Math ap Mathonwy
> Knew no more than I. (Cooper 108)

Reading the book is like picking a fern. Aesthetic beauty is gained, but a kind of material beauty is destroyed. The disappearance of the material book brings mastery, but there is also a sense of elegy that the physical Book of Gramarye will itself be no more, concomitant with the thrill of Will having managed to be the last to read so rare a book. Notably, the quatrain itself, although of impeccable Celtic pedigree—it is attributed to the bard Taliesin, and Math ap Mathonwy is a figure in the *Mabinogion*—is in fact a quote form Robert Graves's *The White Goddess*. Though, as Catherine Butler notes, the Book of Gramarye is "clearly more than a poetry anthology" (227), it is striking that its conclusion is a quote from an individual author living at the time Cooper wrote the novel, as if the textual situation of the Book of Grammarye is like Will Stanton's own—splayed in time, between the medieval and the twentieth century, but impossible to see in the past. Dimitra Fimi has recently castigated Cooper's sequence for "outdated scholarship" (250) as it relates to Celtic myth, but if the goal is less a replenishment from a mythic source than an awareness of the fugitive status of the archive, Cooper's sourcing may not seem so scattershot. Analogously, it is not just the content of the book that means Will must travel back in time to read it, but its mode of transmission. In the twentieth century, the Book of Gramarye could be copied, and in the twenty-first all Will would need is a camera phone and the Book of Gramarye would be immortalized in a thousand JPEGs. It is not just the archive that Will reads but the way he reads it that make it medieval.

In the Middle Ages, books were scarce, and, though our idealized image of cloistered monks is that they have all the time they need to sequester themselves and immerse themselves in learning, often reading itself was hurried and fugitive. Consider this example from the sixth century:

> Truly a hard command and imposed by one who seems unwilling to realize the burden of the task. Nor do you note this, that my utterance is too slight to fill so magnificent a trumpet of speech as his. But above every burden is the fact that I have no access to his books that I may follow his thought. Still—and let me lie not—I have in times past read the books a second time by his steward's loan for a three days' reading. The words I recall not, but the sense and the deeds related I think I retain entire. (Mierow 51)

The writer is Jordanes, at the beginning of his *Getica*. The *Getica* is a history of the Goths, the people whose migrations made such an impact upon the Roman Empire from the fourth to sixth centuries, and the writer is a man of Gothic descent who has become resident in, and loyal to, the imperial capital of Constantinople. Jordanes bases his history on the far larger work of Cassiodorus, a more renowned writer of whom Jordanes's history is an epitome and, in effect, an abridgement. Yet Jordanes does not have an ideal relationship to his source. He has read it once, at, it is implied, a remove reasonably remote, and then had only three days with it, in his second reading, to refresh his memory.

In the age of late print culture of which Will Stanton, a 1970s boy, was a member, and in the age of digital culture in which many of us are now natives or near-natives, we see the art of reading, and especially of archival research, as close reading, scrupulous scrutiny of the *ipsissima verba*. Medieval writers like Jordanes did not have that luxury. Manuscripts were rare, arduous and time-consuming to copy by hand, and not liberally distributed. People in the situation of Jordanes were compelled to memorize as much as they could. Thus, as Mary Carruthers has pointed out, the *ars memoriae* is not just a tactical tool in that era but an essential imaginative framework.

Like Will Stanton, Jordanes had to read quickly and yet discerningly, for his future depended upon it. Will's memory-dependent future is as a doer of deeds, as knowledge of the Book of Gramarye will help him turn the tide against the rising dark. Jordanes's memory-dependent future is as an author, and he rests his reputation as a chronicler upon knowledge of this fugitive text, no longer available to him, as much as Will does his as a wielder of white magic. Jordanes's tales may seem less important in the cosmic scale; but for a historian, reliability matters as much as esoteric knowledge does to a wizard. The general neo-medieval cast of fantasy means that the reading conditions of Jordanes will have much in common with those of Will Stanton. Unless a fantasy is set totally within the parameters of modern print culture (as is true of J. K. Rowling's *Harry Potter* books, Susanna Clarke's *Jonathan Strange & Mr Norrell*, and, interestingly enough, considering their very different ideological vantage-point, of China Miéville's Bas-Lag novels), the default assumption of most fantasy worlds is that written knowledge is transmittable by manuscript only. Indeed, one might hazard that a distinction between worlds where information is hard to transmit and worlds where information is easy to transmit is very nearly a generic distinction between fantasy and science fiction as such. Thus, Jordanes's speed-reading is, in mode, characteristic of what might be asked of a fantasy character such as Will Stanton.

But there is a second connection between Jordanes's act of reading and fantasy fiction: the fact that the effective founder of modern fantasy, J. R. R. Tolkien, was an eminent medievalist scholar and, as an Anglo-Saxonist, would have known Jordanes (who talks early on about the history and settlement of Britain) as an author. T. A. Shippey has pointed out that the Goths and the Gothic language were highly influential on Tolkien's fictional and linguistic heterocosm (16–17), Sandra Bailey Straubhaar has said it is likely Tolkien read Jordanes, and Miryam Librán Moreno has conjectured some more specific connections between Tolkien and Jordanes. Yet in the very possibility that Tolkien read Jordanes is the difference between Tolkien's situation, as a modern reader with access to the finest print libraries, and Jordanes's, as a scholar necessarily on the sly and on the run. Tolkien had all the hours of a long life to do research, and this is perhaps reflected in the key scene in which an archive figures in *The Lord of the Rings*, Gandalf's research into the archives of Gondor to find out just what happened to the Ring after Isildur took it from the hand of Sauron. The hunt for the Ring is, on the side of the Good, largely an archival hunt, a process of identifying the Ring Frodo Baggins possesses as that made by Sauron; and indeed,

Gandalf and Saruman's exchanges about the Ring have an air of donnish rivalry of the sort with which Tolkien was thoroughly familiar with in his professional capacity. As David Oberhelman points out, the "scrolls and documents of Men" stored in the archives of Minas Tirith are "seldom used" (162). When Gandalf goes to Minas Tirith and reads the scrolls, he finds Denethor, the Lord Steward of that city, dismissing his interest as one of mere scholarly minutiae:

> 'If indeed you look only, as you say, for records of ancient days, and the beginnings of the City, read on!' he said. 'For to me what was is less dark than what is to come, and that is my care. But unless you have more skill even than Saruman, who has studied here long, you will find naught that is not well known to me, who am master of the lore of this City.'
>
> So said Denethor. And yet there lie in his hoards many records that few now even of the lore-masters now can read, for their scripts and tongues have become dark to later men. (Tolkien II.2.252)

Archives in any fantasy world are going to be obscured, as their use in the plot depends on their providing information previous unknown on a mass scale. In addition, the overt power of Evil in most fantasy worlds mean that archives are going to, at worst, be in danger of erasure or misappropriation, or at best, be under the sway of the incuriosity shown by Denethor. But, as compared to Will Stanton's brief flash of presence in the archive, Gandalf takes many years to conduct research into Ring-lore; indeed, one of the most fascinating aspects of the hunt for the Ring is how long, in represented time, it takes: almost twenty years following Bilbo's disappearance from the Shire. That is not to say that there is no time pressure, as every year that passes increases the chances the Enemy will find out the whereabouts of the Ring, and Gandalf's search definitely has an element of hurry. Still, the process here seems more leisurely, and, even if the archives Gandalf seeks are discounted in terms of their importance, his perusal of them is not obstructed — indeed enabled by the society's very sense of their triviality and superfluity.

George R. R. Martin's fantasy sequence *A Song of Ice and Fire*, considered by many the contemporary successor to Tolkien, takes, in its most notable archive scene so far, perhaps a middle position between the fugitive hurry of Will Stanton and the more prolonged research of Gandalf. Eddard Stark, trying to find out why his predecessor as Hand to King Robert I Baratheon, Jon Arryn, had been murdered, finds a book by Maester Malleon (the maesters are the men of learning in Martin's world) about the lineages and histories of the great houses of the Seven Kingdoms. Through painstaking and somewhat laborious research —

Ned Stark is not a maester nor, particularly, a reader or intellectual—Stark finds out the secrets the book contains. The black-haired King Robert and his golden-haired queen, Cersei Lannister, have three blonde children. Stark finds Malleon recording two previous marriages between Lannisters and Baratheons yielding "a large and lusty boy born with a full head of black hair," and then "three daughters and a son, each black-haired" (469). Thus, Stark realizes that the ostensible children of Robert and Cersei must not be Robert's, as their hair color broke with the genetic pattern.

But the process of finding this out is hurried, must be kept secret from the Lannisters and their allies, and must not be liberally shared. Notably, though Ned Stark finds out the truth, he is not totally able to put the truth in its full picture or comprehend its relationship to other truths including the secrets he himself keeps. He is not a magician like Gandalf or even the young Will. Interestingly, though, as with Gandalf, we are told the archival research only in retrospect. Gandalf relates his manuscript foraging in the Gondorian archives much later as he is testifying to the Council of Elrond. The reader only hears of the result of Ned Stark's researches when he himself confronts Cersei with them. In Tolkien and Martin, archival research is supplementary and told in flashback. In Cooper, though, it is at the center of the action, the key element in the fashioning and transfiguration of the hero. In all cases, though, archives and research into them are, as Jordanes found too in his own day, fugitive.

To go back to Dimitri Fimi's castigation of Cooper for not only being outdated in her sourcing but overly stereotypical and organicist and vulnerable to "popular clichés" (250) in her reading of Celtic mythology, it is interesting that this problem arises in Jordanes as well, or at least in our latter-day reception of him. As Walter Goffart has pointed out, Jordanes was misread as somebody extolling the inherent virtue of the Gothic, and therefore Germanic race; even though, as Goffart points out, his history ends with a hope of a Gothic-Roman synthesis. In both the cases of Cooper's perhaps too-idealized Celticity and Jordanes's misinterpreted Germanic afflatus, the fugitive nature of the archival materials operates as an antidote. Michael Drout comments that Cooper's preference for order and hierarchy is "profoundly conservative" (244), yet the fount of this social order cannot, unlike most hierarchical sacred texts, be either promulgated as propaganda or hoarded as a permanent textual reserve. In both Cooper and Jordanes, the fugitive nature of the archive is a bar against placing too much credence in history and the chimerical consolations it may have to offer us. As Oberhelman points out, the archive is a place where the written, and the vulnerability and fallibility of its textual traces, are more important than the bardic certainty of "oral culture" (155). The more fleeting our encounter with the book, the less ideological hold the book may have over us.

The Fugitive Archive in Science Fiction

In fantasy worlds, the archive is always in the past of a world that the readers themselves do not know, as we only have access to the past of a fantasy world through its iteration in its projected present. Even in a book that takes place in a world close to our own, such as Susanna Clarke's alternate-Regency England, the revelation that the Raven King, John Uskglass, ruled the northern half of England as a separate magical kingdom from the Norman Conquest to the Renaissance, presents us with a past we never knew. In science fiction, the situation is different, as in a future world the archive is nearly always our own knowledge. As Joseph Hurtgen has written, authors of near-future science fiction explore such themes as "the corporate use of changed cultural archives to manipulate people" (56). Hurtgen points out that Ray Bradbury, in *Fahrenheit 451*, depicts "archival erasure" (56)—the banning of books in favor of faux-solitary televisual media that in fact enforce social conformity. With printed books banned, their ephemeral and severely impinged-upon availability becomes a model for resistance and memorization of books as a subversive gesture. Guy Montag's memorization of parts of the Biblical book of Ecclesiastes (Qoheleth) is significant not just because he has managed to make mnemonically permanent a necessarily evanescent encounter with the text, but because the wisdom of the text itself lauds the fleeting and evanescent, is resistant to hard-and-fast, overly anchored truths. Although Montag seeks resistance against authority rather than the consolatory, revivifying authority at least ambiguously sought by Jordanes and by Will Stanton in Susan Cooper's novel, the emphasis on the combination of the fleetingly encountered and transformative wisdom within the archive is similar.

Yet all the books mentioned in *Fahrenheit 451* are books that the reader of the novel in its publication year of 1953 might have known. So the thought of their loss in a hypothetical future ends up privileging their meaning for the present. Thus what in both Jordanes's chronicle of hazy migrations in the Gothic past and Will Stanton's momentary glimpse of the archive of Gramarye are things that the reader by definition does not know, in science fiction the fleeting archive is, precisely, us. We feel more thrill at its preservation and rediscovery, more peril at its disregard and attempted erasure, but typically the near-future science-fiction archive does not represent objects beyond our cognitive grasp. If Bradbury had invented a text produced between 1953 and the action's probable date of a then-future 1999, then that text would be both perishable in the lens of the depicted society and an object of mystery in our own. In Frank Herbert's *Dune* novels, set in the relatively far future, the Orange Catholic Bible, a future hybrid of various current terrestrial devotional texts, is presented as the basis for the spirituality of the books' interplanetary diaspora; this is not a text the reader actually sees or knows, but which is merely presented in snippets, representative or not we cannot tell, appended or affixed to sections of the books. Absent positing this kind of future-intermediate text, though, the archive of science fiction is an archive that to the reader of science fiction is not at all mysterious. There can admittedly be variants of this. Hurtgen, in discussing the near-future work of Neal Stephenson and William Gibson, examines how earlier forms of technology that might have seen, in Bradbury's day, as dangers to the archive are in these books engrafted or incorporated into it. (These books make it clear how much Susan Cooper's Will Stanton exists in late print culture, even though just a few chronological years away from a widely available digital culture). In Bernard Beckett's *Genesis*, real-world events of the early twenty-first century lead to the made-up story of Adam Forde, a human being who rebels against conformism; his story is presented as part of the archive, a backstory to what turns out to be the robotic elimination of all human life and attempted obliteration of humanoid affect. But the fundamental formula remains the same: occultation of the archive in the near-future, availability of the same archive in our own minds.

Some science fiction narratives, though, contain both elements. I will examine a classic American male author and two contemporary Latin American women authors to show how this can be. In Isaac Asimov's original *Foundation* trilogy, there are two different archival hunts. One is for the origin of the human species, in the far-future world of a declining Galactic Empire. In one of the opening episodes, the Imperial chancellor, Lord Dorwin, also operates as an amateur archaeologist, speculating whether the origin of the human species took place on Alpha Centauri, "Sol" or "61 Cygni" (Asimov 56). Whereas even the learned Lord is open to conjecture on this point, we, the reader, have a sense of dramatic irony, as we know what the origin planet, and as of this date sole planet, of humanity is. Indeed, if in fantasy the fugitive archive can radicalize fundamentally conservative universes such as in Cooper, in science fiction it has quite the reverse effect, as knowing that the answer is Sol gives us a sense of cognitive control in a universe otherwise filled with, to use Darko Suvin's well-known term, cognitive estrangement.

But later on in the Foundation trilogy, Asimov gives us an example of an archive we cannot control. The entire action of the Foundation series revolves around two Foundations set up to preserve knowledge during an era of galactic decline. The First Foundation is well-known to be located on Terminus, and is a very obvious participant in much of the action. But the whereabouts of the Second Foundation are unknown. When the First Foundation is conquered by the Mule, a megalomaniacal mutant, the location of the Second Foundation becomes an urgent need. The conquered Foundation's leading scientist, Ebling Mis, begins a frantic search through the archives of the deserted library of the fallen Empire's ruined capital planet in order to find the answer. Aided by a young couple, Bayta and Toran Darell, and a pitiable clown, Magnifico, Ebling Mis finds the secret. But, before he can reveal it, Bayta kills him—because it turns out Magnifico is the mutant dictator in disguise, and if Mis had lived he would have revealed the secret to just who he had not wanted to give it up to.

But it is not just Mis who does not find out the object of his archival research. We, the reader, are denied it as well (at least until the final book of the trilogy) and this supplies a moment of transcendence, disorientation, and cognitive estrangement far more like what happens with the Book of Gramarye than with Ecclesiastes in *Fahrenheit 451*. We experience the thrill of archival evanescent not-knowing. Part of this may well be because Asimov based the concept of the Foundation series on Gibbon's *Decline and Fall of the Roman Empire*, which touches on the half-accessible early history of the Celtic and Germanic peoples, and therefore possesses that same fugitive sense of an archive occulted from the archive that we know, projected by Asimov into the far future and not the dead past.

Dominican writer Rita Indiana (who also writes as Rita Indiana Hernández) and Argentine author Pola Oloixarac both set their works in a near-future world much closer to our own than Asimov's Galactic far-future. In Oloixarac's *Savage Theory*, Rosa Ostreech—a narrator who manifests herself on two levels and under two different names, being "Kamtchowsky" in the strand of the novel set in the past—is a researcher in the near-future. Ostreech is obsessed with her elderly professor, August Roxler, who himself is obsessed with a long-dead Dutch anthropologist, Johan Van Vliet. Van Vliet had proposed a theory of "egoic transmission" which claims that our cells store an ancestral memory of *homo sapiens* being once preyed upon by wild animals. Thus the search for the archive—Rosa's obsession with Rozler, Rozler's with Van Vliet—is also a search for the epistemically inaccessible, that which precisely because it is conjectural and unknowable provides a sublime object. "Formal records, chronicles, obituaries—Van Vliet held them all in high esteem, believing each to be part of a single unifying Act" (179). His diary was "dense with bibliographic scribbles" that, given "how casually" the references were introduced, he must have memorized "by heart" (180). The remembrance of what is conjectural, made-up, or just plain false presents a different sort of archival thrill than retrieving data that are important to use in our world but lost in a nightmarish science-fiction future.

Rita Indiana's *Tentacle* is set in the mid twenty-first century after a devastating ecocatastrophe has destroyed much of the Malecón in Santo Domingo and, even worse, made the Caribbean devoid of life. A transgender man, Acilde, is sent back in time by a wise Santeria practitioner, and with the tacit knowledge of the evil president Said Bona, in order to avert the catastrophe. Acilde, in other words, originates in a near-future mid-twenty-first century, and is set back to a historic early twenty-first century that the reader already knows. Here, he meets Argenis, an art dealer who travels back to a far earlier time, of the Caribbean in the early modern era of colonization. (This not only has political and racial valences, but comes tantalizingly close to a triptych of early print culture/late print culture/digital culture). Much like Asimov's galactic future that is also the early Middle Ages, Indiana's tripartite time-travel tableau allows the future to both mirror the past and question the present. But the twist is that Acilde, having gone back in time to in effect, play the role of Giorgio Maricucci, finds he enjoys that role (the role more than the gender, since he had already transitioned in the future time). Acilde ends up "becoming" Giorgio, forgetting the identity of Acilde, and leaving it up in the air whether the ecological crisis is averted or reversed. Here, the future becomes the fugitive archive, and the present to which Giorgio 'escapes' is somewhat like Will Stanton's present in Cooper's novels, if he had not the disruptive knowledge of Gramarye. In other words, science fiction can make the future an archive in a way that fantasy does with the past, although admittedly here the fantastic element of time travel is present.

It is when science fiction posits other archives than merely the knowledge we in the present assume that archival plots within the genre become most interesting, approaching the way fantasy creates a spectra of "fabled storehouses of knowledge" which can become the "stuff of legend" because of the peril of them becoming "forever lost" (Oberhelman 157). The fugitive archive makes clear in its evanescence, the value that archives have—in worlds present, future, or fantastic.

Works Cited

Asimov, Isaac. *The Foundation Trilogy*. 1951–1953. Heinemann, 1983.

Beckett, Bernard. *Genesis*. 2006. Text, 2011.

Bradbury, Ray. *Fahrenheit 451*. 1953. Harper Voyager, 2018.

Butler, Catherine. *Four British Fantasists: Place and Culture in The Children's Fantasy of Penelope Lively, Alan Garner, Diana Wynne Jones, and Susan Cooper*. Scarecrow Press, 2006.

Carruthers, Mary. *The Book of Memory: A Study of Memory in Medieval Culture*. 2nd ed., Cambridge UP, 2008.

Cooper, Susan. *The Dark Is Rising*. McElderry, 1973.

Drout, Michael D. C. "Reading the Signs of Light: Anglo Saxonism, Education and Obedience in Susan Cooper's *The Dark Is Rising*." *The Lion and the Unicorn*, vol. 21, no. 2, 1997, pp. 230–50.

Fimi, Dimitra. *Celtic Myth in Contemporary Children's Literature: Idealization, Identity, Ideology*. Palgrave Macmillan, 2017.

Goffart, Walter. *The Narrators of Barbarian History: AD 551–800*. Princeton UP, 1988.

Graves, Robert. *The White Goddess*. Faber and Faber, 1948.

Indiana, Rita. *Tentacle*. Translated by Achy Obejas, And Other Stories, 2018.

Hurtgen, Joseph. *The Archive Incarnate: The Embodiment and Transmission of Knowledge in Science Fiction*. McFarland, 2018.

Jordanes. *The Gothic History of Jordanes, in English Version*. Translated and edited by C. C. Mierow, Princeton UP, 1915.

Librán Moreno, Miryam. "J. R. R. Tolkien and Jordanes. Some Resemblances in Spiritual Outlook." *Littera Aperta*, vol. 1, no. 1, Cultural Association Littera Aperta, Dec. 2013, pp. 64–76, doi.org/10.21071/ltap.v1i1.10817.

Martin, George R. R. *A Game of Thrones*. Harper Voyager, 2011.

Oberhelman, David D. "A Brief History of Libraries in Middle-earth: Manuscript and Book Repositories in Tolkien's Legendarium." *Loremasters and Libraries in Fantasy and Science Fiction: A Gedenkschrift for David Oberhelman*, edited by Jason Fisher and Janet Brennan Croft, Mythopoeic Press, 2022, pp. 155–65. Originally published in *Truths Breathed Through Silver: The Inklings' Moral and Mythopoeic Legacy*, edited by Jonathan B.

Himes, with Joe R. Christopher and Salwa Khoddam, Cambridge Scholars, 2008, pp. 81–92.

Oloixarac, Pola. *Savage Theories.* Translated by Roy Kesey, Soho Press, 2018.

Shippey, T. A. *The Road to Middle-earth.* Allen and Unwin, 1982.

Suvin, Darko. *Metamorphoses of Science Fiction: On the Poetics and History of a Literary Genre.* Yale UP, 1979.

Straubhaar, Sandra Ballie. "Jordanes." *J. R. R Tolkien Encyclopedia: Scholarship and Critical Assessment,* edited by Michael Drout, et al., Routledge, 2006, pp. 311–13.

Tolkien, J. R. R. *The Lord of the Rings.* 50th Anniversary Edition, Houghton Mifflin, 2004.

Books Within Books in Fantasy and Science Fiction: "You are the Dreamer and the Dream"

Phillip Fitzsimmons

T HIS CHAPTER DISCUSSES BOOKS that exist only within works of science fiction and fantasy—what the "List of Fictional Books" on Wikipedia calls a "fictional book" and what Claire Fallon calls "invented books" in her article for the *Huffpost* website, "Fictional Books Within Books We Wish Were Real."[1] When done well, these books can act as keystones[2] to the structure of both the stories and the worlds in which they appear. Some books become elements of their stories and imaginative worlds comparable to other story-telling elements such as character development, plot, dialogue, or scene. An interesting commonality of the "invented books" mentioned above is that they have heroes who are each engaged with books that describe the worlds in which the heroes are living and the books exist.

Examples include the works of H. P. Lovecraft, such as the novella *The Dunwich Horror* [*Dunwich*] in which the contents of the *Necronomicon* are studied and quoted by both sorcerers and heroes, the former to destroy the world and the latter fighting to protect it. In *The Man in the High Castle* [*High Castle*] by Philip K. Dick, the reader sees a world in which the Axis powers won World War II and Japan occupies the West Coast while Germany occupies the East Coast of the United States. In this world there is a popular underground novel titled *The Grasshopper Lies Heavy* that is an alternative history in which the Allies

---

[1] For alternatives to the *Wikipedia* page "List of Fictional Books," George A. Kennedy in Chapter 1 *An Overview of Fictional Fiction* expresses his indebtedness to www.invisiblelibrary.com, which cites "Over one thousand imaginary writers and titles" (Kennedy 18). The page describes itself as "a collection of books that only appear in other books. Within the library's catalog you will find imaginary books, pseudobiblia, artifictions, fabled tomes, libris phantastica, and all manner of books unwritten, unread, unpublished, and unfound." Another source for such books is a contemporary blog, *The Invisible Library*.

[2] It is appropriate to credit Verlyn Flieger as the inspiration for this use of the keystone and arch metaphor, which she used to describe J. R. R. Tolkien as the keystone supporting the contradictions in his written and spoken words in her keynote address "The Arch and the Keystone" at Mythcon 50, now published in *Mythlore* #135.

won the war, and, as with many other Philip K. Dick stories, characters slip between realities.

Finally, there are the novellas of the 1950s story-character and aspiring science fiction writer Benny Russell, who first appears in the *Star Trek: Deep Space Nine* [*DS9*] television episode "Far Beyond the Stars" ["Beyond"]. Russell writes stories about his imaginative creation, Captain Benjamin Sisko, who commands the space station Deep Space Nine. In the episode Russell is confused by his experience of being the alter-ego of his creation Sisko throughout an extended ordeal of racism, assault, and professional disappointment. He asks a street preacher about his own identity, and the answer he receives is, "You are the dreamer and the dream" ("Beyond"). In the frame story of the episode, when Benjamin Sisko is revived from a seizure, he is equally disturbed by the thought that he, Benjamin Sisko, a Star Fleet officer and commander of the space station, could be the product of an author's imagination. Both items, "invented books" and heroes living within the worlds they have dreamed about, satisfy J. R. R. Tolkien's standards of good fantasy writing as described in his essay "On Fairy-stories." His standard requires that the writer make ideas that are equivalent to a phrase, such as "the green sun," go beyond being a mere imaginary concept but instead develop into an integral part of a world that is so consistent that it inspires "secondary belief" within the reader. Tolkien called this "a kind of elvish craft" and wrote that "when [such difficult tasks] are attempted and in any degree accomplished then we have a rare achievement of Art: indeed narrative art, story-making in its primary and most potent mode" (61). This chapter argues that the "invented books" described above meet Tolkien's high standard for good fantasy writing in the stories in which they reside and the worlds they create.

It is necessary to include a word about George A. Kennedy's academic work *Fictitious Authors and Imaginary Novels in French, English, and American Fiction from the 18th to the Start of the 21st Century* [*Authors*], which is both an erudite and witty treatment of imaginary authors and their "invented books." Kennedy compares earlier examples with contemporary uses of stories within stories, which were:

> set in a narrative framework that supplies an occasion for their being told. The imaginary work [...] allegedly taken from a *printed* source [...] is a development in a different direction, in that the larger narrative framework into which it is inserted is the more important part of the book, to whose plot, characterization, theme, or meaning in the built-in story may contribute in some way. (6)

He goes on to explain that the "built-in fiction" of today is "realistic," often functions as satire, and raises questions about the primary narrative voice or reality of the work (1–7). Kennedy delves much more deeply into the topic of "built-in fiction," what this chapter refers to as "invented books," than is appropriate here. The authors described in this study are not addressed in Kennedy's book, but this quotation still sets up the question of what the function of "invented books" are for H. P. Lovecraft, Phillip K. Dick, and the writers of *Deep Space Nine*. For example, in Lovecraft, there was always an underlying puckish humor in his enumeration of obscure occult authors and titles in his stories, though I would not say that it was intended as satire or blatant humor, or any of the other functions described by Kennedy. Any of these functions would have distracted the reader from the frightful seriousness and experience of personal endangerment for the characters in the world Lovecraft created. Any such distraction from the horror and impending doom that his stories present would have made Tolkien's "secondary belief" impossible for the reader.

The use of "invented books" in real-world novels is a story-telling device used for a variety of purposes;[3] as Kennedy states above, they also represent degrees of significance within their story-worlds and are found in a variety of genres of fiction. The following list of titles represents this variety. Some are works in which the "invented books" are integral to their stories and their worlds, while others are mentioned in passing by narrators but are not necessary to the story or world in which they reside. Examples of works that are integral to their story-worlds include: Italo Calvino's *If on a Winter's Night a Traveler* (magical realism); Arthur Conan Doyle's Sherlock Holmes stories (mystery, presented as case studies written by the character Dr. John H. Watson); William S. Burroughs's *The Ticket That Exploded* (experimental fiction, composed using the cut-up technique); Samuel R. Delany's *Dhalgren* (experimental science fiction, with a circular text that concludes where the novel began); Douglas Adams's *The Hitchhiker's Guide to the Galaxy* (humorous science fiction); Herman Hesse's *The Glass Bead Game: Magister Ludi* (futuristic traditional fiction, an invented biography and bildungsroman of the hero); Frank Herbert's *Dune* books (science fiction space opera, contains epigraphs from other works of the narrator, Princess Irulan); Adam Rex's *The True Meaning of Smekday* (YA science fiction, an invented book-length school essay contest entry including a comic book created by the heroine); and, finally, J. R. R. Tolkien's principal works (fantasy, represented in the fictive Red Book of Westmarch).

---

[3] See also Fisher in this volume.

In contrast, other novels contain "invented books" that are only mentioned in passing. They are props needed for the plot and add texture to the story-world but do not contribute as a keystone to the stories or to the worlds in which they exist. Examples include Owen Barfield's *Excerpta* in *The Silver Trumpet*: C. S. Lewis's *Is Man a Myth?*, *Nymphs and Their Ways*, and other titles on Mr. Tumnus's bookshelf in *The Lion, the Witch and the Wardrobe*; and Arthur Conan Doyle's many titles of books written by Sherlock Holmes on topics of interest to crime investigators, especially *On the Study of Tobaccos and their Ashes*, mentioned throughout the Holmes canon.

As stated above, "invented books" found in real-world novels vary in function and significance to their story-worlds. H. P. Lovecraft, Philip K. Dick, and *Deep Space Nine* offer examples of such outstanding uses of the "invented book" and "the dreamer being the dream" tropes in 20th-century science fiction and fantasy that the stories do engender "secondary belief" in their readers. Together, these three examples represent a century's use of these devices in science fiction and fantasy: H. P. Lovecraft, the early part of the century (1890–1937); Philip K. Dick, the middle (1928–1982); and *Deep Space Nine*, the end (1993–1999). It should be noted that *Deep Space Nine* originally presented its stories through the media of television, and, in doing so, it represents a later stage in the evolution of storytelling technology, from the early days of pulp magazines to the present time of multi-media fantasy and science fiction productions.

H. P. Lovecraft

A search for the *Necronomicon* in the *Complete Collection of H. P. Lovecraft* [*Lovecraft*] returns sixty-nine instances of the title from throughout his canon, and the *Necronomicon* is only one of nineteen invented book titles referenced throughout his works according to the "List of Fictional Books" on Wikipedia. A reading of Lovecraft reveals many functions of having his characters refer to and quote from the *Necronomicon* in his stories. Within the story-world, the characters reading the *Necronomicon* are either innocent scholars interested in the occult, or they are sorcerers intent upon personal power, immortality, or the destruction of the world. Two of Lovecraft's stories that contain both heroic and villainous scholars and who consult and recite from the *Necronomicon* are *The Dunwich Horror* (1929) and "The Thing on the Doorstep" ["Doorstep"] (1937).

The Dunwich Horror is the story of the villain Wilbur Whateley, born of an unknown father in the country out near Dunwich village,

Massachusetts. He is raised and educated by his grandfather who has the ambition that his grandson will call evil creatures into their dimension to destroy the world. The boy grows quickly and becomes known as the Wizard Whateley. A description of the ancient books, course of study, and mysterious preparations for the developing magic of young Wilbur Whateley make up the beginning of the story. Lovecraft's skill in describing these preparations gives depth and realism to the world of his story. The sixteen-year-old Wilbur Whateley's purpose is to discover and use the magical "formula or incantation containing the frightful name *Yog Sothoth*" (*Dunwich* 111) found in the *Necronomicon* to call forth monstrous creatures from another dimension for the destruction of humanity.

His purpose comes to the attention of Dr. Henry Armitage of the Miskatonic University Library, when Wilbur Whateley visits the library to consult its Latin copy of the *Necronomicon* to compare it with his grandfather's imperfect English translation. Armitage comes to understand Whateley's purpose when he sees which passages the young scholar consults. The librarian refuses Whateley's request to allow him to take the book home for consultation in the work of perfecting his occult experimentations. At that point, Armitage realizes that much more is at stake and that he is not seeing mere rustic superstition. Lovecraft outlines the hero's actions:

> (His t)alks with several students of archaic lore in Boston, and letters to many others elsewhere, gave him a growing amazement which passed slowly through varied degrees of alarm to a state of really acute spiritual fear. As the summer drew on he felt dimly that something ought to be done about the lurking terrors of the upper Miskatonic valley, and about the monstrous being known to the human world as Wilbur Whateley. (113)

By this time there are reports of a destructive invisible monster lurking in the Dunwich region. The first phase of the incident described by the narrator as the "Dunwich Horror" occurred during the night several weeks after Wilbur Whateley's visit to the Miskatonic University Library. Whateley is killed by a guard dog while attempting to steal the *Necronomicon* from the library. The dying Wilbur Whateley is described as follows:

> The thing that lay half-bent on its side in a foetid pool of greenish-yellow ichor and tarry stickiness was [...] [a]bove the waist [...] semi-anthropomorphic [...]. Below the waist, though, [...] all human resemblance left off and [...] from the abdomen a score of long greenish-grey tentacles with red sucking mouths protruded limply [...]. Their arrangement was odd, and seemed to follow the

symmetries of some cosmic geometry unknown to earth or the solar system. (111–15)

Wilbur Whateley dies reciting the *Necronomicon*: "These fragments, as Armitage recalls them, ran something like *'N'gai, n'gha'ghaa, bugg-shoggog, y'hah; Yog-Sothoth, Yog-Sothoth...'* They trailed off into nothingness as the whippoorwills shrieked in rhythmical crescendos of unholy anticipation" (115).

The whippoorwills are psychopomps excited as they prepare to carry off Wilbur Whateley's soul, while the recitations from the book have the same feel as Gandalf's reading from the One Ring at the beginning of *The Fellowship of the Ring*. In this passage, he explains that, "The letters are Elvish, of an ancient mode, but the language is that of Mordor, which I will not utter here" (I.2.50). Gandalf's comment leaves the sound of the language of Mordor to the imagination of the reader (until it is later recited in the original Black Speech in Rivendell), which would probably have a family resemblance to the last death recitations of the Wizard Whateley from the floor of the Miskatonic University Library. The ritual recitation in Lovecraft's story and the description of the language of Mordor in Tolkien's novel contribute to the depth of the world-building of their stories. That depth arises from the sense engendered in the reader that the words originate from a real and living people, language, and literature, resulting in "secondary belief" in the story-world.

After the death of Wilbur Whateley, law enforcement authorities find a ledger in his house written in an unknown syllabary and language. Armitage's research at this point focuses upon cracking the code of the symbols and discovering in what language the ledger is written so that he can understand the plans of the late Wilbur Whateley. When he cracks the code of the ledger, he finds it to be encrypted English. He assembles a study group of three students of folklore to do bibliographic and chemical research. They help him to plan, prepare, and carry out a response to the newly discovered threat Wilbur Whateley has unleashed. After the death of the young sorcerer, there are increased reports of an invisible monster raging through the Dunwich countryside, leaving giant footprints, eating livestock, destroying houses, and killing their occupants. *The Dunwich Horror* ends with the four scholars and local residents confronting the invisible monster while it is on a killing spree. A chemical spray allows them to briefly see where the monster is, and then Armitage recites incantations that result in its destruction. Visible upon its death, the monster is seen to be a giant creature with a proportionally large duplicate of Wilber Whateley's head and face. Fortunately, only one creature was released into their dimension before

Wilbur Whateley's death put an end to his plans. In this story, the use of the *Necronomicon* provides information about the imagined world to both the characters and the reader. It informs the characters about the meaning of what they see and explains the workings of the extraordinary phenomena they perceive. Descriptions of the process of research, study, and use of information, first by the Wizard Whateley, to bend the world to his will, and then by the hero and his team to protect the world, provide a lesson in the value and power of words, books, and research. This presentation of empowerment through scholarship rings true with the reader's experience from our world and is another detail that contributes to the reader's "secondary belief" in the imaginary world.

Two other Lovecraft stories that include characters who study "invented books" are "The Thing on the Doorstep" (1937) and *The Case of Charles Dexter Ward* (1941) [*Ward*]. Each tells the story of a bright young man who has been drawn into the study of the occult and ultimately led to the *Necronomicon*. In "The Thing on the Doorstep," Daniel Upton narrates the story of how he avenges his best friend, the gifted but naive Edward Derby, whose life is undone as a result of his occult studies. Derby becomes involved with Asenath Wait, literally falls under her magical spell, and marries her. By the end of the story, the reader discovers that Asenath's father, Ephraim Wait, psychically possesses her. He animates her physically to attract and marry Derby and then discards her when he moves on to the next stage of his plan to take the body of Edward Derby as his own so that he can continue his immortal existence as a man. In this story, the victims and the villain are all three students of the occult and use the information within the books, including the *Necronomicon*, to bend the world to their wills. At one point, Ephraim Wait flaunts who he really is to Daniel Upton, the narrator, while in possession of the body of Edward Derby in an asylum, as he patiently waits to be released by the hospital doctors. Daniel Upton resolves the story with a description of how he ends the immortality of Ephraim Wait and avenges his friend.

The novella *The Case of Charles Dexter Ward* has similarities to the previously discussed stories. It describes the discovery, research, and actions of Dr. Marinus Bicknell Willett, the family friend and physician of the young Charles Dexter Ward. In this story, the victim falls under the influence of the spirit of his ancestor, the wizard Joseph Curwen, whom he discovers while doing antiquarian and genealogical research. Under the influence of the evil spirit of his ancestor, Charles Dexter Ward does extensive, international bibliographic and laboratory study to recreate the underground research of his ancestor with the aim of resurrecting Joseph Curwen and establishing his ancestor's immortality. Much like *The Dunwich Horror*, the family friend and physician Dr. Willett responds to what he sees by performing his own research of occult books, and, with the help of Ward's father, he confronts and defeats the evil spirit. He uses lengthy incantations that are reproduced in the novella. All three stories do an excellent job of using the "invented book" as a keystone to support the imaginary world of the stories of H. P. Lovecraft.

Another story about the greed for immortality that begins with a youthful love of antiquities and genealogical research is *The Shadow Over Innsmouth*. It describes the decline of the people of the remote town of Innsmouth, who have given in to the temptation of seeking immortality. The story shows the reader that the cost of immortality is to be transformed physically and mentally into fish-like creatures. The unnamed hero of the story discovers through his extensive research that he is related to Captain Obed Marsh, the patriarch of the original family that made the pact to become immortal. Interestingly, the hero is drawn to join the people of Innsmouth despite knowing the costs of that decision.

A story that shows a combination of the study of occult books and of dreams shaping reality is "The Dreams in the Witch House" (1933). It tells the story of the mathematics student Walter Gilman of Miskatonic University who studied "Non-Euclidean calculus and quantum physics" and folklore in an attempt to "trace a strange background of multi-dimensional reality behind the ghoulish hints of the Gothic tales" (296). The direction of his studies is inspired by the mysteries of the antiquated city of Arkham, his reading of many occult books listed in the story—the *Necronomicon* among them—and his study of local court records. Gilman moves into a house that was inhabited in the 1700s by the witch Keziah Mason and her familiar Brown Jenkin, a rat with the face of a bearded old man having four hands in the place of paws. Gilman reads in the court records that, during Keziah Mason's witchcraft trial, she "told Judge Hathorne of lines and curves that could be made to point out directions leading through the walls of space to other spaces beyond [...]. Then she had drawn those devices on the walls of her cell and vanished" (297).

Gilman examines the walls of Keziah Mason's former living quarters for evidence of the "lines and curves" that she used to transcend space. Gilman suffers from a fever but pushes forward with his studies despite the illness. He progresses in his research and receives visitations from Keziah Mason and her familiar. Gilman learns the answers to his questions about mathematical constructs and the ability to pass through to other dimensions. Keziah Mason manipulates Gilman while he is weakened by fever and takes him with her during night-time ramblings of the city. Her goal is to indoctrinate him into all of her secrets if he will submit to her demonic master. The story ends with a physical confrontation between Gilman, the witch, and her familiar when he learns that he has attended the death of a child during their night-time ramblings while mesmerized. He fights the witch when she attempts to force him to participate in the ritual sacrifice of another child. Later, as is seen in other Lovecraft stories, a library of occult books and paraphernalia is discovered by workmen when the house is being demolished.

Impossible lines and angles are often descriptors of the architecture of buildings, places, and objects throughout the work of Lovecraft. They indicate a connection to other occult dimensions. Such impossible geometries are part of the description of an entryway between dimensions in "The Call of Cthulhu," and they are included in descriptions of the architecture of the ancient, deserted city in *At the Mountains of Madness*, of jewelry in *The Shadow Over Innsmouth*, and the body of Wilbur Whateley, as seen in the quotation above from *The Dunwich Horror*. Unusual geometries are recurring details within the works of Lovecraft that become a structural touchstone, which makes his world magical, multi-dimensional, and self-consistent, and which also gives it a frightening and believable depth.

Similar to the way in which Sisko's alter ego Benny Russell is both the "dreamer and the dream" in the episode "Far Beyond the Stars" ["Beyond"] from *Deep Space Nine*, most of Lovecraft's Randolph Carter Stories describe the hero as an "old dreamer" who has the ability to physically explore different levels of dreamlands and then return to the waking world. These stories include "The Silver Key," written in 1926 and published in 1929; the novella *The Dream-Quest of Unknown Kadath*, completed in 1927 but unrevised and unpublished until 1943, after Lovecraft's death; and "Through the Gates of the Silver Key," co-written during 1932 and 1933 and first published in 1934. "The Silver Key" is the most satisfying of the Randolph Carter dream stories. It describes his abilities as an "old dreamer" to explore dreamlands, explains how he lost his gift by accepting a modern scientific understanding of the world, and recounts the process he goes through to regain his former ability. "The Silver Key" dramatizes a character who is both the dreamer and the dream and shows a connection between dreaming, scholarship, and the shaping of the world of the hero with his dreaming.[4]

Related to the phenomenon of the "invented books" of story-worlds are books from the real world that add to or support the imaginative world of authors such as H. P. Lovecraft. Among them are the works of Charles Fort (1874–1932), mentioned twice in Lovecraft's works—in a minor work, "The Descendent," and in a novella, *The Whisperer in the Darkness*. In both cases, Fort's books are described as an example of the type of occult or fringe books Lovecraft's characters read. On the face of it, these passing references should not be significant. However, reading his work reveals that this slightly older contemporary of Lovecraft described essential characteristics of the world that Lovecraft created in his stories. Similar strange phenomena described in Fort's work also appear in Lovecraft's writings. Both writers include unconventional ideas, such as the belief that objects and creatures pass through thin places in our universe from other dimensions. Lovecraft's stories that include this idea are *The Dunwich Horror*, "Dreams in the Witch House," "The Colour Out of Space," and the novella *The Whisperer in the Darkness*. This novella opens with a description of newspaper reports of the discovery of the bodies of unearthly creatures found in Vermont rivers during historic floods. The character Albert N. Wilmarth, literature professor, folklorist, and rationalist, is drawn into the frightening reality that the Earth is being mined for a "rare metal" by interstellar aliens. This revelation occurs at the end of a series of events that begins when he writes rationalist responses to newspaper reports about the strange dead creatures. Another similarity of Lovecraft's stories to the works of Charles Fort is the idea that there is evidence that our planet was once habited by creatures from other worlds and that one day they will return to mete out our destruction.

Charles Fort's *The Book of the Damned* [*Damned*] presents to the reader a world of strangeness that could have been written by Lovecraft. Fort gives verisimilitude to his claims by paraphrasing articles from science periodicals and newspapers and providing informal citations to the items. His data are stories that describe the purported phenomena of falling fish, frogs, blood, black snow, and other items coming from the sky like rain all over the world. He describes found items having odd properties that suggest they were made by aliens or giants. He theorizes that there are other worlds near our own, but in other dimensions, and that the things falling from our skies came through

---

[4] See Fisher in this volume.

weak spots in space where the dimensions meet. In chapter twelve of *The Book of the Damned,* he explicitly voices the cynical opinion that the aliens are so advanced in comparison to humanity that treating us as equals would be equivalent to humans establishing "diplomatic relation(s)" with farm animals (163). He continues to assert that the extra-terrestrials own our planet:

> I think we're property.
> I should say we belong to something:
> That once upon a time, this earth was No-man's Land, that other worlds explored and colonized here, and fought among themselves for possession, but that now it's owned by something:
> That something owns this earth—all others warned off. (*Damned* 163)

Fort continues a tongue-in-cheek list of the many ways aliens might have come to Earth and gives a list of things they might have done while visiting, such as "hunting, trading, replenishing harems" (*Damned* 164). He speculates that there will come a time when our owners will return and that humanity will be defenseless against whatever they desire to do with us and our planet.

It is fruitful to include Charles Fort when discussing the works of Lovecraft because his books appear to have contributed to the shape of Lovecraft's story-world. This is seen in both of the authors' portrayals of our doomed and myopic humanity—Fort's paraphrasing of articles from newspapers and journals and Lovecraft's fictional stories—and in how Lovecraft's "ancient Elder Things" will return to threaten our temporary peace. In both Fort and Lovecraft's works, humanity as a whole does not wake up to the threat to which we are blind. Only a few unfortunates and students of the occult, especially of the *Necronomicon,* stumble upon the truth, usually leading to insanity and death.

Philip K. Dick

The Man in the High Castle presents a story in which the characters live in an alternative world where the Axis Powers won World War II and divided the United States among them. The East Coast states are ruled by the Nazis, the West Coast states by the Japanese, and the Rocky Mountain states are a neutral area in the center of the country. In the culture of this alternative world, the Japanese victors are obsessed with collecting pre-WWII American historical artifacts. The most popular items are firearms from the American Civil War and from the era of the Old West. The collectors are also interested in items from popular culture such as movie posters, Mickey Mouse watches, Horrors of War, Gum Inc. collecting cards, and even old milk bottle caps, because pre-

WWII era children collected them and played games with their collections of the various items.

The novel opens with Frank Frink, a machinist in a shop that builds reproductions of the western guns that are sold by dealers as genuine antiques. He has just lost his job because he stood up to his boss. The novel shows the process by which Ed McCarthy, his foreman, convinces him to become partners at setting up an independent shop and going into business together to create original jewelry, a move contrary to the known demands of the market. The novel then introduces Robert Childan, a shop owner and dealer of pre-WWII antiques who is persuaded to carry the jewelry on a trial consignment basis. The reader sees the effects of the original artistry upon two of Childan's Japanese customers. Each progresses from dismissal of the jewelry, due to the prejudiced belief that post-WWII Americans cannot create anything of artistic value, to responding to the aesthetic spirit of the new American works of art.

The story of one of the customers is relevant to the thesis of this chapter. Mr. Nobusuke Tagomi, a high Japanese trade official, has just killed a Nazi operative in self-defense during an attack upon his office. He enters Childan's shop with the idea of selling him the antique gun and ammunition that he used in his act of violence. During a scene of painfully artificial courtesy, he listens to Childan's sales pitch of the new American jewelry. Tagomi, in distress over taking a life, makes an impulse purchase of the jewelry while leaving the shop. It is a desperate attempt to try anything that may restore his peace of mind from his distress. He ends up on a park bench probing the jewelry with all of his senses. In an act of frustration, he throws the jewelry away. Tagomi instantly finds himself in the alternative reality in which the Allied Powers won WWII. He sees a freeway that did not exist in his version of reality, and, in confusion, he goes into a diner where a Caucasian man confronts and argues with him when he demands that the Caucasian customers make a space for him to sit. He returns to his version of reality upon finding the piece of jewelry back at the park bench.

Mr. Tagomi redeems himself after his display of racial chauvinism in the diner, when he returns to work. He stands up to Freiherr Hugo Reiss, the Nazi official, who approaches Mr. Tagomi in his office to deny Nazi responsibility for the attack on the Japanese Trade Mission offices. Mr. Tagomi is insulted, uncharacteristically expresses his outrage, and refuses Reiss's request for the transfer of Frank Frink, who was arrested and being held for a graft charge, from Japanese to Nazi detention. Not only does Mr. Tagomi refuse the transfer, but he writes and signs a new order to release Frink from jail and drop all charges.

As mentioned earlier, in this imaginative world of Philip K. Dick, there is a popular underground novel titled *The Grasshopper Lies Heavy* that describes the alternative history that Mr. Tagomi briefly experienced. The author of the book, Hawthorne Abendsen, lives in the neutral states along the Rocky Mountains. His book is seen by the Japanese and Nazi leadership alike as a threat to their mutual annexation of the United States. A story-thread in Dick's novel shows Juliana Frink, the ex-wife of Frank Frink, after she has moved from the West Coast to the Rocky Mountains. She supports herself as a martial arts instructor. She unknowingly becomes involved with a Nazi operative named Joe Cinnadella, who is posing as a truck driver and was sent to assassinate the author of *The Grasshopper Lies Heavy*. He introduces her to the book and tricks her into believing that he wants to take her on a trip to meet the author. In reality, she is part of Cinnadella's strategy for getting close to Abendsen. He knows from party records that Abendsen is attracted to women of Juliana's type. She uncovers his plans and then kills him in self-defense when he attempts to force her to continue with him on his mission.

Julianna travels alone to Abendsen's home to warn him to protect himself from future assassination attempts. She discovers while visiting Abendsen that the version of reality in which the Allied Powers won WWII is his real world. She also learns that Abendsen consulted the *I Ching* at every stage of writing *The Grasshopper Lies Heavy*. Julianna upsets the Abendsen household by advising them to arm themselves, telling them that she killed a Nazi whose mission was to assassinate the author as well as revealing to the author's household and party guests that he used the *I Ching* in the creation of his famous novel. The last is upsetting to Abendsen, he explains, because the truth reduces him to little more than a typist. After a tense conversation, Julianna leaves the Abendsen house in the dark of the evening with no plans for what she will do next. She considers returning to her ex-husband, Frank Frink, but she hasn't decided yet. She leaves on foot with confidence because she knows that she can do anything.

This presentation of characters who believe they live in the real world but are living in a dream or an imaginary construct is a recurring idea in the works of Dick. *Eye in the Sky* is an early novel of his in which the characters, victims of an industrial accident, find themselves in a group dream that changes when each world-imagining dreamer loses consciousness. Throughout the novel, they find themselves moved from one dream-world to the next, each one worse than the one before. The dream-worlds are projections of each person's superstitions, prejudices, and fears. First, they are in the world of an elderly man who is the member of a fundamentalist Chicago cult from the 1930s. In his world, miracles and prayer replace science, and his racism has humiliating results for the African American tour guide. The title of the book refers to a scene in which two of the characters see the eye of God, which is the size of a lake. Next, the members of the group find themselves in the world of a middle-aged woman, a privileged culture-seeking busy-body who banishes anything she doesn't like. The other members of the group escape her world by provoking her to banish things she needs to remain conscious. Then, the group finds themselves in the terrifying world of a paranoid young woman. Objects within a house are hurtled at them. Eventually, they must flee when the house itself attacks them. The process of passing from bad to worse mental worlds ends when they find themselves in the world of a Communist Party mole. They must survive an armed confrontation between Communist Party Workers and gangster-style Capitalists. An observation Dick developed throughout the novel is that all of the characters—consequently, each of us—live in fantasy worlds without realizing how often they are fantasies or understanding that these fantasies tend to enable superstitions, fears, and prejudices, in addition to empowering the belief that a person is the center of the universe.

As with the connection between the real-world works of Charles Fort and the stories of H. P. Lovecraft, the *I Ching* is a real-world divination text that is significant within the fictional world of *The Man in the High Castle*. In the novel, Frank Frink consults the *I Ching* to help him decide if he should go into business with Ed McCarthy. Frink compulsively consults the book for all decisions and uses it to help him understand events in his life such as the loss of Julianna Frink, his ex-wife. In one section of the novel, two characters simultaneously consult the *I Ching*: Frank Frink receives an encouraging reading about his new business opportunity, while Mr. Tagomi tries to find out how a business deal of his own will turn out. The reader also sees Julianna Frink turning to the oracle throughout her scenes in the novel. The Japanese hero of the book explains:

> "We are absurd," Mr. Tagomi said. "because we live by a five-thousand-year-old book. We set it questions as if it were alive. It *is* alive. As is the Christian Bible; many books are actually alive. Not in metaphoric fashion. Spirit animates it. Do you see?" (*High Castle* 72)

The *I Ching* was an important book to Dick, who was known to consult it often himself, much like Frank Frink. In the following quotation from *The Exegesis of Philip K. Dick* [*Exegesis*], the editors describe the book in the glossary:

> *I Ching:* An ancient Chinese text used as a tool for divination […] Dick, […] consulted the *I Ching* frequently and claimed to have used it to resolve turning points in the plot of *The Man in the High Castle* (1962), which also features an oracular book written using the *I Ching*. (925)

It is scarcely possible to overstate the significance of the *I Ching* to Dick, personally and within his story worlds. The Wilhelm/Baynes translation, which he owned and consulted (*Exegesis* 925), contains a foreword by C. S. Jung (1947) [Jung] in which the prominent psychologist explains the legitimacy of using the book as an oracle for sincere seekers. He explains that it is a tool to reveal the user's subconscious knowledge of the answers to questions they have about the world around them. He describes his experience of consulting the *I Ching* throughout every step of composing his Foreword to the Wilhelm/Baynes translation (Jung). Dick's use of the *I Ching*, mentioned above, when writing *The Man in the High Castle* and his character Hawthorne Abendsen's similar consultations of the oracle while writing *The Grasshopper Lies Heavy* are identical to Jung's consultations of the Oracle just mentioned.

The *I Ching*, as it appears in the works of Philip K. Dick, is an example of a real-world book used as an oracle that has affected the lives of its readers for thousands of years. Thus, it is world-shaping in our reality as well as in Dick's imagined realities. At the same time, it is a structural keystone of the story and world of the novel, *The Man in the High Castle*, and in its alternative history, *The Grasshopper Lies Heavy*.

Benny Russell

Star Trek: Deep Space Nine, in both its television episodes and associated novels, includes a number of "invented books" that figure prominently in the fictional lives of the characters. They include the Bajoran religious texts, *When the Prophets Cried* and the evil *The Book of the Kosst Amojan*, *The Ferengi Rules of Acquisition*, and three titles from the Cardassian culture — the mystery genre of the Enigma Tales; the epic *The Never-Ending Sacrifice* [*Sacrifice*]; and their religious text, the *Hebitian Records*. I include *Deep Space Nine* [*DS9*] in this chapter because the television series and related novels repeatedly examine the many cultures in its fictional universe as they both clash and co-exist. In order to live side by side, the characters often must learn about and tolerate the religions, literature, customs, and other forms of expression of many different peoples. At the center of these exchanges is Benjamin Sisko, a Starfleet commander at the beginning of the series who is promoted to captain at the end of season three and whose position requires him to negotiate or interact with the many races on the station. On top of that, Sisko is seen as a religious figure, the Emissary, to the natives of the planet Bajor who own the station. He is believed to be the Emissary because of his direct experience with the Prophets, a nontemporal alien race whom the Bajorans worship as gods. Many episodes involve Sisko mediating conflicts among the residents of and visitors to Deep Space Nine. Just as in the real world, peaceful co-existence in that fictional corner of the universe can be difficult, but—once again mirroring reality—shared experiences and understanding can achieve what is initially thought to be impossible.

How that achievement occurs is perhaps best reflected in the episode "Far Beyond the Stars," which chronicles the attempts by Benny Russell, a 1950s African American science fiction writer, to publish his story about an African American captain of the space station Deep Space Nine. What seems fantastical in 1950s Earth is reality in the 24th century, as, by then in the episode's story arc, Captain Benjamin Sisko experiences Benny Russell's reality while suffering from seizures induced by the Prophets. In Russell's world, after many setbacks, he is told by a street preacher that he is both "the dreamer and the dream" ("Beyond"). Russell's dream—his novella—describes the adventures of Captain Sisko and his crew on the space station Deep Space Nine; meanwhile, Sisko's dream—his seizure-induced hallucination—is that Russell will persevere in a time when African American achievement was denigrated and thwarted. Near the end of the episode, Russell is beaten by the police, learns his novella has been pulped, and is told he has been fired from his magazine job. Even so, Russell insists, his dream cannot be destroyed. The editor Douglas Pabst tells him to calm down, or they will call the police. Russell's response is among the most significant and moving speeches in the entire television series.

> BENNY. You go ahead! Call them! Call anybody you want. They can't do anything to me. Not anymore. And nor can any of you. I am a human being, damn it. You can deny me all you want but you cannot deny Ben Sisko. He exists! That future, that space station, all those people, they exist in here. In my mind, I created it. And every one of you know it. You read it. It's here. You hear what I'm telling you? You can pulp a story but you cannot destroy an idea. Don't you understand? That's ancient knowledge. You cannot destroy an idea. That future, I created it, and it's real. Don't you understand? It is

real! I created it and it's real! It's real! Oh, God. (Benny collapses, sobbing.) ("Beyond")

At the end of "Far Beyond the Stars," the revived Sisko ponders his identity, asking "who is the dreamer and who is the dream?" He wonders if, in fact, he is the product of the writer Benny Russell's imagination, or if things are as they seem, with Captain Benjamin Sisko being the fount of his existence and Russell being a vision sent to him by the Prophets to help him decide what he will do next during an intergalactic war.

During the television show's last season, Sisko struggles with a crisis in which the Prophets are defeated by their enemies, the Pah-wraiths. This defeat severs the Prophets' connection with the people of Bajor. In the midst of this crisis, Sisko again experiences visions of being Benny Russell. In the hallucinations, Russell is confined to an asylum, and his doctor tells him he can be cured of his delusions of Benjamin Sisko if he will paint over the story that he has written on the walls of his cell. As Sisko grapples with how best to help Bajor, Russell agonizes over whether to paint over his fictional world or not. Finally, he chooses his created world and continues to write and completes the *DS9* story. The result is that Sisko is able to release the Prophets from their confinement by the Pah-wraiths, allowing the Prophets to reconnect with Bajor. All of the Sisko/Russell storyline is an explicit presentation of the power of written stories, in reality or within fictional worlds, to change the worlds in which they exist.

As the Emissary, Sisko becomes well-versed in the Bajoran religious prophecies. As the station administrator, he also becomes familiar with the central text of the Ferengi culture, *The Ferengi Rules of Acquisition*, because the station's most important retail establishment is owned by a Ferengi named Quark, son of Keldar. The Ferengi culture is based entirely on commerce, and *The Rules of Acquisition* are both a social guide and a religious text reflecting their philosophy that business is the primary and even sacred activity for a Ferengi (Behr vi). Representative of the text is the first Rule of Acquisition, "Once you have their money, never give it back" (Behr 2), which appears in the episode "The Nagus." The eighteenth Rule, "A Ferengi without profit is no Ferengi at all" (Behr 11), appears in the episode "Heart of Stone." Three Ferengi—Quark, his brother Rom, and Rom's son Nog—become important characters across the seven-season series, with many stories showing how their values frequently conflict with Sisko's Star Fleet and the United Federation of Planets' sensibilities. One episode, "The Jem'Hadar," concludes with Sisko admitting to and taking a step toward overcoming his own bias against Quark specifically and the Ferengi in general. Throughout the long arc of the series, Sisko develops an appreciation for Quark, Nog, and Rom as individuals as well as a deeper understanding of the ways of the Ferengi as a people. Indeed, Sisko eventually agrees to sponsor the nephew Nog's application to become the first Ferengi member of StarFleet.

Thus, Sisko serves within the context of the DS9 stories as a dreamer who effects justice and peace in his world, motivated in part by his appreciation of two alien religious texts. In addition, he is himself the dream of a fiction writer who wants to bring about those changes within his own time. The role of Benny Russell's invented stories as the possible origin of an entire story-world and of Sisko himself demonstrates the creative power of books to change all worlds. In fact, the long story arc of the *Deep Space Nine* television show ends with the episode "What You Leave Behind" ["Behind"], which shows the destruction of *The Book of the Kosst Amojan*, a book of black magic similar to Lovecraft's *Necronomicon*, used to release the aforementioned Pah-wraiths. In this episode, the Pah-wraiths are released from their own confinement to the Fire Caves by Kai Winn, an embittered religious leader, using recitations of ancient Bajoran incantations from *The Book of the Kosst Amojan*. The scenes of this ritual are akin to the recitations described earlier in the works of Lovecraft. As in Lovecraft's stories, the purpose of releasing the Pah-wraiths is so they will burn and destroy the world of Bajor.

Gul Dukat, the principal villain throughout all seven seasons of the show, describes his purpose of assisting the Kai in releasing the evil spirits: "Soon the Pah-wraiths will burn across Bajor, the Celestial Temple, the Alpha Quadrant. Can you picture it? An entire universe set in flames, to burn for all eternity" ("Behind"). The destruction of the book by Sisko re-imprisons the Pah-wraiths along with Gul Dukat in the Fire Caves for eternity. The Prophets tell Sisko that "the Emissary has completed his task" ("Behind"). They confirm that the book was a "key" to "a door that can never be opened again" ("Behind"). Concluding the series with this solution demonstrates the creative power of books in all story-worlds. It is a fitting way to end a series that repeatedly shows a reverence and value for books and learning.

Hour-long episodes—the television equivalent of short stories— can offer only a glimpse of these cultural impacts on a handful of characters such as Benjamin Sisko, but the franchise novels inspired by the television series go much deeper. One novel building on the fictive Cardassian epic, and sharing its title, is *The Never-Ending Sacrifice* by Una McCormack. She presents the story of the Cardassian boy, Rugal, who first appears in the television episode "Cardassians." He was a war orphan adopted, loved, and raised by a Bajoran couple. He comes to the attention of the authorities during an incident when he and his adopted father are on the station. Rugal is forced by the Federation legal system, due to a decision of then-Commander Sisko, to return him to Cardassia with his biological father, a national politician. The novel picks up where the episode, "Cardassians," leaves off. The Cardassian epic *The Never-Ending Sacrifice,* an invented book, follows the members of a family who sacrifice themselves through several generations to the supposed higher interests of Cardassian Society. Rugal discovers that *The Never-Ending Sacrifice* is also the title of an academic book in which Dr. Natima Lang, a fictional academic who appears in the episode "Profit and Loss," criticizes the Cardassian culture for always sacrificing the individual interests of its own people throughout its history. Dr. Lang's book inspires Rugal to live a life of caring service, and he always acts to make his native world and culture more responsible and compassionate, or, just like Russell and Sisko, he becomes the dreamer building the dream. This wonderful piece of science fiction world-building gives the reader a deep understanding of Cardassian history, including an explanation of how the Cardassians justify the annexation of Bajor to themselves, and describes the disintegration and reconstruction of their society at the end of a devastating intergalactic war. Rugal lives his own epic, attempting to return to his adoptive parents on Bajor, fighting and struggling for survival after their deaths, and finally rebuilding his life despite his many setbacks. Though a rarity, *The Never-Ending Sacrifice* is both a good franchise novel and good science fiction, without qualification, that provides a satisfying fictional world, people, and culture. In doing so it meets Tolkien's requirements for world-building as described in "On Fairy-stories."

The final literary form in this discussion that is part of the *Star Trek: Deep Space Nine* universe comes in the form of the Cardassian Enigma Tales associated with Elim Garak, who was the former Cardassian spy banished by his superior to live on DS9, during the years portrayed in the television show, and who survives by working as a tailor. In the season 3 episode, "Distant Voices," he describes the Enigma Tales to his friend Dr. Julian Bashir as a genre of mystery novel in which everyone is guilty. The genre is brought up again in the relaunch novels about Cardassians, and the Enigma Tales are mentioned often with both disapproval and appreciation by various characters, much as we real-world readers of fantasy and science fiction literature debate our own tastes. For example, Rugal's grandmother spends all of her time reading Enigma Tales ("Sacrifice"). In the final Cardassian novel, *Enigma Tales*, we see once again that Garak loves them and yearns, after returning to his war-torn planet, for time to read the latest volume, months after its publication. The title of the 2017 novel and repeated references to the genre throughout the book series signify the importance of the genre within the world of *DS9*.

Conclusion

This chapter has explored examples of "invented books" and the trope that characters are "the dreamer and the dream" in fantasy and science fiction literature throughout the 20th century. The works of H. P. Lovecraft, Philip K. Dick, and the writers of the *Deep Space Nine* stories were chosen for this discussion because they span the length of the century that saw fantasy and science fiction develop into the genres we know and love today. From that century, J. R. R. Tolkien stands among the giants of fictional world-building in the high standards his stories of Middle-earth have set for other authors. His work has influenced and challenged most fantasy and science fiction writers from his time to the present, inspiring the attempt to equal his achievements. Tolkien's essay "On Fairy-stories" also articulates that the goal of every fantasy writer should be to create fantastic elements in his or her world-building that are so consistent and integral to the imagined world that they will inspire "secondary belief" (61) within their readers. The challenge of fantasy and science fiction is for the fantastical elements to behave as structural keystones to their story-worlds instead of acting only as interesting texture or decoration for the stories in which they appear. The authors discussed here have made these elements integral to the logic of their stories and shown them to be a part of the formation and structure of the worlds in which they exist. In all of the cases described above, these elements are used in a way that adds depth and contributes to the strength of their story-worlds with the result of satisfying the "green sun" standard that J. R. R. Tolkien established in "On Fairy-stories." In addition, I believe that the authors H. P. Lovecraft, Philip K. Dick, and the various writers of the *Deep Space Nine* episodes and novels are all engaged, to varying degrees, in Tolkien's "elvish craft," in "story-making in its primary and most potent mode."[5]

---

[5] I would like to thank Dr. Denise Landrum-Geyer for reading this chapter and making comments for its improvement.

Works Cited

Behr, Ira Steven. *The Ferengi Rules of Acquisition.* Pocket Books, 1995.

Dick, Philip K. *Eye in the Sky.* Vintage Books, 2003.

——. *The Exegesis of Philip K Dick.* Edited by Pamela Jackson and Jonathan Lethem, Houghton Mifflin Harcourt, 2011.

——. *The Man in the High Castle.* Vintage Books, 1992.

Dillard, J. M., et al. *Emissary.* Pocket Books, 1993.

"Distant Voices." *Star Trek: Deep Space Nine,* created by Rick Berman and Michael Piller, season 3, episode 18, Paramount Pictures, 10 Apr. 1995.

Fallon, Claire. "Fictional Books Within Books We Wish Were Real." *Huffpost.* 23 Oct. 2014, huffingtonpost.com/2014/10/23/fictional-books-within-bo_n_6024472.html.

"Far Beyond the Stars." *Star Trek: Deep Space Nine,* created by Rick Berman and Michael Piller, season 6, episode 13, Paramount Pictures, 11 Feb. 1998.

Flieger, Verlyn. "The Arch and the Keystone." *Mythlore,* vol. 38, no. 1, #135, 2019, pp. 1–18.

Fort, Charles. *The Complete Books of Charles Fort: The Book of the Damned / Lo! / Wild Talents / New Lands.* Dover Publications, 1974.

"Heart of Stone." *Star Trek: Deep Space Nine,* created by Rick Berman and Michael Piller, season 3, episode 14, Paramount Pictures, 6 Feb. 1995.

The Invisible Library. 14 July 2006. Archived on the *Internet Archive: Wayback Machine* at: web.archive.org/web/20011215090703fw_/ http://invisiblelibrary.com/index.html.

The Invisible Library. 17 Apr. 2008, invislib.blogspot.com.

Joshi, S. T. *H. P. Lovecraft and Lovecraft Criticism: An Annotated Bibliography.* Borgo Press, 2002.

Jung, C. G. Foreword. *The I Ching or Book of Changes.* by Anonymous. Translated by Richard Wilhelm and Cary F. Baynes, 1967, 3rd ed., Princeton UP, 1949, pp. xxi–xxxix.

Kennedy, George A. *Fictitious Authors and Imaginary Novels in French, English, and American Fiction from the 18th to the Start of the 21st Century.* Edwin Mellen Press, 2004.

"List of fictional books." *Wikipedia.* 7 Nov. 2019. Archived on the *Internet Archive: Wayback Machine* at: web.archive.org/web/20191107042956/ en.wikipedia.org/wiki/List_of_fictional_books.

Loucks, Donovan K. "Lovecraft's Fiction (Publication Order)." *The H. P. Lovecraft Archive.* hplovecraft.com/writings/fiction/publish.aspx.

Lovecraft, H. P. *Complete Works of H. P. Lovecraft.* Delphi Classics, 2013.

——. *At the Mountains of Madness and Other Tales of Terror.* Del Rey, 1985.

——. "The Call of Cthulhu." *The Best of H. P. Lovecraft: Bloodcurdling Tales of Horror and the Macabre*. Ballantine Books, 1982.

——. *The Case of Charles Dexter Ward*. Ballantine Books, 1985.

——. "The Colour Out of Space." *The Best of H. P. Lovecraft: Bloodcurdling Tales of Horror and the Macabre*. Ballantine Books, 1982.

——. "The Descendant." *Complete Works of H. P. Lovecraft*. Delphi Classics, 2013.

——. *The Dream-Quest of Unknown Kadath*. Ballantine Books, 1986.

——. "The Dreams in the Witch House." *The Best of H. P. Lovecraft: Bloodcurdling Tales of Horror and the Macabre*. Ballantine Books, 1982.

——. *The Dunwich Horror*. *The Best of H. P. Lovecraft: Bloodcurdling Tales of Horror and the Macabre*. Ballantine Books, 1982.

——. *The Shadow Over Innsmouth*. *The Best of H. P. Lovecraft: Bloodcurdling Tales of Horror and the Macabre*. Ballantine Books, 1982.

——. "The Silver Key." *The Best of H. P. Lovecraft: Bloodcurdling Tales of Horror and the Macabre*. Ballantine Books, 1982.

——. "The Thing on the Doorstep." *The Best of H. P. Lovecraft: Bloodcurdling Tales of Horror and the Macabre*. Ballantine Books, 1982.

——. *The Whisperer in the Darkness*. *The Best of H. P. Lovecraft: Bloodcurdling Tales of Horror and the Macabre*. Ballantine Books, 1982.

McCormack, Una. *Enigma Tales*. Pocket Books, 2017.

——. *The Never-Ending Sacrifice*. Pocket Books, 2009.

"Profit and Loss." *Star Trek: Deep Space Nine*, created by Rick Berman and Michael Piller, season 2, episode 18, Paramount Pictures, 20 Mar. 1994.

"The Jem'Hadar." *Star Trek: Deep Space Nine*, created by Rick Berman and Michael Piller, season 2, episode 26, Paramount Pictures, 12 June 1994.

"The Nagus." *Star Trek: Deep Space Nine*, created by Rick Berman and Michael Piller, season 1, episode 11, Paramount Pictures, 21 Mar. 1993.

Tolkien, J. R. R. *The Lord of the Rings*. 50th Anniversary Edition, Houghton Mifflin, 2004.

——. "On Fairy-stories." *Tolkien On Fairy-stories*, edited by Douglas A. Anderson and Verlyn Flieger, HarperCollins, 2008, pp. 21–84.

"What You Leave Behind." *Star Trek: Deep Space Nine*, created by Rick Berman and Michael Piller, season 7, episode 25/26, Paramount Pictures, 2 June 1999.

Is there an Index to the Prophecies? Or, Finding the Needle in the Enchanted Haystack

Janet Brennan Croft

> *"You want weapons? We're in a library. Books! Best weapons in the world. This room is the greatest arsenal we could have. Arm yourself."*
> (*Doctor Who*, "Tooth and Claw" 31:02)

WHILE THIS MOMENT FROM *Doctor Who* may make book-lovers cheer wildly,[1] I have to admit a certain skepticism. Yes, it's great to see books so valued, and all those books in that wonderful old library at Torchwood House may be chock-full of exactly the information the Doctor (David Tennant), Rose Tyler (Billie Piper), and his other companions on this adventure need in order to get out of this particular tight spot—but how are they supposed to find it? They pull books off the shelf at random and leaf through them, maybe consulting indexes in the back or alphabetical entries—under biology, zoology, werewolves, and mistletoe—but we don't see a card catalog and they seem to just be pulling uncategorized books off the shelf haphazardly rather than using a logical search strategy or checking to see if the man who put the collection together had perhaps developed a finding aid of some sort. Though this episode was set in 1879, about the time the library card catalog was just beginning to coalesce into its familiar form in the United States,[2] there had been other methods of cataloging and accessing the contents of a library available for centuries—for example, the catalog and index that accompanied Thomas Jefferson's personal library which formed the kernel of the Library of Congress.

All too often, this is the sort of approach we see in popular culture depictions of searches for information, and perhaps especially in science fiction and fantasy. This serendipitous, instinctive, random approach makes for great dramatic reading and viewing, but it does librarians and archivists a disservice in overlooking the hard work we put into creating discovery tools, and glosses over how much time and effort these can save the researcher. As a librarian, I worry that

---

[1] See Larsen in this volume, for example.
[2] See in particular chapters 3 and 4 of Devereaux and Hayden.

users may be coming to us with unrealistic expectations—or even just plain avoiding us—because of media depictions that lead them to expect that they will just have to rummage through piles of material to find what they need. Or users may have the opposite expectation: that we information professionals know the collection so intimately, no matter its size, that we can give answers off the tops of our heads.

In this essay I am going to take a roughly chronological (within the history of the development of libraries) look at collections of information, how they are organized, and how they are accessed in some fictional worlds created by J. R. R. Tolkien, Terry Pratchett, Neil Gaiman, and Joss Whedon. The unifying theme in these examples—faux-medieval and modern alike—is that we seldom see the use of higher-level finding aids like catalogs, indexes, cross-reference lists, and so on. The key to finding anything in the collection seems to exist primarily in the vast memory of the person in charge of it—or the good luck, instincts, and perseverance of the person doing the digging.

Middle-earth

As David Oberhelman has pointed out, "there are many scattered references to libraries, archives, manuscript repositories, and other collections for the preservation of literature, lore, and history" throughout J. R. R. Tolkien's legendarium, as well as additional references to older oral traditions and artistic methods for "the preservation of cultural memory" (155). The melancholy certainty of loss is a major theme in Tolkien's work, and these archives are attempts to hold back the tide. Readers will be familiar with the library at Minas Tirith where Gandalf researches the Ring (*The Lord of the Rings* [*LotR*] II.2.252) and the collection of maps and lore at Rivendell, which members of the Fellowship consulted before their journey (II.2.277), both depicted in the Peter Jackson movies, as well as the mostly-destroyed Chamber of Records in Moria where the account of the annihilation of the ill-fated dwarf-colony is discovered (II.5.321).

As Oberhelman recounts in his essay, our primary-world development from oral culture through the invention of writing to the collecting of archives is paralleled in Tolkien's world. Paralleled also is the way in which great centers of civilization, like his Gondolin and Númenor, amassed cultural collections only to lose them in their inevitable fall, to be succeeded by smaller localized collections recalling the monastic libraries of the Middle Ages. As a noted scholar of European languages and linguistics, Tolkien would have been very familiar with this pattern.[3]

It may come as a surprise, then, to discover that the boisterous, earthy hobbits were also unexpectedly bookish. We see that Bilbo and Frodo have books, maps, manuscripts, and papers in their study, but they are exceptional hobbits, not the norm at all. However, as was pointed out in Tolkien's Prologue to *The Lord of the Rings*, hobbits as a culture "liked to have books filled with things that they already knew, set out fair and square with no contradictions," especially genealogical information (Prologue.7). Merry was not only the author of *Herblore of the Shire*, *Reckoning of Years*, and *Old Words and Names in the Shire*, but kept one of the three largest libraries of historical books and records after the events of *The Lord of the Rings* at Brandy Hall, specializing in the history of Eriador and Rohan. He even travelled back to Rivendell to do research in the archives there. The library at Great Smials, where Pippin was head of the Took family, collected manuscripts about Gondor, and seems to have held many documents not available elsewhere on the history of Númenor and the rise of Sauron (Prologue.15), which were consulted by scholars from outside the Shire. The library at Undertowers, where Sam's descendants lived, held Bilbo's Translations from the Elvish and the Red Book of Westmarch, the historical record started by Bilbo and continued by Frodo and later Sam, which eventually became, in Tolkien's frame-story, *The Lord of the Rings* (Prologue.14).

It is not stated specifically who had access to these materials, though. They were the private collections of wealthy and upper-class families, like the one I referenced from the *Doctor Who* episode earlier, and there is no mention of any sort of public library or professional librarian, or even bookbinding, paper, parchment-making, or printing trades in the Shire (though these necessary industries have been the subject of much playful scholarly speculation; see, for example, Hammond). What we see here is the rise of the gentleman-antiquarian, the private individual with the wealth and leisure to collect and create books, and a culture perhaps on the very brink of adding public libraries to its roster of municipal services along with the Shire Post and the Shirriffs.

---

[3] As a side note, the catalog for the exhibit *Tolkien: Maker of Middle-earth* includes a letter from Tolkien to his fiancée Edith Bratt, dated 3 November 1913, describing the quintessential Oxonian rite of passage of taking the oath at the Bodleian Library and registering as a user, gushing about how "awesome and splendid" the collection is but noting that "they are very rude to some people" (McIlwaine 152–53).

But the Shire is a quite deliberate anachronism in Middle-earth. Tolkien called it "more or less a Warwickshire village of about the period of the Diamond Jubilee," or the late 1890s (*Letters* 230). The archives of Gondor are more what we might expect to find in this medieval-feeling world, and in their neglect more suited to the theme of a major state in its decline in a culture without great churches, monasteries, or universities to serve as alternate paths to preserve records.

Here I want to contrast the way Tolkien describes Gandalf's hunt in these archives with the way it is depicted in the Peter Jackson movies. Tolkien had a good idea of what the archive of a great but declining medieval city might have looked like; as described by Gandalf, it was full of "hoarded scrolls and books," "records that few even of the lore-masters now can read, for their scripts and tongues have become dark to later men" (II.2.252). Faramir, the younger son of the Steward of Gondor, says that in the treasury there are "books and tablets writ on withered parchments, yea, and on stone, and on leaves of silver and of gold, in divers characters. Some none can now read; and for the rest, few ever unlock them" (IV.5.670). Access to these treasures is solely at the will of the Steward, the *de facto* ruler of Gondor. Eventually Gandalf finds the original document detailing how the One Ring was taken from Sauron and telling him how he will need to test Frodo's ring to confirm his suspicions.

In contrast, Jackson presents a dramatic image of a library from the depths of an imaginary Dark Ages (*JFR*, scene 8). Gandalf (Ian McKellen) is led down a steep spiral stair by a man with a dangerously flaring torch, presumably the person in charge of the archives, who points towards a certain niche full of papers that have obviously not been touched in years. We see books piled high in tottering stacks and on overflowing shelves, covered in dust and cobwebs. Gandalf clears a space on a dusty table and puffs furiously at his pipe while he leafs through the pile. He raises clouds of dust as he moves paper around, flickering the open candle flames. He handles the paper roughly and sips from a beaker (probably wine) as he reads. Quills sit in what appears to be an open ink bottle. There are a few concessions to the technology of the time—a glass globe filled with water to concentrate the light[4] and a magnifying lens—but if there can be a globe and a lens, why not hurricane glass around the

---

[4] This is sometimes called a lace maker's lamp, though this particular one looks more like it ought to be used as an oil lamp; see Waters on differentiating between the purposes of different antique glass globes.

---

candles themselves? The whole scene seems designed to make any sane archivist shudder. But this is the sort of cultural ur-image of library research in a quasi-medieval world that is familiar to our users: a messy pile of paper and books with no organization and no dedicated caretaker, where the user is left to hunt on his own.

Discworld

In Terry Pratchett's Discworld, there *is* a great university on the medieval model, which marks a major progression in the organization and retrieval of information. Discworld is a fantasy world where magic works—under certain rules and constraints. Discworld "is flat and rests on the backs of four elephants standing on a giant tortoise swimming through space. But Discworld is also full of ordinary people living relatively ordinary lives without the help of magic, and inevitably developing technology to do the things that magic does for the gifted" (Croft, "Golempunk" 110). It's also very funny; Pratchett "writes the kind of parody which celebrates rather than satirizes," for "to parody a form or an institution effectively one has to understand it to the point of affection" (Sawyer 61–70). Pratchett understood and loved books and libraries.

Over the course of the more than 40 books of this series, written between 1983 (*The Colour of Magic*) and 2015 (*The Shepherd's Crown*), we witness the development of the printing press, paper money, an equivalent of the telegraph, and the steam engine locomotive. Because of this leapfrogging of magic by technology, this is a world that is in some ways making a jump straight from the Middle Ages to a steampunk-inflected Victorian England with just the briefest of stops in the Renaissance.

One place where this tension is especially evident is Unseen University, a tradition-bound medieval holdout in the midst of bustling urban Ankh-Morpork. "Unseen University was founded [...] in part to [keep] young men with magical power where their elders could keep an eye on them [...]. Wizards don't seem to do much practical magic, and indeed the main function of the University is really to keep them from messing about with things" (Croft, "Education" 132–33).[5] UU has, of course, the largest library on

---

[5] There is a gendered division of magic on Discworld: boys with magical talent generally go to the University for training, while girls learn from witches in a one-on-one apprenticeship model.

Discworld, containing some 90,000 magical books and an uncounted number of more mundane volumes.[6]

> The Library [...] is a low, brooding building, with high, narrow, barred windows and a glass dome high above its centre [...] The interior is a topographical nightmare; the sheer presence of so much stored magic twisting dimensions and gravity into the kind of spaghetti that would make M. C. Escher go for a good lie-down [...]. In most old libraries the books are chained to the shelves to prevent them being damaged by people; in the Library of Unseen University, of course, it's more or less the other way around. [There are] Cannibal books. Books which will read you [...] Books which, if left on a shelf with their weaker brethren, would be found in a 'Revised, Enlarged and Smug' edition in the morning. [...]. (Pratchett and Briggs 228–30)

A concept Pratchett developed in parallel with the Unseen University Library was L-Space: the idea that any sufficiently large library (or bookshop) generates a space-time distortion that connects it, for those who know the secret, to all libraries everywhere. "[T]here are strict limits on its use, and the Librarians of Time and Space—that is, [those who have been initiated after they have performed "some valiant act of librarianship" (Pratchett, *Guards! Guards!* 171)]—have developed three simple rules to ensure abuse is kept to a minimum:

1. Silence
2. Books must be returned by the last date stamped
3. Do not interfere with the nature of causality." (Pratchett and Briggs 228)[7]

One of the unique aspects of Pratchett's humor is his economy in not letting a good joke go to waste; what may seem just a one-liner in an early book is quite likely to show up as a fully fleshed-out concept in a later one. Witness the Librarian of Unseen University himself. The librarian is accidentally changed into an orangutan in the second book of the series. He subsequently resists any attempt to change him back; he finds it very convenient for his work to have prehensile toes and extra-long arms, and no needs besides a regular supply of soft fruits and index

---

[6] The second largest library, at Ephebe, was destroyed by the Omnians in a religious war, in a parallel to our Library at Alexandria. Fortunately, the photographic memory of Brother Brutha was used to rescue some key scrolls. When Brutha sets everything back down in writing, he makes the new library of Omnia open to all (*Small Gods*). Additionally, many of the Guilds in Ankh-Morpork maintain libraries, some open to the public or by appointment; most notably, the Guild of Armourers, the Guild of Historians, and the Guild of Assassins (*The Compleat Ankh-Morpork* 34–48). Large private libraries also exist; that of Lady Margolotta of Uberwald plays an important part in *Unseen Academicals*.

[7] See Elise McKenna's essay in this volume for another point of view on the UU Library and L-Space.

cards. "Like most librarians, he is paid peanuts but, finding himself in a physical form where that is more an advantage than not, he is content" (Sawyer 77). A vocabulary limited to "Oook" seems to be no hindrance in communicating with his fellow faculty, and as long as no one says the word 'monkey,' all is well. But his image is a bit problematic:

> The Librarian is, of course, very much in favor of reading in general, but readers in particular get on his nerves. There is something sacrilegious about the way people keep taking books off the shelves and wearing out the words by reading them. He likes people who love and respect books, and the best way to do that, in the Librarian's opinion, is to leave them on the shelves where Nature intended them to be. (Pratchett and Briggs 227)

Here we see the stereotype of the overly-protective hoarding type of librarian—though he has been known to provide exactly the right book at the right time when needed,[8] he does not encourage or teach users how to access materials themselves, and most students avoid the Library altogether. He "serves his clients and defends his library" (Sawyer 74) but he does not give his users the tools of self-sufficiency. On the other hand, the Unseen University Library *is* too dangerous a place to allow the uninitiated to wander about freely, so his attitude may not be entirely without basis.

An example of the leapfrogging of magic by technology is the "thinking machine" Hex. Ponder Stibbons, one of the younger and less stodgy professors, puts together a device with the help of some eager grad students to try to analyze over 500 love charms and determine the common denominator, and the resultant apparatus takes on a life of its own. The "anthill inside" was the research team's design, but then "a lot of it had just … accumulated" (*Interesting Times* 31), like the aquarium, the collection of small religious pictures (icons), the mouse nest, the ram's skull, and the hourglass on a spring that pops out when Hex is working on a query. Eventually it acquires a voice input interface, responds by means of a quill pen, a scroll, and an arrangement of wires (*Hogfather* 92–93), and can handle natural-language queries. In the TV miniseries version of *Hogfather*, the Archchancellor (Joss Ackland) is able to shout "What is that *gling-ing-gling-ing-gling-ing* noise all about?" into its speaking tube and get a coherent answer (*Terry Pratchett's Hogfather*, scene 10). Hex seems sapient, for a given value of sapient; it can believe, when ordered to

---

[8] For example, providing Sam Vimes with a copy of Gen. A. Tacticus's *Veni Vidi Vici: A Soldier's Life* at a key point in *Jingo* (152), or handing a revelatory book about orcs to Glenda in *Unseen Academicals* before she even asks (278).

do so, in the Hogfather (the Discworld equivalent of Father Christmas), and it has desires, writing out a lengthy Hogswatch wish list after asserting its belief (*Hogfather* 241–42).

Hex may be a finding aid, but the model is unrealistic, at least for our unmagical world; we don't see what goes into its database (though it eventually seems to tap into L-Space on its own [Pratchett, Stewart, and Cohen 64–65]), and there does not appear to be a stage between the initial development of Hex and its ability to handle spoken natural-language queries. In spite of poorly phrased questions and arcane error messages like "MELON MELON MELON — OUT OF CHEESE ERROR — REDO FROM START," and an unfortunate incident where it briefly catches insanity from the Bursar (*Hogfather* 91–94), Hex always arrives at the right answer. Our own search engines and databases, alas, do not manage to live up to expectations raised by Hex. But perhaps it is safest if they don't develop quite that level of self-awareness and insist that their FTB (fluffy teddy bear) be present or else refuse to work.

Good Omens

Moving on to the 20th century, *Good Omens: The Nice and Accurate Prophecies of Agnes Nutter, Witch* (1990), is the product of a collaboration between Neil Gaiman and Terry Pratchett. Set roughly contemporaneously with their writing of it in the late 1980s, it is a hilarious, satirical, and deeply profound tale about the end of the world, dealing with "the absurdity of prophecy" and ineffability (Clemons 86) — and in the end, finding that "humans are worth saving, if only because of our utter ridiculousness" (98). (The temptation to just start quoting and not stop is, if anything, even worse than with the Discworld books.)

In 2019 it was released as a six-episode mini-series on Amazon Prime, starring David Tennant as the urbane, sophisticated demon Crowley and Michael Sheen as the book-loving, good-natured angel Aziraphale.[9] The two, as sole permanent representatives of their respective sides on Earth, have developed an appreciation of the planet's pleasures, a well-balanced but clandestine working Arrangement, and more than a hint of actual affection for each other, when it suddenly becomes clear that the Antichrist is due to arrive on Earth and the

---

[9] Perhaps due to ineffability, it was released on May 30 rather than May 31 as expected, so when I heard Gaiman speak on that date at Rutgers University, many of us in the audience had already seen at least the first episode. Gaiman's recounting of his collaboration with the late Sir Terry Pratchett and his intent to honor his memory in the adaptation were quite moving.

countdown clock to Armageddon has already started. The problem is, the Antichrist seems to have been mislaid—and Crowley and Aziraphale can't avert Armageddon without finding him first.

What particularly interests me as a librarian is that there is a great deal of information gathering and use depicted in the book, which is updated in a rather lopsided way for the show set thirty years later. The show is clearly contemporary: characters both mundane and supernatural use cell phones and webcams, cars have Bluetooth, theodolite and ley line readings are confirmed with GPS and entered onto an iPad. Hell even has a Lord of the Files. It is essential, however, that information behavior *not* be evenly updated, since part of the plot hinges on the loss of a particular physical collection of information and how characters compensate for that loss. And in the real world, less efficient or technological methods of information organization and retrieval do of course continue to exist alongside the cutting edge.

For example, the Witchfinder Army—consisting, at this time, solely of Sergeant Shadwell and Private Newton Pulsifer—keeps a very close eye on the news for any evidence of witchy activity and other "Unexplainable Phenomenons. Phenomenatrices. Phenomenice. Things, ye ken well what I mean" (162). In the book, Shadwell receives day-old newspapers from the shop downstairs, which Newt is expected to scour and clip and collate into scrapbooks. The television series retains this method rather than updating it for the internet age and setting up electronic news alerts and so on; it underscores the anachronistic Shadwell's (Michael McKean) abiding parsimony and intensity of focus, and it is just as well since Newt (Jack Whitehall) is kryptonite for computers anyway.[10]

A subtle instance of criticism of information literacy education in the show obliquely acknowledges the different media environment of the updated setting. The child characters, Adam Young (Sam Taylor Buck) and his companions, are great consumers of popular media in all of its formats and cheerfully mash and mangle genres and cultures for their own amusement. When Anathema Device (Adria Arjona) lends Adam a pile of New Age occult magazines called *The New Aquarian*, Adam is fascinated and swallows it all whole, protesting to his father, "It's not rubbish. They wouldn't write about it in magazines if it was rubbish" ("Hard Times," 1.3). When he starts

---

[10] In a scene not included in the television release, Madame Tracy (Miranda Richardson) asks Newt "Wouldn't it be easier to get a computer, dear? It's all on the internet nowadays." But Newt admits "I can't make computers work" (*Script Book* 207).

telling his friends about all the "brilliant" things he's been learning—the existence of Atlantis and the evils of nuclear power, tunneling Tibetan monks and disappearing rainforests, UFOs and government conspiracies and so on—they are a bit hesitant to believe:

> PEPPER (Amma Ris). Adam, I don't think this stuff is, you know… real.
>
> DOG. [growls] [*No one contradicts his Master!*]
>
> ADAM. Things on the Internet can be made up. This is magazines. Of course it's real. ("Saturday Morning Funtime," 1.4)

The most important point for this discussion is that *Good Omens* includes as a major plot device a depiction of the organization and retrieval of essential information in the absence of its primary source. *The Nice and Accurate Prophecies of Agnes Nutter* of the book's subtitle, written in 1655, is the *only* 100% accurate book of prophecies in the world, and only one copy has survived, which has been handed down through Agnes's descendants. "The trouble was that in order to understand the Predictions you had to be able to think like a half-crazed, highly intelligent seventeenth-century witch with a mind like a crossword-puzzle dictionary" (*Good Omens* 85). Additionally, most of Agnes's prophecies "relate to her descendants and their well-being" rather than the world at large (199), making interpretation quite the art. When Agnes's many-times-great granddaughter Anathema, who is also trying to find the spot where Armageddon will take place, loses that single copy early on in *Good Omens*, it seems disastrous.

The person who finds the lost book turns out to be the angel Aziraphale, who runs a bookshop in Soho:

> Aziraphale collected books. If he were totally honest with himself he would have admitted that his bookshop was simply somewhere to store them. He was not unusual in this. In order to maintain his cover as a typical second-hand bookseller, he used every means short of actual physical violence to prevent customers from making a purchase. (*Good Omens* 43)

Aziraphale has, in his back room, a collection of first editions of books of prophecy, mostly signed by the authors, and this particular rarity is one he'd been hunting for years. What he discovers, as he works his way through it, is the exact time and location of the final battle.

Aziraphale's bookshop does have a computer, which he uses solely for "scrupulously accurate" bookkeeping (151), but he does not use this to help him in his research. In the show, he consults a Bible which is on his reference shelf above his desk, then a list of area codes to find the one for Tadfield ("The Book," 1.2); in the book he calls Directory Assistance (161). When Agnes's book later winds up in

Crowley's possession, he complains "Why isn't there an index?" ("The Doomsday Option," 1.5)—but there is one, of a particular sort.

For Anathema, losing the book was *not* the total disaster it seemed to be, because over the generations Agnes's descendants had created an extensively annotated card file interpreting, cross-referencing, and speculating on all 4,000-plus of the prophecies. Anathema is relying not just on archival research in a unique original source, but also on the commentary and interpretation of a line of scholars having a centuries-long conversation about that source. At one point Anathema "leaf[s] through a battered card index" and notes that "I kept meaning to put it all on computer [...]. Word searches and so forth. You know? It'd make it a lot simpler. [...] We've built up quite a concordance over the years, though, and my grandfather came up with a useful cross-referencing system..." (*Good Omens* 201). But with the world due to end in her own lifetime, Anathema just never bothered.

So what happens when this is all updated for a miniseries set in the current day? As it turns out, not too much. For example, Anathema may use a wireless tablet and online maps, but she still gathers information using a pendulum and dowsing rods and writes in a notebook by hand. In keeping with this, in spite of the fact that in the update Agnes's descendants interpreted her predictions about Apple correctly and made pots of money, they still never entered the predictions and annotations into a computerized database—even though, at only 4,000 and some entries, it is not that daunting a task. But Anathema *has* created alarms on her phone to remind her of some major upcoming events, like "Prophecy Alert: Witchfinder will arrive at 12:05" ("Saturday Morning Funtime," 1.4). The information is still not optimally organized; information is found either by rummaging around, through Anathema's recall of specific prophecies, or simply, after the file box is overturned, by picking up a card at random.

In *Good Omens* we have the depiction of a highly specialized, organized, and accessible, but solely personal, database, which could be improved by technology but is reasonably effective as is, even when scrambled (by an incident which could have been prevented by using proper library supplies like hole-drilled cards and a rod-equipped file drawer). The fact that the impending apocalypse makes it seem pointless to create a computer database is a tidy counterpoint to something the child Adam says during the climactic confrontation of the book: "[I]f you stopped tellin' people it's all sorted out after they're dead, they might try sorting it all out while they're alive" (335). As it is, though, this annotated card index is the essential reference source

Anathema uses to figure out what is happening in Lower Tadfield as the world lurches inexorably—or ineffably?—toward Armageddon.

The Buffyverse

Let us move forward a little to the contemporary (for its time) high school library of *Buffy the Vampire Slayer* (aired 1996–2003) and the corporate library and archives of Wolfram and Hart in its spinoff *Angel* (1999–2004). *Buffy*'s first three seasons center around the high school library, run by her Watcher, Rupert Giles (Anthony Head). Many of the plots are driven by books and documents of some sort; demons are imprisoned in books or released by incantations read from books; curses and spells are researched and used or defused; prophecies are translated and interpreted rightly or wrongly; key historical or demonological information needs to be located in order to figure out what they are up against and how to fight it. "We'll hit serious research mode!" is an oft-heard rallying cry for the Scooby Gang, as they call themselves. The Sunnydale High School Library is a mostly real-world setting with the familiar physical apparatus of card catalogs, indexes, file cabinets, and even computers (over Giles's objections). But the collection is highly specialized and is peculiarly supplemented by Giles's own large personal collection of books; as Principal Snyder (Armin Shimerman) sarcastically inquires, "Just how is *Blood Rites and Sacrifices* appropriate material for a public school library? Chess Club branching out?" ("Gingerbread," 3.11).[11]

Is Rupert Giles really a librarian, or is this just a front for his job as Buffy's Watcher? His fictional biography does not list a library degree; he seems to have gotten the job on the strength of his general knowledge, his tweediness, and his English accent—and of course through the behind-the-scenes machinations of the Watchers' Council, which needs to place him in a good position to oversee Buffy. We don't really see him engaging in the activities that would be part of the regular job duties of a typical high school librarian—he checks books in and out once in a while, but we seldom or never see him purchasing and processing books and AV materials relevant to the courses taught at the school, giving general reference help, supervising a study hall, training student volunteers, fixing the photocopier or the overhead

---

[11] "Gingerbread" (3.11) is a particularly interesting episode, dealing with parental hysteria and censorship and climaxing with the near-burning of Giles's books along with Buffy (Sarah Michelle Gellar), Willow (Alyson Hannigan), and Amy (Elizabeth Anne Allen).

projector, or most importantly for this age group, teaching classes in research techniques and information literacy.[12]

And we don't really see him guiding the research of the Scoobies like a librarian would, teaching them efficient search strategies or the use of finding aids—they usually just pile books on the table and hunt-and-peck through them randomly. Of course, using the *Reader's Guide to Periodical Literature* and the card catalog, or their late 1990s CD-ROM or online or demonological equivalents, does not make for exciting and visually compelling TV. And the writers would have to know these things exist in order to include their use in the show. After the destruction of the library and much of the high school at the end of season 3, Giles no longer keeps of the pretense of being a librarian, but sets up his collection first in his home, and then in his storefront The Magic Box, *"Your one-stop spot to shop for all your occult needs."*

Giles was very popular, though, during the show's first few seasons as a largely positive, if sometimes problematic, popular culture representation of librarianship. An article in *American Libraries* praises his ability to "[bridge] the chasm between the information as it lives in the text and [...] transfer [...] that information into a form [Buffy and her team] can actually use" and his respect for the "sacredness of the book" and ability to know and name "the forces of darkness," but admits that his technological ineptitude is a problem, and his "collection-development policy must be an extraordinary document" (DeCandido 41–46). A somewhat humorless rebuttal a few months later takes issue with this "negative and over-simplified [image]" of the profession, but makes the valid point that "[Giles] has no concept of reader service and is always surprised when students enter the library to do real research" (Cullen 42).

Scholars who are not librarians do not seem to see this as a problem as much as we in the profession might. English professor Adriana Estill pointed out as a positive "Giles's near synonymity with the physical library as he directs the students—with nary a glance at a card or online catalog [...]" (241). This physical relationship with the books is something he celebrates, explaining his aversion to the computer:

> Books smell. Musty and, and, and rich. The knowledge gained from
> a computer, is, uh, it ... it has no, no texture, no, no context. [...] If

---

[12] I was working in a small rural college library at the time this show was set, and it's hard to picture Rupert Giles with a set of giant card catalog cards, an easel, and a pointer, trying to hold the attention of a group of two dozen or so bored and hormonal young people. I doubt he would see much point in trying.

> it's to last, then, the getting of knowledge should be, uh, tangible, it
> should be, um ... smelly. ("I, Robot—You, Jane")

It is the "collective and physical search [...] the act of convening at a table piled high with books" (Estill 248), and within the community-centric sanctuary of the library, that is being privileged here in these early seasons. The team works together relatively harmoniously towards a shared and achievable goal. This team feeling is something that is hard to recapture, after the group goes its various ways after graduation and the series gets darker. It is in the celebrated musical episode "Once More, With Feeling" (6.7) that Giles comes to the realization that he has been doing too much for Buffy, that he is the reason why she is "standing still," that he is "standing in her way" by facing and solving her problems for her—and, one might argue, by not training Buffy to do research on her own with as much dedication as he trains her to fight.

The final example I want to look at in some detail is *Angel*, the spin-off from *Buffy: The Vampire Slayer*, which follows the 250-year-old vampire Angel (David Boreanaz) as he sets up shop as a private investigator in Los Angeles to "help the hopeless" and make amends for his past life. One member of the team he gathers around himself is Wesley Wyndam-Pryce (Alexis Denisof), who was trained as a Watcher like Giles, but turned out to be too inexperienced and overconfident and just plain prissy to be effective in Sunnydale. By the end of season 4 of *Angel*, he has been through many traumatic changes but still, at heart, has that Watcher's hunger for knowledge.

In the last episode of season 4, "Home," Angel Investigations has finally penetrated the very center of the evil multinational corporation they've been fighting for years, Wolfram and Hart, and instead of meeting resistance, find themselves offered their deepest desires and the chance to effect change from within the belly of the beast. They are presented with control of the L. A. branch of the company—"the building, assets, personnel, letterhead, paper clips, all of it [...] a turnkey, state-of-the-art, multi-tasking operation"—and more specifically, each member of the team is tempted with the leadership of a division in the company exactly suited to his or her personal desires.

Wesley is shown into an office in which several dozen old leather-bound books are lined up on a table. He's unimpressed until his guide shows him that he can whisper the name of the text he wants into a book, and the pages automatically fill with its contents. Though conceptually not that much different from a tablet hooked up to the Project Gutenberg website, this is somewhat more remarkable because these texts come from the uniquely esoteric archives and files of the company. Wesley winds up saying, and not just about the library, "As much as it pains me to admit it, there's probably a great deal we could accomplish with the resources available here" ("Home," 4.22).

Those resources also include the entire Files and Records Department, which actually has a finding aid, Gwen—personified, amusingly enough, by the actress who plays Flo in the Progressive Insurance commercials (Stephanie Courtney). When Wolfram and Hart employee Lilah Morgan (Stephanie Romanov) asks for all the records on Angel in the episode "Dad" (3.10), Gwen hands her a thick 3-ring binder—which is not the information itself but simply the reference key to the thirty-five filing cabinets full of actual records. While Gwen has a computer interface, she also has direct mental access to everything in her department, and when Lilah voices a question aloud after fourteen hours of searching, Gwen is able to answer it instantly:

> LILAH. How did you…
>
> GWEN. I'm Files and Records. It's my job.
>
> LILAH. [*gets up*] You mean I've been sitting here for the last fourteen hours…
>
> GWEN. Ah-hmm.
>
> LILAH. To find that you know everything that's in this case file.
>
> GWEN. No, Miss Morgan.
>
> LILAH. Oh.
>
> GWEN. I know everything in every case file. I'm Files and Records, it's my—
>
> LILAH. —your job. Unbelievable. ("Dad," 3.10)

This is somewhat encouraging—we do at least see a finding aid and a caretaker who knows how to search. But it is also quite limited, since Lilah's fourteen hours of searching do not turn up the answer she's looking for, and while the magically aided memory of the librarian-figure finds it within seconds, she does not volunteer to help. (Of course, it could also be that Lilah is just not that good at using a finding aid, and the company culture at Wolfram and Hart is every man, woman, and demon for itself…nobody is going to help anybody without some substantial *quid pro quo*.)

Other examples and conclusions

There are many other interesting cases of popular science fiction and fantasy media depictions of information-seeking behavior, offering additional perspectives on what our users may be expecting when they walk in our doors.

For example, Madame Irma Pince in the *Harry Potter* books and movies embodies the worst stereotype of a child's nightmare librarian, and students avoid her at all costs, relying instead on Buffy-ish hunt-and-peck sessions and Hermione's insatiable curiosity and retentive memory when they need to do research. Rowling admits she knows better:

> I would like to apologise for you and any other librarians present here today and my get-out clause is always if they'd had a pleasant, helpful librarian, half my plots would be gone. 'Cause the answer invariably is in a book, but Hermione has to go and find it. If they'd had a good librarian, that would have been that problem solved. So ... sorry. [...] She sprang directly from my childhood fear of scary librarians. The kind who hate kids. (qtd. in "Irma Pince")

It is a good plot device for books and media—but a very bad model for young readers who need to do actual research. As Alison R. Jones points out, Pince is concerning "because librarian stereotypes keep library patrons from fully utilizing library services" (191). Still, students could do far worse than to emulate the way Hermione relies on and treasures her reference books.

On a more positive note, there are successful archival searches in newspapers and microfilm and quests for books on amphibians in the early–1980s public library in the Netflix series *Stranger Things* ("Holly, Jolly," 1.3, and "The Pollywog," 2.3), where librarian Marissa (Christi Waldon) is a relatively sympathetic and helpful character. The BBC America series *Orphan Black,* more contemporary with our own time, features searches in the Cold River Asylum archives, where a caretaker directs Sarah (Tatiana Maslany) to the correct boxes ("To Hound Nature in Her Wanderings," 2.6), and in online newspaper databases ("Gag or Throttle," 5.7).[13]

What I find interesting is that we see here writers who are known library lovers—Tolkien, Gaiman, Pratchett, and Rowling in particular—who know how modern libraries work and have been known to publicly praise librarians, perpetuating this image of the library as either a disorganized place where users must find their own way, or guarded by a fierce protector who would prefer users not to touch the books at all. These authors depict information searches where what is needed is found either by rummaging around or by taking advantage of the prodigious memory of the librarian. This is

---

[13] Further back, viewers of the original *Star Trek* may remember Mr. Atoz, the librarian in the episode "All Our Yesterdays" (3.23), who memorably said that "A library serves no purpose unless someone is using it," or Memory Alpha, the Federation's library planetoid in "The Lights of Zetar" (3.18).

what librarians have to contend with when we try to introduce what libraries and librarians *really* do to an audience who may only have encountered these pop culture images.[14]

I want to close with a comment about how I use this in my own teaching, since the panels where this paper started always concluded with a practical Q&A section on research and publishing. When I teach research on popular culture topics, I talk about using specialized subject and journal indexes, and the difficulties of access for independent scholars not affiliated with a college or university and how to get around them. I touch briefly on evaluating resources and note that a lot of my research is in fan-created book or show-specific wikis, *TV Tropes,* and Pinterest boards that require an extra level of attention to accuracy, reliability, and copyright issues before I cite them or use them in a PowerPoint presentation. I use the fact that people obviously see a need for and create their own reference works to segue into my next suggested strategy, which is organizing and building one's own personal database of research resources. I like to use Anathema's card file when I discuss the benefits of using a citation manager like EndNote to create a personal collection of information. Another topic I talk about is research as a conversation, a conversation you are having with the scholars who have come before you, which requires an awareness of the extent of earlier scholarship and a knowledge of how to find it.

It is too bad that the creation and use of indexes, bibliographies, library guides, and the like does not make for good drama. Just think of the time it would have saved Gandalf if he could have pulled up the catalog record for all documents in the Minas Tirith archives referencing the One Ring....

Works Cited

"All Our Yesterdays." *Star Trek,* created by Gene Roddenberry, season 3, episode 23, NBC, 14 Mar. 1969.

"The Book." *Good Omens,* created by Neil Gaiman, season 1, episode 2, Amazon Prime Video, 31 May 2019. *Amazon,* amazon.com/Prime-Video/b?node=2676882011.

---

[14] I'm not talking here about *using* pop culture references in bibliographic instruction; unfortunately, this just tends to lead to students rolling their eyes at our "lameness" (Marshall 8).

Clemons, Amy Lea. "Adapting Revelation: *Good Omens* as Comic Corrective." *Journal of the Fantastic in the Arts*, vol. 28, no. 1, 2017, pp. 81–101.

Croft, Janet Brennan. "The Education of a Witch: Tiffany Aching, Hermione Granger, and Gendered Magic in Discworld and Potterworld." *Mythlore*, vol. 27, no. 3/4 (#105/106), 2009, pp. 121–42.

——. "The Golempunk Manifesto: Ownership of the Means of Production in Pratchett's Discworld." *Discworld and Beyond: Essays on the Works of Terry Pratchett*, edited by Kristin Noone and Emily Lavin Leverett, McFarland, 2020, pp. 111–23.

Cullen, John. "Rupert Giles, the Professional-image Slayer." *American Libraries*, vol. 31, no. 5, 2000, p. 42.

"Dad." *Angel*, created by Joss Whedon and David Greenwalt, season 3, episode 10, WB Television Network, 10 Dec. 2001.

DeCandido, GraceAnne A. "Bibliographic Good vs. Evil in *Buffy the Vampire Slayer*." *American Libraries*, vol. 30, no. 8, 1999, pp. 41–47.

Devereaux, Peter, and Carla Diane Hayden. *The Card Catalog: Books, Cards, and Literary Treasures*. Chronicle Books, 2017.

"The Doomsday Option." *Good Omens*, created by Neil Gaiman, season 1, episode 5, Amazon Prime Video, 31 May 2019. *Amazon*, amazon.com/Prime-Video/b?node=2676882011.

Estill, Adriana. "Going to Hell: Placing the Library in *Buffy the Vampire Slayer*." *The Library as Place: History, Community, and Culture*, edited by John Buschman and Gloria J. Leckie, Libraries Unlimited, 2007, pp. 231–50.

"Gag or Throttle." *Orphan Black*, created by Graeme Manson and John Fawcett, season 5, episode 7, BBC America, 22 July 2017.

Gaiman, Neil. *The Quite Nice and Fairly Accurate* Good Omens *Script Book*. HarperCollins, 2019.

Gaiman, Neil and Terry Pratchett. *Good Omens*. Ace, 1990.

"Gingerbread." *Buffy the Vampire Slayer*, created by Joss Whedon, season 3, episode 11, WB Television Network, 12 Jan. 1999.

Hammond, Wayne. "Papermaking in the Shire." *Amon Hen*, iss. 94, Nov. 1988, pp. 11–18.

"Hard Times." *Good Omens*, created by Neil Gaiman, season 1, episode 3, Amazon Prime Video, 31 May 2019. *Amazon*, amazon.com/Prime-Video/b?node=2676882011.

"Holly, Jolly." *Stranger Things*, created by the Duffer Brothers, season 1, episode 3, Netflix, 15 July 2016. *Netflix*, netflix.com.

"Home." *Angel*, created by Joss Whedon and David Greenwalt, season 4, episode 22, WB Television Network, 7 May 2003.

"I, Robot—You, Jane." *Buffy the Vampire Slayer*, created by Joss Whedon, season 1, episode 8, WB Television Network, 28 Apr. 1997.

"Irma Pince." *Harry Potter Wiki*. https://harrypotter.fandom.com/wiki/Irma_Pince#cite_note-26. 14 Aug. 2019. Accessed 5 Sept. 2019.

Jones, Alison R. "A Librarian's View of Madam Pince." *Harry Potter for Nerds II: Essays for Fans, Academics, and Lit Geeks*, edited by Kathryn N. McDaniel and Travis Prinzi, Unlocking Press, 2015, pp. 191–204.

Larsen, Kristine. "'Books! Best Weapons in the World': How Libraries Save the World in Popular Culture." (In this volume.)

"The Lights of Zetar." *Star Trek,* created by Gene Roddenberry, season 3, episode 18, NBC, 31 Jan. 1969.

The Lord of the Rings: The Fellowship of the Ring. 2001. Special Extended DVD Edition, New Line, 2002.

Marshall, Jerilyn. "What Would Buffy Do?: The Use of Popular Culture Examples in Undergraduate Library Instruction." Annual Meeting of the PCA/ACA, 11–16 Mar. 2002, Toronto.

McIlwaine, Catherine. *Tolkien: Maker of Middle-earth*. Bodleian Library, 2018.

Oberhelman, David D. "A Brief History of Libraries in Middle-earth: Manuscript and Book Repositories in Tolkien's Legendarium." *Loremasters and Libraries in Fantasy and Science Fiction: A Gedenkschrift for David Oberhelman*, edited by Jason Fisher and Janet Brennan Croft, Mythopoeic Press, 2022, pp. 155–65. Originally published in *Truths Breathed Through Silver: The Inklings' Moral and Mythopoeic Legacy*, edited by Jonathan B. Himes, with Joe R. Christopher and Salwa Khoddam, Cambridge Scholars, 2008, pp. 81–92.

"Once More, With Feeling." *Buffy the Vampire Slayer*, created by Joss Whedon, season 6, episode 7, United Paramount Network, 6 Nov. 2001.

"The Pollywog." *Stranger Things*, created by the Duffer Brothers, season 2, episode 3, Netflix, 27 October 2017. *Netflix*, netflix.com.

Pratchett, Terry. *Guards! Guards!* Harper, 1989.

——. *Hogfather*. Harper, 1996.

——. *Interesting Times*. Harper, 1994.

——. *Jingo*. Harper, 1997.

——. *Small Gods*. HarperCollins, 1992.

——. *Unseen Academicals*. Harper, 2009.

Pratchett, Terry and Stephen Briggs. *Turtle Recall: The Discworld Companion…So Far*. Harper, 2013.

Pratchett, Terry and The Discworld Emporium. *The Compleat Ankh-Morpork*. Doubleday, 2014.

Pratchett, Terry, Ian Stewart, and Jack Cohen. *The Science of Discworld*. Anchor, 2014.

"Saturday Morning Funtime." *Good Omens*, created by Neil Gaiman, season 1, episode 4, Amazon Prime Video, 31 May 2019. *Amazon*, amazon.com/Prime-Video/b?node=2676882011.

Sawyer, Andy. "The Librarian and His Domain." *Terry Pratchett: Guilty of Literature*, edited by Andrew M. Butler et al., The Science Fiction Foundation, 2001, pp. 31–50.

Terry Pratchett's Hogfather. Directed by Vadim Jean, The Mob, 2007.

"To Hound Nature in Her Wanderings." *Orphan Black*, created by Graeme Manson and John Fawcett, season 2, episode 6, BBC America, 24 May 2014.

Tolkien, J. R. R. *The Letters of J. R. R. Tolkien: A Selection*. Edited by Humphrey Carpenter and Christopher Tolkien, 1st Houghton Mifflin paperback ed., Houghton Mifflin, 2000.

——. *The Lord of the Rings*. 50th Anniversary Edition, Houghton Mifflin, 2004.

"Tooth and Claw." *Doctor Who*, season 2, episode 2, BBC America, 6 Oct. 2006.

Waters, Laurie. "Collecting: Lighting for the Lacemaker." *Lace News*. 12 Apr. 2011, updated 23 Sept. 2017. lacenews.net/2011/04/12/collecting-lighting-for-the-lacemaker.

Part 3: Topics in Tolkien Studies

Legal Precedent and Noldorin History: Míriel's Weaving

Cami Agan

J. R. R. TOLKIEN'S EXTANT WRITINGS about his created world, known collectively as *The History of Middle-earth*, have revealed the author's processes of writing and revision, his shifting positions regarding the framing structures of the major narratives, and his developing interests in historical, cultural, and philosophical issues related to his Secondary World, Arda. In particular, his work now collected in *Morgoth's Ring*, which Tolkien returned to following the publication of *The Lord of the Rings,* contains a treasure trove of Tolkien's considerations and revisions of his foundational First Age narratives. As he returned his attention to the First Age, Tolkien revised and expanded earlier versions of the *Quenta Silmarillion*, but he also crafted new essays, dialogues, judgments, and debates concerning metaphysical, philosophical, and anthropological systems of the Eldar. As Christopher Tolkien explains,

> Meditating long on the world that he had brought into being and was now in part unveiled [by the publication of *LotR*], he had become absorbed in analytic speculation concerning its underlying postulates. [...] [H]e must satisfy the requirements of a coherent theological and metaphysical system, rendered now more complex in its presentation by the supposition of obscure and conflicting elements in its roots and its tradition. (Foreword viii)

The volumes of *The History of Middle-earth* thus reveal Tolkien's later concern with both the overall vision/scope of the Elder Days, as well as the minutiae of cultural practices, such as Elven marriage and legal debate, that would (or should) conform to "a coherent theological and metaphysical system." In these "meditations," Tolkien often worked through several, at times incomplete, versions of texts that analyze problems springing from decisions and events of the Elder Days. For example, developed in several versions and part of the larger treatise entitled "The Customs of the Eldar," the "Story of Finwë and Míriel" explores the thematic concerns vital to Tolkien in the period: "the immortality (and death) of the Elves; the mode of their reincarnation; [...] and above all, the power and significance of Melkor-Morgoth [...]" (viii). In the process of exploring these vital thematics, the "Story of Finwë and Míriel," and specifically the portions known as "Doom of Finwë and Míriel" or "Statute of Finwë and Míriel," foregrounds Míriel as a central figure in the Noldor's history, particularly as a source for and creator of historical and aesthetic materials recounting/documenting that history.

Thus, although Míriel quickly recedes from the published *Silmarillion's* narrative of the Noldor's fall and exile once she decides to leave her body and never return, exhausted from the spiritual cost of giving birth to the "Spirit of Fire" (Silm 63), *Morgoth's Ring* centers Míriel's particular positions as first to "die" in Valinor and as uniquely gifted artist-craftsperson. As Christopher Tolkien explains, the "Story of Finwë and Míriel" "would assume an extraordinary importance in my father's later work on *The Silmarillion*" (205). Because of its ramifications for the Noldor's tragic exile in Middle-earth, Míriel's choices and the tales that flower from it grow, arguably, as significant as the Great Tale of Tinúviel, for just as "Unchanged, imperishable, [Lúthien's song] is sung still in Valinor beyond the hearing of the world [...]" (Silm 187), Míriel's artistic creations continue and endure, apart and eternal in the Blessed Realm. In fact, Míriel's position and her aesthetic skill not only affect the unfolding of the Noldor's history, but, like Lúthien's song, result in astonishing artistic representations of those events. In Tolkien's later conception of the Eldar, Míriel thus emerges as far more than first wife of Finwë and mother/namer of Fëanor. The judgments and debates that arise from her decision to die provide the catalyst for a vast collection of queries, responses, and judgments that reflect the unique "death" of Míriel and that define Elven marriage from that point forward; as such, Míriel reflects both the problematic nature of Elven immortality and its far-reaching ramifications for the Eldar. Subsequently, as resident chronicler of the Noldor's post-exile history, she also reflects the vital role of the collector, creator, and craftsperson who preserves the history of her people in the imperishable Halls of Vairë.

"The Story of Finwë and Míriel" as Legal Precedent

As detailed in "Laws and Customs Among the Eldar," and particularly in the "Story of Finwë and Míriel" (209ff), Míriel's resignation of her body raised serious debate regarding Elven marriage (or remarriage), both for the Eldar and the Valar,[1] in that the question of Míriel's death,

---

[1] In his editorial introduction to the Second Phase of the *Later Quenta*, Christopher Tolkien calls the sections detailing the "Laws and Customs of the Eldar" "a major independent disquisition concerning the nature of the Eldar.

her decision about rebirth, and the resulting marital status of Finwë force the Valar to confront the ways in which Melkor has perverted their creation of Arda. "Of the Severance of Marriage" indicates, for example, that "death and the sundering of spirit and body was one of the griefs of Arda Marred [...]" (225), and although Elven marriage was naturally permanent, the death of one spouse marred this permanence, so that the Elves "did not know what should be done or thought" (225).[2] Even before the darkening of Valinor and the death of the Two Trees, Míriel's "death" points to the dissonance Morgoth has sewn into the very Creation. In response to the question of whether Finwë might remarry, and after a significant time in consultation with the other Valar—rendered as a fascinatingly detailed debate (233-50)—Mandos's "Doom of Finwë and Míriel" stands: "If Míriel, thy wife, will not return [from the dead] and releases thee, your union is dissolved, and thou hast leave to take another wife" (237). According to the Doom, then, if the dead spouse does not wish or is not permitted to be reborn, the surviving spouse might remarry after a period of ten years.[3] This particular judgment regarding Finwë and Míriel thus becomes a general law for the Eldar and, interestingly, acknowledges the inevitability of future deaths of the Eldar, consequences of the Marring of Arda. As a result, the "Story of Finwë and Míriel" reveals layers of debate, concern, and anxiety regarding her unique decision to pass out of even the Blessed Realm. From a primary world perspective, the debate and doom regarding Míriel and Finwë points to Tolkien's concern, so evident in the Great Tale of Tinúviel, with death, immortality, and marriage.

Arising out of an account of their marriage laws and customs, this discussion extends into a lengthy analysis of the meaning of death, immortality and rebirth in respect of the Elves" (199).

[2] Manuscript A's passage goes further: the Valar "perceived that this was a grave matter, and a portent, in that Míriel had died even in Aman, and had brought sorrow to the Blessed Realm, things which they before had believed could not come to pass" (239). Elizabeth Whittingham notes that the debate concerning Finwë and Míriel reveals that "The fall [...] is in the very process of creation, and everything is tainted from the beginning" (145–49). In *Arda Reconstructed*, Douglas Kane expresses regret that the debate of the Valar was not included in the published version of *The Silmarillion* (82), and David Bratman offers a reading of the debate in his detailing of Tolkien's style (76).

[3] Amelia Rutledge calls this sequence "the conclusion of a quasi-legal debate in the absence of precedents" (59); in my reading, it *sets* the legal precedent and leads to the layers of later commentary. For a helpful summary of Tolkien's various versions regarding Finwë and Míriel, all now contained in *Morgoth's Ring*, and the order in which they might have ultimately been organized, see Whittingham (141–49).

Consistently through the various versions of the "Story and Doom of Finwë and Míriel," there are numerous references to records, texts, and lore books that contain and preserve the pronouncement about the death of a spouse and the possibility for remarriage. Such references point to Míriel's role as a kind of irritant that results in the pearl of a vast legal collection. In the section entitled "The Statute of Finwë and Míriel and the Debate of the Valar at its Making" (209ff), for instance, the text characterizes the "The Doom of Finwë and Míriel" (226ff) as legal precedent that prompts subsequent additions, queries, and scholarly commentary: "there are many commentaries that record the explanation of points arising from its consideration" (226), so that the Doom/later commentaries "was preserved among the chief of their books of law [...]" (254). Míriel's death and her sundering from Finwë thus result in the creation-development of what must be a large collection of legal texts (and subsequent commentaries) documenting the possible problems resulting from the death of one marital partner, and echoing repeatedly the lament of Arda Marred.[4]

Further, in Tolkien's notes following "Laws and Customs," he adds that "the Eldar were permitted to attend all conclaves [of the Valar] and many did so (especially those that so deeply concerned them, their fate, and their place in Arda, as did this matter)" (250). Far from the image in the published *Silmarillion* of the Ring of Doom where the Valar declare and judge (see Silm 71–9, 82), here Tolkien details a working community of Vala and Eldar, debating, discussing, and, eventually, codifying and cataloguing. Viewed through the lens of the debates and statutes in *Morgoth's Ring*, Valinor becomes a scholarly community with the Valar welcoming witnesses and commentary on their judgments. Those Elvish observers would then record the conclave, comment on it, and leave a document for later discussion/commentary, as with the documents surrounding Míriel and Finwë. Because the Valar's debate regarding Míriel and Finwë is preserved and "was among the documents of lore most deeply studied and pondered" (251), it is safe to assume that those documents would then rest with the "loremaster-librarians"

---

[4] Given the subsequently tragic events of the Noldor's rebellion, the Doom of Míriel and Finwë portends the Doom of Mandos to Fëanor after the Kinslaying: "For though Eru appointed to you to die not in Eä, and no sickness may assail you, yet slain ye may be, and slain ye shall be: by weapon and by torment and by grief [...]" (Silm 88). The numerous losses of the Noldor and all the Eldar in Middle-earth as a result of Morgoth's return justify the concern and the necessity to revisit the question of remarriage for the Eldar.

(Oberhelman 160), initially in Aman, to be organized, catalogued, and re-catalogued as new commentaries emerge. While references to collections of Elvish wisdom are common throughout Tolkien's extant materials—in the form of tales related by Pengoloð and detailed in various framing devices by Ælfwine—the legal nature of the "statute" and the use of the term "books of law" potentially gestures to a different set of holdings: a vast and ever-expanding collection of decrees, judgments, and debates that later Eldar might consult as a system for guiding their decisions and lives.

"Of the Severance of Marriage" (225–27) reads as one of those legal "books of lore" and offers clear evidence of the kinds of textual layers that a series of legal volumes would contain. As the section opens, it dutifully cites extant material detailing Elven immortality: "Much has now been said concerning death and re-birth among the Elves. It may be asked: of what effect were these upon marriage?" (225). With a reference to the original conclave and earlier commentary, "much has been said," the passage then self-consciously refers to new queries it will entertain, "It may be asked," and organizes the new analysis through questions about the resulting effects on Elven marriage. Soon after, the account directly cites precedent, known as the Doom of Finwë and Míriel: "Manwë delivered his ruling through the mouth of Námo Mandos, the Judge" (225); this citation serves to open up the text for further commentary on the statute. In the last part of the section, which is incomplete, the existence of later editorial commentary becomes clear: "Upon this pronouncement ["The Doom of Finwë and Míriel"] [...] there are many commentaries that record the explanation of points arising from its consideration, some given by the Valar, some later reasoned by the Eldar. Of these the more important are here added" (226). With the phrase "the more important are here added," we get a brief glimpse of a curator-editor, gleaning previous commentaries and presenting only those most central to the argument. Initial judgment, following by further explanation from the Valar, and yet more details developed by the Eldar, then curated by a later scholar, all form part of this compilation, a book or series of volumes growing from the original oral pronouncement, "The Doom of Finwë and Míriel." In its organization, then, the account models the kinds of layers that develop from a legal judgment over time, and thus also gestures to a library or collection of such volumes. Subsequently, the account uses the formula "It was asked / It was answered" (226–27) to frame the relevant queries about Elven spirit and body in marriage. The sense of layers and depth, so clear in the development of the major tales of the First Age, here suggests a similar trove of documents, or layers of voices within documents, surrounding crucial questions of mores among the Eldar.[5] In addition to the scribes recording and bards reciting tales, then, "Laws and Customs of the Eldar" indicates there must also be scholars of the law—working in special libraries or collections—who consult these ancient precedents, read, re-copy, analyze, and comment on them.

In the debate surrounding the Doom of Finwë and Míriel, Nienna's observation that "The severance of the *fëa* was in Míriel a thing special" (242), resounds both in the context of Elven history and in the context of ages long textual production. The Doom and her decision to remain in the Halls of Mandos results in the loss of one who could curb Fëanor's fiery will, in Finwë's remarriage, in the birth of Fingolfin and Finarfin, and the resulting history of exile and tragedy the *Quenta Silmarillion* recounts. The tales that Fëanor boasts as the legacy of his choice to leave Valinor spring at least partially from his mother's inability to recover from giving birth to him. Interestingly, her decision also results in the development of layers upon layers of legal texts: records of Valarin statutes, queries and responses to those statutes, later citation of those statutes in books of lore, and the creation of vast holdings, living documents that later Eldar consult, engage with, and account for in their own judgments. Likely, the memory of those statutes and commentaries continued to influence the Noldor in exile in Middle-earth, as socio-political events often brought the Eldar into fraught relations with each other. What was Aredhel's recourse, for instance, once she escaped Ëol with Maeglin and returned to Gondolin? The Doom appears to indicate she remains married to him, at least for the short time they lived. However, might there have been consultation of these statutes and their commentary, arguments regarding the extent of Aredhel's freedom of choice to marry the Dark Elf, and might her particular "marriage" alter or reframe the precedent of Míriel and Finwë with yet more commentary?[6] As with Míriel's decision to renounce her body, Ëol's decision to seduce Aredhel into Nan Elmoth and "[take] her to wife" (Silm 133) evokes Arda Marred, and particularly, the evil fruits of the Kinslaying and exile of the Noldor. Given Gondolin's reputation as a repository of lore, we can safely assume the presence of scholars familiar with these "books of

---

[5] Whittingham also notes that the Question-Answer format "introduces it as a historical text that is based on a combination of information from the Valar and the interpretation of the Eldar" (151).

[6] For a full discussion of the rape of Aredhel, see Whitaker.

law"/precedent who could advise and develop the statute in Aredhel's particular case. No less than the well of story developed in the First Age informs later dwellers in Middle-earth, Aredhel's example suggests that the Doom of Finwë and Míriel establishes a well of precedent, a vast and ancient collection of texts that inform and instruct the later inhabitants of Arda.

Míriel as chronicler of Noldorin history

Once Finwë arrives at the Halls of Mandos, Míriel's position grows even more significant to the notion of a "collection," specifically a collection eternally preserving the history of the exiled Noldor. In the *Later Quenta*, Míriel, known as Serendë,[7] the Broideress, is referenced alongside Rúmil as among the chief early artists-craftspeople of the Noldor:

> her hands were more skilled to fineness than any hands even of the Noldor. By her was the craft of needles devised; and were but one fragment of the broideries of Míriel to be seen in Middle-earth it would be held dearer than a king's realm, for the richness of her devices and the fire of their colours were as manifold and as bright as the glory of leaf and flower and wing in the fields of Yavanna. Therefore was she named Míriel Serendë. (185)

Her needle, like Rúmil's pen, produces a new art form—in her case embroidery or needlecraft—and results in aesthetic productions that align her with the finest of the Noldor's creators, and even with the Vala Yavanna. The account also suggests that her creations preserve and reflect an ideal, in color, depth, and likeness, to "real" creation, a capacity that later tapestries, such as those in Menegroth, Gondolin, and later Lothlórien, can only dimly reflect. Thus, in addition to the crafting of jewels and runes, Míriel's creative powers point to an early positive form of sub-creation of the Noldor in Aman. In contrast to her son Fëanor's "greedy love" (Silm 69) for his sub-created Simarils, Míriel's weaving/embroidery appears to be a communal offering, visible to those in Aman and closely echoing the creation of Yavanna herself. While not reflected in the published *Silmarillion*, Tolkien's later attention to Míriel's role and labor point to a curative sub-creation for her and for the Noldor, in contrast to Fëanor's destructive and obsessive craft. In adding her epithet, Serendë the Broideress, the passage also aligns her with heroic and/or artistic action that a new name warrants; her identity and her cultural contribution are bound up in her hands, her making, and in the creation of fine aesthetic production.

---

[7] The alternate spelling, Serindë, is also used.

In the earliest version of the "Story of Finwë and Míriel," Míriel declines to be reborn following the pronouncement of the Doom and thus opens the possibility for Finwë to marry Indis. Significantly, the decision also reorients Míriel to her creative power source, the needle: "And Míriel has dwelt ever since in the house of Vairë, and it is her part to record there the histories of the kin of Finwë and all the deeds of the Noldor" (207). Her prodigious skills allow her to contribute "her part," the significant role of creating beauty out of the tragedies of Noldorin exile. While this passage does not indicate Míriel returns to her body, later versions of the tale expand to include her reincarnation, uniquely in the history of the Elves, to her original body; significantly, this reincarnation aligns with her return to her art: the recording of history via her needle.[8] Additionally, Míriel's habitation in the halls of Vairë locates her in a space already marked out for sub-creation, as Vairë's task, too, is weaving: "[she] weaves all things that have ever been in Time into her storied webs [...]" (Silm 28). While Vairë is master weaver of "all things", the unfolding of the drama of Arda, Míriel specializes in her people's particular contributions to that drama. Like the scribes and scholars, or Elven "loremasters" (271) as Christopher Tolkien calls them, Míriel's weaving represents another method of artistic preservation of the events of mythic import to Arda. In this role, Míriel works as an artist-chronicler, contributing her records, her sub-creation, to the halls of Vairë; rather than an illuminated manuscript, she illuminates the halls with her handiwork, recounting and preserving the events of her people.

A later version of the episode notes that Míriel enters her body once again, and is permitted to do so for one particular purpose: to use her skills to create and to represent the long tale of the Noldor's exile.

---

[8] See Tolkien's notes regarding Míriel's unique position; because her body remained preserved in Aman, she was able to return to it, rather than be reborn (250). See also in Christopher Tolkien's discussion about this detail and the complex and often contradictory nature of Míriel's body, the location of the House of Vairë and its relation to the Halls of Mandos in Tolkien's various revisions (263–65n9). Whittingham refers to Míriel as "a unique exception for all time" (151) in returning to her original body. She also notes the changes regarding Míriel returning to her body in the "Shibboleth of Fëanor" (166). The "Shibboleth of Fëanor" claims that "Míriel was condemned to remain forever discarnate" (Peoples 335), and there is no mention of her weaving historical accounts of the Noldor. It is unclear whether Tolkien viewed possessing a body as *necessary* for the labor of embroidery-weaving, but the notion of her skill (and the Noldor's skill) so often linked to "handiwork" (*Morgoth's Ring* 92) or "dexterity of hand" (*Peoples* 333) seems to suggest so.

That is, in this version, assigning her the role of chronicler-artist *requires* re-embodiment. Reincarnated, she seeks entry to the halls of Vairë:

> [...] Míriel was accepted by Vairë and became her chief handmaid; and all the tidings of the Noldor down the years from their beginning were brought to her, and she wove them in webs *historical* [emphasis mine], so fair and skilled that they seemed to live, imperishable, shining with a light of many hues fairer than are known in Middle-earth. This labour Finwë is at times permitted to look upon. And still she is at work, though her name has been changed. For now she is *Fíriel*, which to the Eldar signifies, 'She that died', and also 'She that sighed'. As fair as the webs of *Fíriel* is praise that is given seldom even to works of the Eldar. (250)

As handmaid to Vairë, Míriel works as a kind of apprentice to the Vala, developing the Noldorin collection with great skill and with direct access—"tidings"—to events occurring in Middle-earth. Separated from the action of the narratives of the Noldor, she is positioned as a scholar-artist, crafting "webs historical" to recount, preserve, frame, and display those narratives. Thus, the events known as the *Quenta Silmarillion* unfold in time in Middle-earth and in art in the Halls of Vairë, with Míriel in the role of historian-artisan who crafts the tapestries-histories. In their various versions, the accounts of the Elder Days feature the labor of "loremasters" compiling Elven history into tales of the First Age: the Exile of the Noldor and the Kinslaying, the Siege of Beleriand, its battles, and the major narratives of Gondolin, Lúthien, and Túrin, for example. Likewise, in Valinor, Míriel's tapestries compile and document these vital events in ever-expanding weavings. As the events of Middle-earth "are brought to her," she compiles and crafts them as they happen, and she remains documentarian of the Noldor as their history continues to unfold, "for still she is at work."

In fulfilling her role as broideress and chronicler, Míriel's ability to "see" events unfolding for the Noldor in Middle-earth parallels the Valar's experience of Arda, both in their vision of the *Ainulindalë* and upon later consultation, referenced in the debate of the Valar as "the Tale of Arda" (240). Numerous times, the Vala consult that vision and its unfolding to guide their decisions and in their attempts to heal the hurts of Arda Marred. Just as the Valar hearken back to their vision while the history of Arda unfolds, in order to best fulfill their roles as caretakers, Míriel attends to the history and events of her people to document their tales, all tied to Morgoth's treachery, in her assigned role as caretaker of the Noldor's history. Míriel, the first to "die" in Aman, now employs her skill to preserve the Noldor's tale, upon which her husband Finwë, the first slain in Aman, "is at times permitted to look." That is, Finwë visits the library of the halls of Vairë and reads "news" of the Noldor in Middle-earth, thanks to the artistic production of Míriel. Míriel's works become living, ongoing documents of the events of the Noldor that both she and Finwë experience as Art. Those events, with their inevitably tragic arc, potentially transform into recuperative works through the beauty of her creation.

While the Halls of Vairë might be considered the "library of Arda"—replete with the Vala's weavings of all "the Tale of Arda"— Míriel's tapestries represent a kind of special collection, the archives of the history of the Noldor as recorded-created by one re-gifted her physical body for that very purpose. With her proximity to the Vala Vairë, we can assume Míriel improves and deepens her already prodigious craft, so that the tapestries reflect the Noldor's history with a skill that, the passage suggests, cannot be equaled beyond these holdings. Míriel's significant role as creator and curator of the "Noldorin collection" may also function as both process of atonement and reward offered to her in the unique situation that was her "death" and reincarnation. She becomes the witness and the preserver of the events that she, at least partially, has set in motion. Although her decision to leave her body contributes to the eventual tragic events of the Noldor's exile, Míriel's position as the handmaid of Vairë and her ongoing work in the halls offer a kind of compensation for that role, in the form of restorative art. When Fëanor responds to his exile with the claim that "the deeds that we shall do shall be the matter of song until the last days of Arda" (Silm 88), Manwë responds by recalling Morgoth's original Marring. In his response, perhaps Manwë foresees not only the Great Tales of Beleriand preserved even into the Fourth Age, but also envisions Míriel's task to weave her special collection: "Dear-bought those songs shall be accounted, and yet shall be well-bought. For the price could be no other. Thus even as Eru spoke to us shall beauty not before conceived be brought into Eä, and evil yet be good to have been" (Silm 98). This "beauty not before conceived"— the Great Tales of the Eldar—also finds representation in Míriel's weavings of those great deeds. With each event that marks Arda's marring, from the *Ainulindalë,* to Míriel's death, to Fëanor's rebellion, Tolkien inscribes the necessity for artistic creation as a response to those events: new themes, new tales/songs, and new weavings to account for and make beautiful the Tale of Arda.

Considering Míriel's weaving as part of the Noldorin collection in the library of Arda expands the notion of the "textual" representations, or sub-creations, of the Eldar in Tolkien's created world. The framing techniques that reference Pengoloð and Ælfwine consistently reference "loremasters" such as Rúmil, who record the great tales of the Eldar, and these tales survive in textual holdings and oral tales reaching down through the Ages to the Hall of Fire and the holdings of Rivendell.[9] Míriel's "imperishable" tapestries, recounting in "many hues fairer than are known in Middle-earth" like the imperishable song of Lúthien before Mandos that recounts the Marring of Arda, offer an additional example of work that records and preserves the central events of the First Age. To Oberhelman's "loremaster-librarians" (160) of the Eldar, then, we must add "weaver-broideress," sub-creators like Míriel whose art preserves the beauty and history of the Elves.[10] Because her tapestries are in Aman—specifically housed in the library of Arda and therefore "imperishable"—they may also represent a kind of ideal collection, beyond the effects of time and decay to which all libraries and artifacts are subject, for unlike the famed libraries of Gondolin, Menegroth, Rivendell, and Moria, the "webs historical" of Míriel are safe; isolated, yet "imperishable." As a result, Míriel's "Noldorin collection" stands as a unique example of Elven sub-creation that escapes the most damaging effects of the great Marrer, Morgoth. Although the contents of her collection recount the cycle of Morgoth's violence upon her people, his ensnarement of the Noldor in his webs of deceit, her creations construct a restorative web and remain apart from that tragedy, perfectly captured and preserved in Art.

Reaching back as far as the *Ainulindalë*, the unfolding of Arda develops not merely through narrative events, but also through the skill and labor of creators, sub-creators, compilers, and preservers of those events: the tales, histories, and artifacts of the great drama of Arda. Míriel's weaving, her "webs historical," provides another example of the importance of using aesthetic skill to record and detail history, particularly the history of the First Age. Her tapestries also center the Noldor's particular gifts—words, tales, works of the hand—as specifically fitting to the task of crafting a vast collection or record of history. Further, as Tolkien developed her tale in *Morgoth's Ring*,

---

[9] As Oberhelman details, "In the Hall of Fire the ancient songs, tales, and other oral traditions of the First and Second Ages are replayed, but Imladris also holds a large cache of maps, books, and manuscripts the Noldor have managed to retain after the destruction of Beleriand and Eregion in the Second Age" (161–62).

[10] Indeed, if Míriel's webs represent a collection, then perhaps Galadriel's weaving in Lóthlorien reflects that same skill, so that as Oberhelman suggests, there may not be libraries of texts (161), given Galadriel's skill, there are surely collections of tapestries that weave of the tales of the Galadhrim in her halls.

Míriel's narrative—resulting in both the legal precedent of the "Doom/Statute of Finwë and Míriel" and in the woven history of the Noldor—centers her choices and her particular gifts to suggest that her decisions and role as Serindë affect the Tale of Arda no less powerfully than Tinúviel herself. While she does not participate directly in the great tales of the First Age so central to Tolkien's conception of his created world, Míriel's task remains as vital: to employ the fineness of her craft to preserve in Art the unfolding of those tales. Although she renounces the experience of living out her immortal being amongst her own people, Míriel *can* catalogue the experiences of her people in a vast and ongoing representation of their deeds. In becoming Fíriel, she who died, Míriel can turn to the crucial work of sub-creation, preserving the life and history of the Noldor with her imperishable webs historical.

Post-script

The fact that Míriel's account of the Noldor comes in the form of *weaving/tapestry* may reflect particular (Primary World) historical creations, such as the Bayeux Tapestry, and her work certainly aligns her with numerous literary precedents—instances of women weaving works that recount or reflect a central narrative, or figures such as the Fates whose role is to spin the thread of life—going back to ancient times. Finally, the interconnectivity of meaning between the craft of weaving and the craft of poetry/telling, down to the linguistic connections between the two activities, may explain most fully why Tolkien develops Míriel's sub-creation of the history of her people in the form of weaving.

Perhaps the most famous surviving text of the Middle Ages, the Bayeux Tapestry offers an intriguing potential source of inspiration for Míriel's weavings. In reality an embroidery, the Bayeux Tapestry visually recounts the Norman victory over the English in vast detail: "it displays a long and developed narrative which flows uninterruptedly for its entire seventy metres" (Brown 23). Although its exact origins are uncertain, there is general agreement that women stitched the extraordinary work, "created in England within a generation of the events it depicts" (1). While the assumption that women produced the work might reflect gendered or cultural assumptions about needlecraft, according to Andrew Bridgeford, "From surviving texts it is known that Anglo-Saxon women, in particular, were renowned for their skill at embroidery" (156).[11]

---

[11] Bridgeford also notes that "The widow of the Anglo-Saxon warrior Byrhtnoth, who died in 991 at the Battle of Maldon, is known to have produced

Interestingly, it appears Tolkien was aware of the famous Bayeux Tapestry's origins, when in a letter to Rhona Beare he notes that "The styles of the Bayeux Tapestry (made in England) fit [the Rohirrim] well enough, if one remembers that the kind of tennis-nets [the] soldiers seem to have on are only a clumsy conventional sign for the chain mail of small rings" (*Letters* #281, p. 281). Although the aesthetic of the historical Bayeux work does not reflect the stunningly beautiful "webs historical" that Míriel constructs in the Halls of Vairë, the existence of a textile that recounts "one of the most significant monuments from the history of England" (Brown 8) certainly points to ways in which a collection of tapestry-embroideries might do the work of commemoration for a people.

Of course, in his academic work, Tolkien was just as familiar with the descriptions of wall hangings adorning the literary halls of Hrothgar's Heorot, Arthur's Camelot, and Bertilak's castle in *Sir Gawain and the Green Knight*. These aristocratic productions, "embroidered and bound with the brightest gems" (SGGK stanza 4) and constructed by ladies of the Court, register the worth and standing of the community as much as the weaponry laden with runes or the song of the bard who recounts its great tales. Like weaponry and song, the tapestries and intricately embroidered garments were complex, valuable, and symbolic representations of the values of their bearers. Thus, to develop the narrative of Míriel as a master "broideress" continues the symbolic import of weaving and creating representations of a people, in this case, the Noldor. That Míriel's collection of "webs historical" reside in Aman, far from the ravages of Middle-earth or the kind of devastation that *Beowulf* recounts of Heorot, perhaps points to a concern for preservation of the Tale. Like Lúthien's song, the weavings are "imperishable" in the Halls of Vairë and thus, presumably, the tale-tapestries of the Noldor live on.

In her work *Weaving the Word: The Metaphorics of Weaving and Female Textual Production*, Kathryn Sullivan Kruger examines the oft-repeated and fascinating associations between the creation of cloth and the creation of text. Before her more specific reading of episodes from Ovid, William Blake, and Tennyson, Kruger establishes provocative associations between women's weaving/cloth making and the creation

---

an important stitchwork to commemorate her husband's death and to have given it to the church at Ely" (11). While the textile does not survive, it is safe to assume that Tolkien would be aware of the creation referenced in the *Liber Eliensis*, given his knowledge of the period and affinity with the poetic Battle of Maldon.

of language, textual production, and tale or song.[12] Indeed, her claims about the relationship between text and textile evoke, with intriguing clarity, Tolkien's conception of Creation generally and particularly Míriel's role as chronicler: "Weaving has long been a metaphor for the creation of something other than cloth, whether a story, a plot, or a world" (23). Míriel weaves-embroiders cloth, but that cloth is simultaneously history-tale. In the *Ainulindalë*, at the very moment of Arda's conception, Tolkien consistently employs the analogy of cloth-as-creation when the Ainur begin to sing, "and a sound arose of endless interchanging melodies *woven* in harmony" (Silm 15, emphasis mine).[13] The Valar's "fashioning" (Silm 22) of Arda, then, parallels the creation of a vast tapestry, the world, which they construct from a memory of the Vision—the perfected tapestry—Eru offers them prior to the making of Arda. In her sub-creation, Míriel, too, has the accounts of the Noldor brought to her, and "fashions" her tapestry that is also the tale of her people. Music, song, tale, weaving, and fashioning meld together so that singing is creation, weaving is making, and fashioning the world becomes a vast aesthetic task.[14]

With Vairë, Míriel's master teacher, Tolkien suggests the unfolding of the drama of Arda is simultaneously in the process of being represented as tapestry: "Vairë the Weaver [...] weaves all things that have ever been in Time into her storied webs, and the halls of Mandos that ever widen as the ages pass are clothed with them" (Silm 28). Vairë's role thus evokes the classical Fates, the Greek Moirai or the Scandinavian Norns, but rather than attending to the specific fates of individuals, Vairë's labor weaves the Story of Arda itself. The making

---

[12] Kruger's particular methodology, developed fully in chapter two, rests with Julia Kristeva's treatment of Jacques Lacan's theory of language and the Symbolic: "[Lacan and Kristeva's] models for the development of language and how identity is established through entry into the Symbolic finds a striking analogue in the metaphor of weaving and the language of textiles" (13).

[13] Tolkien continues his use of "woven" or weaving for the creation of Arda throughout the account: Melkor's rebellious ideas "he now wove into his music" (16); Eru's third theme harmonizes two dissonant melodies so that "its most triumphant notes were taken by the other and woven into its own solemn pattern" (17); and perhaps the Vision that Eru offers the Ainur (11–18) might be considered a tapestry "unfolding." As the Ainur prepare to enter into Arda, the account notes "Of the fabric of the Earth had Aulë thought" (19), continuing the parallel between textile-world creation.

[14] Kruger cites David Jongeward's excellent observation: "Every weaver, when engaged in the act of interlacing one thread with another, participates in a process that for countless generations has been a primal metaphor for creation, including creation of the world itself" (26).

of Arda and the making of Arda *as art* grow nearly indistinguishable. From the harmonies woven like threads in the *Ainulindalë*, Tolkien envisions Arda to contain cascading layers of weaving-creation-song-tale, down to Míriel's creation in the Halls of Vairë. Míriel employs her skill to make permanent the history-tales of the Noldor as a kind of "bard" who creates, communicates, and preserves, and this labor is part of a larger community of makers-creators-bards reaching back to the Ainur and to Arda's conception. Her choice to remove herself from the action of the Noldor's history allows her the opportunity, through her weaving-creation, to become a primary artist representing those events, no less than Rúmil or Lúthien were masters of tale and song. As Kruger deftly explains, "By participating in the production of textiles [...] women took part in the first textual practices, recording their society's stories, myths, and sacred beliefs in symbols woven or embroidered on their textiles" (22). Further, because Míriel's weaving resides in Aman, her "webs historical" fully suggest that "the woven material becomes a metaphor for something written, and thus permanent, unchanging" (Kruger 55), or in Tolkien's words, "imperishable."

Finally, the linguistic connections between text-textile and weaving-sewing-writing would have presented an aesthetic "rightness" for Tolkien's conception of his created world as a whole, and for Míriel's task in weaving the tale of the Noldor in particular. As Ann Bergren explains, in Greek, "the utterance of poetry or prophecy is described as 'weaving'" (72). A woman passes the shuttle across the loom; the bard entwines events and images through a poem. Linguistically, then, textile work functions as a primary image pattern for the creation of language:

> In many languages, including English, the verb *to weave* defines not just the making of textiles, but any creative act. Likewise, the noun *text* comes from the Latin verb *texere*, also meaning "to construct or to weave." In Greek this verb, *tekhne*, refers to art, craft, and skill. Therefore, a weaver not only fashions textiles but can, with the same verb, contrive texts. Roland Barthes states that "etymologically the text is a cloth; *textus*, meaning 'woven.'" (29)

Given Tolkien's primary academic work in philology and his love for the aesthetic relationships between words, it seems likely that he not only understood these linguistic parallels between textile and textual creation, but also sought to emphasize them in his world-making. As the text is cloth, the weaving—whether Vairë's or Míriel's—is a text, a work of literature recounting events in Time.[15] Going further, the instances of weaving and recording tale-story-history, and preserving these creations

---

[15] In Kruger's words, "texts as textiles constitute another form of literature" (16).

in a library-like space, may point to Tolkien's belief that crafting and tending to the tales-weavings, particularly as time passes or the Tale of Arda unfolds, may be among the most vital role his heroes can perform.

Works Cited

Bergren Ann L. T. "Language and the Female in Early Greek Thought" *Arethusa*, vol. 16, no. 1/2, 1983, pp. 69–95.

Bratman, David. "The Literary Value of *The History of Middle-earth.*" *Tolkien's Legendarium: Essays on* The History of Middle-earth, edited by Verlyn Flieger and Carl E. Hostetter, Greenwood, 2000, pp. 61–91.

Bridgeford, Andrew. *1066: The Hidden History of the Bayeux Tapestry.* Walker, 2005.

Brown, Shirley Ann. *The Bayeux Tapestry; History and Bibliography.* Boydell, 1988.

Kane, Douglas Charles. *Arda Reconstructed; The Creation of the Published* Silmarillion, Lehigh UP, 2009.

Kruger, Kathryn Sullivan. *Weaving the Word: The Metaphorics of Weaving and Female Textual Production.* Associated University Presses, 2001.

Oberhelman, David D. "A Brief History of Libraries in Middle-earth: Manuscript and Book Repositories in Tolkien's Legendarium." *Loremasters and Libraries in Fantasy and Science Fiction: A Gedenkschrift for David Oberhelman*, edited by Jason Fisher and Janet Brennan Croft, Mythopoeic Press, 2022, pp. 155–65. Originally published in *Truths Breathed Through Silver: The Inklings' Moral and Mythopoeic Legacy*, edited by Jonathan B. Himes, with Joe R. Christopher and Salwa Khoddam, Cambridge Scholars, 2008, pp. 81–92.

Jongeward, David. *Weaver of Worlds: From Navajo Apprenticeship to Sacred Geometry and Dreams—A Woman's Journey in Tapestry.* Destiny Books, 1990.

Rutledge, Amelia A. "'Justice is not Healing': J. R. R. Tolkien's Pauline Constructs in 'Finwë and Míriel.'" *Tolkien Studies*, vol. 9, 2012, pp. 51–74.

Sir Gawain and the Green Knight; Pearl; and Sir Orfeo [SGGK]. Translated by J. R. R. Tolkien, Houghton Mifflin, 1978.

Tolkien, Christopher. Foreword. *Morgoth's Ring: The Later Silmarillion, Part 1*, by J. R. R. Tolkien, edited by Christopher Tolkien, Houghton, 1993. Vol. 10 of *The History of Middle-earth.*

——. Notes. *Morgoth's Ring: The Later Silmarillion, Part I*, by J. R. R. Tolkien, edited by Christopher Tolkien, Houghton, 1993. Vol. 10 of *The History of Middle-earth.*

Tolkien, J. R. R. *The Letters of J. R. R. Tolkien*. Edited by Humphrey Carpenter, with the assistance of Christopher Tolkien, Houghton Mifflin, 2000.

——. *Morgoth's Ring: The Later Silmarillion, Part I*. Edited by Christopher Tolkien, Houghton, 1993. Vol. 10 of *The History of Middle-earth*.

——. "The Shibboleth of Fëanor." *The Peoples of Middle-earth*, edited by Christopher Tolkien, Houghton, 1996. Vol. 12 of *The History of Middle-earth*.

——. *The Silmarillion*. Edited by Christopher Tolkien, 2nd ed., Houghton, 2001.

Whitaker, Lynn. "Corrupting Beauty: Rape Narrative in the *Silmarillion*." *Mythlore*, vol. 1–2, no. 111–112, 2010, pp. 51–68.

Whittingham, Elizabeth A. *The Evolution of Tolkien's Mythology; A Study of the* History of Middle-earth. McFarland, 2008. Critical Explorations in Science Fiction and Fantasy 7, Donald E. Palumbo and C. W. Sullivan III, series editors.

Recovering Lost Tales: Found Manuscripts in the Works of J. R. R. Tolkien

Jason Fisher

Introduction and Context

> [I]t was no long while ago that I ventured into the captain's own private cabin, and took thence the materials with which I write, and have written. I shall from time to time continue this journal. It is true that I may not find an opportunity of transmitting it to the world, but I will not fail to make the endeavor. At the last moment I will enclose the MS. in a bottle, and cast it within the sea. (Poe, "MS. Found in a Bottle" 123)

THIS SURPRISING DECLARATION FROM the narrator, coming about midway through Edgar Allan Poe's short story, "MS. Found in a Bottle" (1833), reveals that we are reading the very journal of a dead man, that the story itself is a lost manuscript. Ostensibly cast overboard by its author—the narrator of the tale, not Poe—it would eventually be found in its bottle, washed ashore somewhere, tidied up and perhaps edited, brought to a publisher, and put before readers' eyes. Of course, it's not *actually* a lost manuscript; this is a trick of Poe's to enliven the tale, to increase the sense of loss, to introduce irony, lend an air of authenticity, or perhaps to comment on authorship itself. Whatever Poe's motives, he was hardly unique in adopting the convention of supposedly real documents, letters, diaries, or maps, being lost, hidden, or cast aside by their "authors" and then rediscovered long after and brought to us, readers hungry for tales of the bygone, the exotic, the heroic. This particular tale isn't even unique for its found manuscript among the works of Poe. *The Narrative of Arthur Gordon Pym of Nantucket*, Poe's only novel and published only five years after "MS. Found in a Bottle," utilizes the same technique. It too purports to be an authentic manuscript, with an introductory note by its "author," Pym, in which "Mr. Poe" (the novel's real author) features as a character. The novel breaks off suddenly and a postscript claims that the final two or three chapters were lost, along with Pym, in a sudden accident but that "if ultimately found, will be given to the public" (882).

Any attempt to survey the found manuscript topos across the history of literature would be either of prohibitive length or else capriciously selective. To provide a narrower focus, this exploration will be limited to just one author, J. R. R. Tolkien, in whose works this literary conceit appears again and again. We will examine a wide range of examples of the found manuscript in Tolkien's writings. Then, from the questions of *what* and *where*, we will turn to questions of *how* and *why*, exploring some of the effects of this motif and speculating on the possible reasons behind Tolkien's liberal use of it. Do supposedly found manuscripts lend an air of verisimilitude to his fiction? What attempts does Tolkien make to authenticate these manuscripts as genuine, even though we know they are not? Do Tolkien's lost and rediscovered manuscripts echo those of the real Middle Ages and perhaps underscore Tolkien's wish to restore to England a literary and mythological tradition that it had lost in the wake of successive invasions and displacement by the Romans, the Vikings, the Normans?

But before we dive deeper into Tolkien, some additional context may prove useful, as the literary convention of the found manuscript pervades western literature. It was especially popular in the adventure fiction and "penny dreadfuls" of the 19th century. This was a time when the modern novelistic tradition was really firming up, and authors experimented with various techniques for injecting credibility and authenticity into their fantastic fiction. The more fantastic, the more the apparent need for some reassurance readers should take a tale seriously. In addition to found manuscripts, authors embedded poetry in their prose, collected letters into epistolary novels, moved from one narrator to another, and offered up treasure maps or other artifacts. A forgotten manuscript might accidentally fall into an author's or character's hands, setting an adventure in motion. In other tales, the search for a lost manuscript forms the foundation of the plot. Sometimes manuscripts are lost in plain sight and only rediscovered or appreciated by the lettered wise. And in still other cases, like Poe's and, as we will see, like Tolkien's, the very book we are reading is itself a found manuscript. In such cases, the author makes himself a character in a sense. In claiming that a fictional manuscript is authentic, he makes himself, an authentic author, fictional.

A few brief examples of the found manuscript from the century of so preceding Tolkien will help establish context for the ensuing discussion. We know for sure that Tolkien read and enjoyed some of these—and it's likely enough he knew them all.

Mary Shelley's *Frankenstein* (1818) begins with a series of letters from polar explorer and failed poet, Robert Walton, to his sister, Margaret. Walton describes how his crew discovered Victor Frankenstein in the Artic pursuing the creature he had made, and the bulk of the novel is Victor's tale, recounted to and recorded by Walton. As if that weren't enough, the memoir also contains an extended narrative from the point of view of the monster. Interestingly, while *Frankenstein* begins in the Artic and looks back, Poe's "MS. Found in a Bottle" and *Pym* end in the Antarctic, looking forward. Jules Verne's *Journey to the Center of the Earth* (1864) opens with the discovery of a runic message hidden in an original manuscript of Snorri Sturluson's *Heimskringla*, describing how one can reach the center of the earth through a crater in Iceland. Verne provides the runes in facsimile, much as Tolkien would go on to do in his own works.[1] H. Rider Haggard's *She* (1886) purports to be a found manuscript, which, along with other physical artifacts like the Sherd of Amenartas, Haggard claims were sent to him by someone called Horace Holly. Haggard describes himself as the editor of the account, not its author. Much as in *Journey to the Center of the Earth*, readers are offered a transcription of the "original" ancient Greek text, along with a facsimile illustration of the potsherd. Runes and facsimile manuscript pages turn up in Tolkien's work as well, as we will soon see. And finally, John Buchan also claims to be the editor, not the author, of *Midwinter* (1923), a manuscript said to have been found "among a mass of derelict papers" after "a very drastic clearing out of the cupboards and shelves in the old house in Lincoln's Inn Fields" (Buchan vii). The claim that a manuscript was rescued from the garbage may remind readers of Tolkien as well. We will return to this similarity in due course.[2]

It bears mentioning that the conceit of the found or fictional manuscript goes well beyond Tolkien, proliferating to this day. Every chapter in Frank Herbert's *Dune* (1965) begins with an epigraph from a variety of fictive books by the prolific Princess Irulan. Other novels purport to be their narrators' memoirs—Vladimir Nabokov's *Lolita*, published the same year as *The Return of the King*, is a notable example, as is Gabriel García Márquez's *One Hundred Years of Solitude*, published in 1967. Another of Nabokov's novels, *Pale Fire*, published in 1962,

---

[1] Mark Hooker has discussed parallels between *The Hobbit* and *Journey to the Center of the Earth*, including the significance of their respective runic texts.

[2] Once again, Mark Hooker has discussed extensive parallels between the novels of Buchan and Tolkien.

purports to be a 999-line poem by a fictional poet, framed by a foreword, commentary, and index by a fictional academic. Mike Bryan's minimalist 2003 novel, *The Afterword*, is written in the form of an extensive afterword to a novel that doesn't exist. In addition to novels that present themselves as lost manuscripts, other novels feature lost or found manuscripts as plot devices. Umberto Eco's *The Name of the Rose* (1980) and Nicholas Christopher's *The Bestiary* (2007) revolve around the search for lost texts—Aristotle's lost commentary on comedy and the medieval Caravan Bestiary, respectively—a real lost manuscript in one case and a fictional one in the other. Bookending Poe's "MS. Found in a Bottle" is Stanisław Lem's *Memoirs Found in a Bathtub* (1961). In Chuck Palahniuk's *Lullaby* (2002), the protagonists search for, and eventually find, a lost grimoire that contains a "culling song" fatal to anyone it is recited to. Deborah Harkness's *A Discovery of Witches* (2011) begins in the Bodleian Library at Oxford, where her central character, Diana Bishop, finds a lost alchemical manuscript, *Ashmole 782*, the rediscovery of which awakens her own background and reveals a magical underworld. And the examples go on and on.

Tolkien's Found Manuscripts

Returning to J. R. R. Tolkien, let's begin with *The Hobbit*, which, as everyone knows, is the memoir of Bilbo Baggins. Isn't it? Well, we may be getting slightly ahead of ourselves. It's never claimed in *The Hobbit* that the book we are reading is *itself* Bilbo's memoir. We might infer this. The subtitle of the published novel is *There and Back Again*, a phrase Bilbo uses in reference to the memoir he is writing at the story's conclusion:

> One autumn evening some years afterwards Bilbo was sitting in his study writing his memoirs—he thought of calling them "There and Back Again, a Hobbit's Holiday"—when there was a ring at the door. (H XIX.316)

In Tolkien's first draft, by the way, it was just "There and Back Again"—no "Hobbit's Holiday" (Rateliff 692).

Another clue appears in the Anglo-Saxon runes running along the border of Tolkien's cover art for the novel, which read:

> THE HOBBIT OR THERE AND BACK AGAIN BEING THE RECORD OF A YEARS JOURNEY MADE BY BILBO BAGGINS OF HOBBITON COMPILED FROM HIS MEMOIRS BY J. R. R. TOLKIEN AND PUBLISHED BY GEORGE ALLEN & UNWIN LTD. (Hammond and Scull, *Art of* The Hobbit 139)[3]

---

[3] It should be noted that Tolkien developed the dustjacket design for *The Hobbit* quite late, and indeed he had already begun *The Lord of the Rings*. It is

But this doesn't go quite so far as to claim that Tolkien's novel *is* the preserved manuscript of Bilbo Baggins—only that Tolkien was beginning to imagine that there *was* a memoir and that the novel was based on it. But Tolkien certainly envisioned it as such by the time he was finishing its sequel.

In the first edition foreword to *The Lord of the Rings*, Tolkien begins with this very conceit:

> This tale, which has grown to be almost a history of the great War of the Ring, is drawn for the most part from the memoirs of the renowned Hobbits, Bilbo and Frodo, as they are preserved in the Red Book of Westmarch. This chief monument of Hobbit-lore is so called because it was compiled, repeatedly copied, and enlarged and handed down in the family of the Fairbairns of Westmarch, descended from that Master Samwise of whom this tale has much to say.
>
> I have supplemented the account of the Red Book, in places, with information derived from the surviving records of Gondor, notably the Book of the Kings; but in general, though I have omitted much, I have in this tale adhered more closely to the actual words and narrative of my original than in the previous selection from the Red Book, *The Hobbit*. That was drawn from the early chapters, composed originally by Bilbo himself. If 'composed' is a just word. Bilbo was not assiduous, nor an orderly narrator, and his account is involved and discursive, and sometimes confused: faults that still appear in the Red Book, since the copiers were pious and careful, and altered very little. (*Fellowship*, 1st ed 7)

There is a lot to unpack here. First, this novel, *The Lord of the Rings*, and its predecessor, *The Hobbit*, are in fact said to be based on ancient manuscripts that Tolkien discovered, set in order, and edited. Moreover, Tolkien hints at the existence of more than one manuscript, also naming The Book of the Kings, as well as others to come, as we'll see in a moment. With "pious and careful copiers," Tolkien alludes to the medieval scribal tradition which we have to thank for the survival of most of the texts of the Middle Ages. He also offers an explanation for why *The Hobbit* might not sound quite like the authentic manuscript

---

problematic as evidence for whether Tolkien conceived of *The Hobbit* as Bilbo's memoir while he was writing it, but it clearly shows that he was beginning to think of it this way by late in 1937. My thanks to Janet Brennan Croft for reminding me of this important paratextual element; see also her essay on Tolkien's introductions, prefaces, and forewords. In addition, the title page of *The Lord of the Ring* contains a similar runic paratext: "THE LORD OF THE RINGS TRANSLATED FROM THE RED BOOK [in Cirth] OF WESTMARCH BY JOHN RONALD REUEL TOLKIEN HEREIN IS SET FORTH THE HISTORY OF THE WAR OF THE RINGS AND THE RETURN OF THE KING AS SEEN BY THE HOBBITS [in Tengwar]" (quoted in Flieger 284, and see the surrounding discussion). See also Hammond and Scull, *The Art of* The Lord of the Rings 207–08).

in places—for instance, in the appearance from time to time of a narrator who is obviously not Bilbo. The explanation given is that Tolkien didn't follow the original manuscript as closely as he now does with *The Lord of the Rings*. And finally, Tolkien very cleverly accounts for the differences between the first edition of *The Hobbit* and subsequent revisions to bring it into accord with the new story.

The first edition foreword was not carried on into the second edition of *The Lord of the Rings*. In the new foreword Tolkien makes no mention of the Red Book of Westmarch and instead dons an authorial mantle quite conspicuously. "[*The Lord of the Rings*] was begun soon after *The Hobbit* was written and before its publication in 1937; but I did not go on with this sequel, for I wished first to complete and set in order the mythology and legends of the Elder Days" (*Lord of the Rings*, 2nd ed [*LotR*], Foreword.xxii). Tolkien goes on to comment on aspects of his writing process: "the composition of *The Lord of the Rings* went on at intervals during the years 1936 to 1949" (xxii), he writes, and "[t]hen when the 'end' had at last been reached the whole story had to be revised, and indeed largely re-written backwards" (xxiii). He refers to himself as the "author" more than once, discusses the origins of the novel and its connection to *The Hobbit*, and deflects assumptions of allegory. Indeed, on one of Tolkien's own copies of the first edition of *The Lord of the Rings*, he wrote next to the original foreword: "This Foreword I should wish very much in any case to cancel. Confusing (as it does) real personal matters with the 'machinery' of the Tale is a serious mistake" (quoted in Tolkien, *Peoples* 26).

That Tolkien so clearly positions himself as the author in the second edition of *The Lord of the Rings*—not the discoverer, translator, or editor—might be partly explained by his wish to assert a clear claim of authorship—and ownership—in the wake of the unauthorized edition published in America by Ace Books earlier that same year, 1965. David Bratman has also raised the possibility that Tolkien's change of heart about the persona of discoverer, translator, and editor and his adoption of a more protective role is less about any concern over the Ace Books controversy and more about "his intervening experiences with [film and radio] adaptations of his work [...]. Tolkien had thought that drama was a separate art and didn't affect the reading of the text being adapted. Here is where he found that this view was wrong" (Bratman, email message).[4]

---

[4] See also David Bratman's essay, "The Artistry of Omissions and Revisions in *The Lord of the Rings*."

Be all this as it may, in both the first and second editions of *The Lord of the Rings*, a prologue follows the foreword, and in that prologue, much the same claim is made as in the first edition foreword. The opening text of the prologue is identical in the first and second editions:

> This book is largely concerned with Hobbits, and from its pages a reader may discover much of their character and a little of their history. Further information will also be found in the selection from the Red Book of Westmarch that has already been published, under the title of *The Hobbit*. That story was derived from the earlier chapters of the Red Book, composed by Bilbo himself, the first Hobbit to become famous in the world at large, and called by him *There and Back Again* [...]. (*Fellowship*, 1st ed 11)

Here too, Tolkien cleverly explains the discrepancies between the first edition of *The Hobbit* and the second, which he revised in the mid-1940s to better fit the developing sequel. He writes:

> Bilbo set down [the original account, now shown to be false] in his memoirs, and he seems never to have altered it himself, not even after the Council of Elrond. Evidently it still appeared in the original Red Book, as it did in several of the copies and abstracts. But many copies contain the true account (as an alternative), derived no doubt, from notes by Frodo and Samwise, both of whom learned the truth, though they seem to have been unwilling to delete anything actually written by the old hobbit himself. (23)

It's worth noting that elsewhere in the prologue, Tolkien alludes to and even quotes from another invented manuscript, *Herblore of the Shire*, one of several works "composed or begun" by Meriadoc Brandybuck (15).[5] And to the second edition prologue Tolkien added a "Note on the Shire Records," in which he makes the only references to libraries in Middle-earth, of which the Shire, surprisingly enough, had several.[6] It is here that Tolkien explains why the Red Book is so-called and declares again that "[i]t was in origin Bilbo's private diary" (*LotR* Prologue.14), extensively expanded by Frodo and, to a much lesser degree, by Samwise. Here too, he refers again to Merry's *Herblore*, and he attributes

---

[5] Composed or only begun? Perhaps Tolkien is winking at his own tendency to begin works he would later abandon. Or perhaps he had in mind his notion of "draw[ing] some of the great tales in fullness" but "leav[ing] many only placed in the scheme, and sketched" for "other minds and hands" to complete (*Letters* 145). Or still another possibility is that Tolkien was already feeling the anxieties of dwindling time to set his legendarium in order; as he would write to his son, Michael, in the last years of his life, "when you pray for me, pray for 'time'! I should like to put some of this stuff into readable form, and some sketched for others to make use of" (404).

[6] See also David D. Oberhelman's essay in this collection for a closer look at libraries, scriptoria, and literacy in Middle-earth, and see also Note 8 below.

---

the authorship to Merry of two additional manuscripts, *Reckoning of Years* and *Old Words and Names in the Shire*, material that Tolkien partly represents as appendices to *The Lord of the Rings*. Tolkien's reference in the first edition foreword to another found manuscript, The Book of the Kings, containing some of "the surviving records of Gondor" (7) is nowhere carried forward into the second edition.[7] There are references here and there in the novel to other manuscripts—the Thain's Book, Yellowskin,[8] Bilbo's *Translations from the Elvish*, and the Book of Mazarbul, to which I will return in due course. There are also occasional references to arcane manuscripts *inside* the narrative, as opposed to its appendices and paratexts—for example, the aforementioned Book of Mazarbul and the scroll of Isildur that Gandalf consults at Minas Tirith.[9]

---

[7] The Book of the Kings appears again in Appendix A of the first edition of *The Lord of the Rings* (*Return* 313), alongside the Akallabêth (later to be published as part of *The Silmarillion*) and The Book of the Stewards (to my knowledge, mentioned here and nowhere else in *The Lord of the Rings*). Appendix A in the revised edition of *The Lord of the Rings* differs at many points, including dropping the references to these fictive manuscripts. In drafting the material that would become Appendix A, Tolkien at one point combined two of these manuscripts as "The Book of the Kings and Stewards," said here and nowhere else to be "now lost" (*Peoples* 255).

[8] Yellowskin, or the Yearbook of Tuckborough, appears only once in *The Lord of the Rings*, in Appendix D on the Shire calendar. This was one of the few ancient documents preserved in the Shire, and likely the oldest, "recording births, marriages, and deaths in the Took families, as well as [other] matters, such as land-sales, and various Shire events" (1111). In the published *Lord of the Rings*, Tolkien tells us that "not many ancient documents were preserved in the Shire" by the end of the Third Age (loc.cit.), but Tolkien had originally imagined the situation to be rather different. In draft material for the appendix on languages, Tolkien had written:

> In the Shire, which proved a rich and comfortable country, the old lore was largely neglected; but there were always some Hobbits who studied it and kept it in memory; and copying and compilation, and even fictitious elaboration, still went on. In Bilbo's time there were in the book-hoards many manuscripts of lore more than 500 years old. The oldest known book, The Great Writ of Tuckborough, popularly called Yellowskin, was supposed to be nearly a thousand years old. It dealt in annalistic form with the deeds of Took notables from the foundation of the Shire, though its earliest hand belonged to a period at least four centuries later. (*Peoples* 40)

Remarkably, Tolkien ascribes his own tendency to "fictitious elaboration" to at least certain Hobbits and refers to "book-hoards" (i.e., libraries) in the Shire with an abundance of old manuscripts. But somewhere along the way, Tolkien obviously reconsidered.

[9] The appendices also purport to quote from other Middle-earth manuscripts, but these are not usually named or identified. In Appendix A, Tolkien writes that "actual extracts from longer annals and tales are placed within quotation marks. Insertions of later date are enclosed in brackets. Notes within quotation marks are

Origins and Timing of the Conceit

Before moving on from *The Lord of the Rings*, I think it's worth taking some time to consider when and how Tolkien may have first arrived at the idea of claiming the novel was a found manuscript, a point that will be relevant later. As I have said, it is nowhere made explicit in *The Hobbit* that we are reading a found manuscript, although it is hinted to the attentive that we may be. It is easy to see this as established canon in hindsight, but if *The Lord of the Rings* had never been written, would anyone assume *The Hobbit* was in fact Bilbo's memoir? Maybe, maybe not. In looking more closely at the history of the composition of *The Lord of the Rings*, we can observe the development of the idea. The first form of the prologue actually comes quite early in Tolkien's writing—which isn't too surprising, considering that parts of it are analogous to the narrator's digressions in the opening of *The Hobbit*. In the first version, written in 1938 or 1939 and called a foreword at the time, Tolkien refers to *The Hobbit* as a source of more information about Bilbo Baggins, but he doesn't describe that book as Bilbo's memoir. In a typescript of that draft made not long after, or so Christopher Tolkien supposes, Tolkien now writes that *The Hobbit* was "based on [Bilbo's] own much longer memoirs" (*Peoples* 15). But this is still not quite the same as asserting that the novel *is* Bilbo's memoir.

In contrast with the prologue, the *foreword* was evidently written quite late, with the bulk of the work on the novel already finished (*Peoples* 24). We don't have an exact date, but it would have fallen somewhere between the end of Tolkien's writing the main text of the novel around 1948 and its publication, beginning in 1954. The foreword and parts of Appendix F were largely derived from a late, hastily written and fragmentary text which begins:

> This tale is drawn from the memoirs of Bilbo and Frodo Baggins, preserved for the most part in the Great Red Book of Samwise. It has been written during many years for those who were interested in the account of the great Adventure of Bilbo, and especially for

---

found in the sources" (1033). In the first edition, these quoted extracts are said to be from the Red Book, but this detail was dropped in the second edition. Is that change significant? We can only wonder. In some cases, Tolkien probably pretends to quote sources but is actually engaging in "fictitious elaboration" (see Note 8 above). But in other cases, he may be quoting material of his own in various drafts of his legendarium still unpublished at the time. For example, Tolkien's "quotation" on Malvegil of Arthedain in Appendix A (1040) echoes rather closely, but not exactly, draft material in "The Heirs of Elendil" (*Peoples* 193–94). There is more work to be done here in attempting to source Tolkien references to his own unpublished legendarium, but such comparisons fall outside the immediate scope of this paper.

> my friends, the Inklings (in whose veins, I suspect, a good deal of Hobbit blood still runs), and for my sons and daughter. (*Peoples* 19)

Like the runic inscription on the dustjacket of *The Hobbit*, the claim here is that *The Lord of the Rings* is drawn from a found manuscript, but we haven't quite reached an unambiguous claim that it *is* that manuscript—a few details remain to be worked out.

Within the main narrative of the novel, the conceit is strongly hinted several times. Readers may recall mention of Bilbo's memoir early in the narrative of *The Lord of the Rings*. Before Bilbo departs from Bag End after vanishing from his birthday party, he rhapsodizes about traveling and finding a place to finish his memoir (*Fellowship*, 1st ed 41). A little later, when the hobbits' conspiracy to accompany Frodo from the Shire is unmasked, Merry reveals that he has had a look at "the old fellow's secret book" (*LotR* I.5.105). Still later, Tolkien quotes (or rather, closely paraphrases) the description of Rivendell in *The Hobbit*: "That house was, as Bilbo had long ago reported, 'a perfect house, whether you like food or sleep or story-telling or singing, or just sitting and thinking best, or a pleasant mixture of them all'" (II.1.225). As far as Christopher Tolkien traces the development of these references, they are much the same, and not explicitly equated with the notion that the novel is a found manuscript (*Return of the Shadow* 240, 300).[10] Within the main narrative of *The Lord of the Rings*, it is also several times hinted that Bilbo (and later Frodo) *will* write down the account of the War of the Ring and the quest to destroy the Ring. Perhaps the clearest admission within the novel itself that we are reading a found manuscript or a text closely based on one comes during the denouement of the novel. Frodo is preparing to depart from Bag End:

> There was a big book with plain red leather covers; its tall pages were now almost filled. At the beginning there were many leaves covered with Bilbo's thin wandering hand; but most of it was written in Frodo's firm flowing script. It was divided into chapters but Chapter 80 was unfinished, and after that were some blank leaves. The title page had many titles on it, crossed out one after another, so:
>
> *My Diary. My Unexpected Journey. There and Back Again. And What Happened After.*
> *Adventures of Five Hobbits. The Tale of the Great Ring, compiled by Bilbo Baggins from his own observations and the accounts of his friends. What we did in the War of the Ring.*
>
> Here Bilbo's hand ended and Frodo had written:

---

[10] In the early drafts, there is, in fact, no conspiracy among Frodo's friends at all.

THE DOWNFALL
OF THE
LORD OF THE RINGS
AND THE
RETURN OF THE KING

(as seen by the Little People; being the memoirs of Bilbo and Frodo of the Shire, supplemented by the accounts of their friends and the learning of the Wise.)

Together with extracts from Books of Lore translated by Bilbo in Rivendell. (*LotR* VI.9.1027)

The title is a dead giveaway, closely mirroring the title of the book in our hands.[11] The number of chapters is interesting. One would expect it to corroborate the found manuscript conceit precisely, but it doesn't. *The Hobbit* and *The Lord of the Rings* together contain 81 chapters, not 80, and the text quoted above occurs in the last one. Did Tolkien miscount or perhaps fail to update the number of chapters during years of revision? In draft form, Tolkien gave different numbers here too, 72 or 77. But whatever the case, it is quite close enough to be taken as corroborative.[12]

So, somewhere between the claim that *The Hobbit* was loosely based on Bilbo's memoirs in 1938 or 1939 and the claim that it and *The Lord of the Rings* really *are* the Red Book of Westmarch in the foreword lies the birth of this idea. But we can marshal a little more evidence to trace its origins. At the same time he was finishing principal work on *The Lord of the Rings*, Tolkien retconned *The Hobbit* to bring it into line with new elements in the sequel's plot, particularly with the now sinister nature of the Ring. Tolkien made these changes around 1944 (Rateliff 731), sent them to his publisher, George Allen and Unwin, in 1947, and they were published as the second edition of *The Hobbit* in 1951. The revisions Tolkien made to the novel, most substantially to the account of Bilbo's finding the Ring and escaping Gollum, were originally intended only as an experiment and not meant for publication. Due to a misunderstanding, the publisher moved forward with the changes, surprising Tolkien with page proofs, and Tolkien had to make his peace with it. "I have now made up my mind to accept the change and its consequences" (*Letters* #128, p. 141), he wrote to Stanley Unwin in August 1950, adding in his next letter, "[s]uch people as I have consulted think that the alteration is in itself an improvement" (*Letters* #129, p. 142).

---

[11] Recall that Tolkien refers to *The Lord of the Rings* as *The Downfall of The Lord of the Rings* in the preface to *The Adventures of Tom Bombadil*.

[12] For further discussion of this point, see Hammond and Scull's *The Lord of the Rings: A Readers Companion* 669.

In September 1950, Tolkien wrote two versions of a new prefatory note to be included in the second edition of *The Hobbit* to explain the alterations to readers. One draft was longer; one was shorter. In the event, the shorter one was used, and indeed it was shortened still further. In the final text published with the fifth printing of *The Hobbit* in 1951, it is said that the reason for the change to the text "lies in the history of the Ring, as it is set out in the chronicles of the Red Book of Westmarch, and it must await their publication" (qtd. in Anderson, *Annotated Hobbit* 28). This is the first published reference to the Red Book of Westmarch.[13] Here, it seems Tolkien is finally thinking of *The Lord of the Rings*, finished, more or less, but not yet published, *as* the Red Book of Westmarch. But the longer draft of the prefatory note says more: "If ever it proves possible to arrange extracts from the Red Book and present them in English to students of hobbit-lore" (Rateliff 752), then this will explain Bilbo's departing from the true story of how he found the Ring. Tolkien goes on:

> For the Red Book of Westmarch, not long ago rediscovered and deciphered, contains a chronicle (of great length and by many hands) of that perilous time, as it was seen by hobbits; and its earlier parts are largely made up of extracts from Bilbo's writings, including the various secret or private papers that he gave to his heir. (Rateliff 752)[14]

So, there it is at last, quite clearly. *The Lord of the Rings* (forthcoming) and *The Hobbit* (newly revised) were equated by Tolkien with a fictive manuscript called the Red Book of Westmarch in September 1950 — that is, on paper, but possibly earlier in Tolkien's mind. The foreword to the first edition of *The Lord of the Rings might* predate this text, but we can't be sure about that.

By way of one final coda on *The Lord of the Rings*, we would do well to recall the words of Samwise beneath the shadows of Cirith Ungol: "Still, I wonder if we shall ever be put into songs or tales. We're in one, or course; but I mean: put into words, you know, told by the fireside, or read out of a great big book with red and black letters, years and years afterwards" (712). This is, of course, a physical description of Tolkien's intentions for *The Lord of the Rings* from inside the novel itself: "a great big book with red and black letters." Tolkien wanted the Ring inscription (among other elements) to appear in red, just as some of his runes had been printed in red in *The Hobbit*, but it proved impractical

---

[13] See also Croft.

[14] There are some variations between the manuscript and typescript, but these are of no great moment.

in the end (see *Letters* #171, #183, #186). With deluxe and anniversary editions, we've arrived at Tolkien's—and Sam's—vision at last.

Found Manuscripts in Other Works by Tolkien

Having spent a good deal of time on *The Hobbit* and *The Lord of the Rings*, let's turn next in our survey of found manuscripts in Tolkien's works to *Farmer Giles of Ham*. I'll return in a little while to Middle-earth, but I have a reason for interjecting *Farmer Giles* at this point: it fits in with the timing of Tolkien's development of the found manuscript conceit in his Middle-earth writings. We've narrowed down the point at which Tolkien first explicitly claimed that *The Hobbit* and *The Lord of the Rings* were found manuscripts to the late summer of 1950, but there are implicit reasons to suppose the idea may have been growing on him for some time. One of these is the publication of *Farmer Giles of Ham* in 1949. After several successive enlargements of the text, it was finally accepted for publication by George Allen and Unwin in the second half of 1946. Around that date, Tolkien drafted a mock foreword, the earliest draft of which dates to October 1946 or not too long after. In it, "Tolkien pretends to be the editor and translator of an ancient text" (*Farmer Giles* viii), just as he would shortly do again in *The Lord of the Rings*. Tolkien writes in the foreword to *Farmer Giles*:

> Of the history of the Little Kingdom few fragments have survived; but by chance an account of its origin has been preserved: a legend, perhaps, rather than an account; for it is evidently a late compilation, full of marvels, derived not from sober annals, but from the popular lays to which its author frequently refers. For him the events that he records lay already in a distant past; but he seems, nonetheless, to have lived himself in the lands of the Little Kingdom. Such geographical knowledge as he shows (it is not his strong point) is of that country, while of regions outside it, north or west, he is plainly ignorant.
>
> An excuse for presenting a translation of this curious tale, out of its very insular Latin into the modern tongue of the United Kingdom, may be found in the glimpse that it affords of life in a dark period of the history of Britain, not to mention the light that it throws on the origin of some difficult place-names. Some may find the character and adventures of its hero attractive in themselves. (*Farmer Giles* 7)[15]

So, it would seem that the idea of equating his writings with found manuscripts was heavily on his mind in the second half of the 1940s. In

---

[15] Tolkien also refers in his mock foreword to a "fragmentary legend of Georgius son of Giles and his page Suovetaurilius (Suet)" (8), a reference in the text of *Farmer Giles* to a sequel Tolkien had planned. Although the sequel was abandoned, Tolkien refers to it in the foreword "as if it were a real artifact, a fragment from ancient days" (xiii).

Farmer Giles, it's made explicit in 1946 or 1947, in the *The Hobbit* in 1950, and likewise in the foreword to *The Lord of the Rings*, which we must surmise was also written around this time or perhaps a bit later. Earlier works, such as *Roverandom* and "Leaf by Niggle" make no mention of this conceit and begin like classic fairy tales. *Roverandom*: "Once upon a time, there was a little dog, and his name was Rover" (3). "Leaf by Niggle": "There was once a little man called Niggle, who had a long journey to make" (*Tree and Leaf* 93). I might mention that a much later tale, *Smith of Wootton Major*, also returns to this fairy tale form: "There was a village once, not very long ago for those will long memories, nor very far away for those with long legs" (*Smith* 5).[16]

Another work by Tolkien from around this same time, The Notion Club Papers, also utilizes the found manuscript convention. This is a curious piece of writing, initially having little to do with Middle-earth, but eventually pulled into its orbit to comment on the history of Númenor. It has one thing in common with many of Tolkien's writings: it's unfinished. But in many other respects, it's quite unique. It's Tolkien's only use of the motif of time travel (through the mode of "true dreaming"); his only work in an academic setting (other than one poem, "Knocking on the Door"); his only work structured as the meeting minutes of a fictional literary club modeled on the Inklings, making it something like an epistolary novel; and the only work he set in his own future! Christopher Tolkien dates the work to between the end of 1945 and the first part of 1946. Tolkien referred to the work in a letter to Stanley Unwin on July 21, 1946, just a few months before he drafted the mock foreword to *Farmer Giles*.

Here, as with the other works we have examined, Tolkien writes a fictional foreword to the minutes of the Notion Club, and invents an editor other than himself this time, Howard Green. The foreword begins:

> These Papers have a rather puzzling history. They were found after the Summer Examinations of 2012 on the top of one of a number of sacks of waste paper in the basement of the Examination Schools at Oxford by the present editor, Mr. Howard Green, the Clerk of the Schools. They were in a disordered bundle, loosely tied with red string. The outer sheet, inscribed in large Lombardic capitals: NOTION CLUB PAPERS.
> [...] It remains unknown how the Papers reached the waste-paper sack. It seems probable that they had at some time been prepared for publication, since they are in many places provided with

---

[16] It is nothing more than a coincidence, of course, entirely unrelated to the Red Book of Westmarch, but it is delightful nonetheless that *Smith of Wootton Major* was first published in the magazine, *Redbook*.

notes; yet in form they are nothing more than an elaborate minute-book of a club, devoted to conversation, debate, and the discussion of 'papers', in verse or prose, written and read by its members, and many of the entries have no particular interest for non-members.

The minutes, or reports, covered probably about 100 meetings or 'nights' during the years of last century, approximately 1980 to 1990. It is, however, not the least curious fact about these Papers that no such club appears ever to have existed. (*Sauron Defeated* 155)

This is quite mysterious, isn't it? An unknown club, and for some reason Tolkien pushes the discovery of its records out more than 60 years into his own future. And tied in *red* string, perhaps a telling detail in reference to the Red Book of Westmarch, or perhaps not? Tolkien—writing as the fictional editor, Howard Green—goes on to describe and inventory the fictional manuscript—the number of pages, the kind of paper, missing sections, the handwriting of their scribe, and so on. This is unique in Tolkien's treatment of found manuscripts in his writings, and verges on the kind of descriptions he wrote of actual manuscripts in the course of his career at Oxford—a point to which I will return later. Moreover, Tolkien declares The Notion Club Papers to be a second edition, which is also unique in his handling of found manuscripts. Where is the first edition? I will have more to say about this later too.

Let's review before moving on. We've established that there was a cluster of instances in which Tolkien introduced the found manuscript motif into his tales during the mid to late 1940s—the prefatory note to the second edition of *The Hobbit*, along with other paratextual elements, such as Thror's Map and the dustjacket illustration; the foreword and prologue to *The Lord of the Rings*, along with scattered references in the main narrative to Bilbo's memoirs; The Notion Club Papers, along with its foreword; and *Farmer Giles of Ham*, the only text discussed so far that is not directly tied to Middle-earth. Any attentive reader is bound to be wondering about the "Silmarillion" writings. The earliest form Tolkien's mythology took, The Book of Lost Tales, does not refer to itself as a found manuscript; however, there is a frame narrative, in which Eriol, a sea voyager, meets the Elves in Eressëa, learns their legends, and carries them back to England. These writings could therefore be construed implicitly as a found manuscript as well. At this early stage of Tolkien's mythography, Eriol is connected with genuine English history, a point that will be relevant when we come to examine Tolkien's underlying motives. The mature *Silmarillion*, as published, is not equated within its own pages with a found manuscript; however, in

The Lord of the Rings, it is strongly implied that Bilbo's *Translations from the Elvish* comprise at least some of this material from the Elder Days.[17]

But there's one more Middle-earth text we need to discuss. *The Adventures of Tom Bombadil and Other Verses from the Red Book,* published in 1962, brought together sixteen poems, most of which originally had nothing to do with Middle-earth, as a final coda to *The Lord of the Rings.* Here, as before, Tolkien penned a preface, in which he maintains the conceit that the collected poems originated in Middle-earth, often invented by Bilbo or Frodo themselves. He writes in the preface:

> The Red Book contains a large number of verses. A few are included in the narrative of the *Downfall of the Lord of the Rings,* or in the attached stories and chronicles; many more are found on loose leaves, while some are written carelessly in margins and blank spaces. Of the last sort most are nonsense, now often unintelligible even when legible, or half-remembered fragments. [...]
>
> The present selection is taken from the older pieces, mainly concerned with legends and jests of the Shire at the end of the Third Age, that appear to have been made by Hobbits, especially by Bilbo and his friends, or their immediate descendants. Their authorship is, however, seldom indicated. Those outside the narratives are in various hands, and were probably written down from oral tradition. (*Bombadil* 29–30)

In Tolkien's discussions with George Allen and Unwin during the planning stages of the book, he commented that

> The various items [...] do not really 'collect'. The only possible link is the fiction that they come from the Shire from about the period of *The Lord of the Rings.* But that fits some uneasily. I have done a good deal of work, trying to make them fit better: if not much to their good, I hope not to their serious detriment. [...]
>
> Some kind of foreword might possibly be required. The enclosed is not intended for that purpose! [...] But I found it easier, and more amusing (for myself) to represent to you in the form of a ridiculous editorial fiction what I have done to the verses, and what their references now are. Actually, although a fiction, the relative age, order of writing, and references of the items are pretty nearly represented as they really were. (*Letters* #237, p. 315)

Because of the lighthearted and comic nature of many of the poems, the mock-scholarly preface makes a much more conspicuous contrast than in *The Lord of the Rings,* rather more like the foreword to *Farmer Giles.* In one early review, the English poet and critic, Anthony

---

[17] There is at least one reference to an apparently fictional manuscript in the pages of *The Silmarillion,* the *Narsilion,* "the Song of the Sun and Moon" (Tolkien, *Silmarillion* 99). I say *apparently* fictional because Christopher Tolkien observes that "if there ever was a 'song of the Sun and Moon' [...] it has disappeared" (Tolkien, *Shaping* 170).

Thwaite, described the conceit as "heavy-footed donnish waggery" not to his taste, "a ponderous joke for those with some knowledge of the editing involved in Old and Middle Eng[lish] Lit." But isn't that exactly Tolkien's point?

The Purpose and Effects of the Conceit

Now that we've pretty thoroughly surveyed Tolkien's use of the found manuscript convention in his writings, the time has come to ask why he might have done it and what effects it has on his work. First, why pretend one's fictions are authentic manuscripts from an earlier time, arranged and translated by a later hand? Why not simply let them be fiction? For one thing, Tolkien had a personal preference for "history, true or feigned, with its varied applicability to the thought and experience of readers" (*LotR* Foreword.xxiv). Tolkien was dismissing allegory here, not fiction outright, but his liking for *feigned* history suggests that the kind of fiction he preferred might include pseudo-historical elements such as manuscripts, maps, and other artifacts. And indeed we know of some of these—for example, Haggard's *She* and Buchan's *Midwinter*. Unlike fiction, history is something that really happened, and feigned history is something that could pass for real history. To pass it off as such, some evidence is called for—even if it, too, was manufactured by the author.

In addition to claiming that several of his works either were themselves found manuscripts or made reference to such texts, Tolkien produced a variety of artifacts to go along with his stories. Perhaps the best known are the three facsimile pages from the Book of Mazarbul, written in runes and carefully weathered and damaged by Tolkien so that they could pass for the actual burned, slashed, and blood-stained pages recovered from the Dwarvish record. Of course, they aren't the *actual* pages, and in fact, they *couldn't* be, because if one decodes the runes, one finds they're in English, not in any "authentic" language of Middle-earth. Tolkien addresses this discrepancy in a very late, mainly philological, text, "Of Dwarves and Men," writing:

> In preparing an example of the Book of Mazarbul, and making three torn and partly illegible pages, I followed the general principle followed throughout: the Common Speech was to be represented as English of today, literary or colloquial as the case demanded. Consequently the text was cast into English spelt as at present, but modified as it might be by writers in haste whose familiarity with the written form was imperfect, and who were also [...] transliterating the English into a different alphabet [...].
>
> This is all very well, and perhaps gives some idea of the kind of text Gandalf was trying to read in great haste in the Chamber of

Mazarbul. It also accords with the general treatment of the languages in *The Lord of the Rings*: only the actual words and names of the period that are in Elvish languages are preserved in what is supposed to have been their real form. Also, this treatment was imposed by the fact that, though the actual Common Speech was sketched in structure and phonetic elements, and a number of words invented, it was quite impossible to translate even such short extracts into its real contemporary form, if they were visibly represented. But it is of course in fact an erroneous extension of the general linguistic treatment. It is one thing to represent all the dialogue of the story in varying forms of English [...]. But it is quite another thing to provide *visible* facsimiles or representations of writings or carvings supposed to be of the date of the events in the narrative. (*Peoples* 298–99)

Tolkien intended these pages from the Book of Mazarbul to be included in the published *Lord of the Rings* and was disappointed when they had to be omitted. These illustrations, which Tolkien labored over in ink, colored pencils, and watercolor, were simply too expensive to reproduce as they were. Rayner Unwin had inquired whether they might be reduced to line drawings, but Tolkien was not satisfied with that. He wrote to Rayner in April 1953:

As for the 'facsimiles' of the burned and torn pages of the Runic Book, originally planned to appear at the beginning of Book II Ch. V [...,] I think their disappearance is regrettable; but in spite of what you have said, I think line-blocks are for this purpose impracticable. A page each is required, or the things will be too illegible to be interesting (or too unveracious to be worth inclusion). I earnestly hope it may be found possible to include them in the 'appendix'. (*Letters* #137, p. 168)

In the end, it was not possible to include them even in the novel's appendices, and these pages remained unseen by most fans for another twenty-five years.[18] Tolkien's choice of words here — "unveracious" — is telling, and it reinforces this major reason for appealing to fictional found manuscripts: they imbue a tale with a greater sense of veracity and realism — that is, again, a feeling that the tale might really have happened.

Tolkien provided other glimpses of this verisimilitude, beyond the facsimile pages of the Book of Mazarbul. Let me give you a few more examples of artifact manuscript pages. One of these is the King's Letter, a document representing a letter from King Elessar to Samwise Gamgee early in the Fourth Age, part of an epilogue drafted and then jettisoned from the story before publication. This manuscript page was more "authentic" than Tolkien's pages from the Book of

---

[18] They were first published in *Pictures by J. R. R. Tolkien* in 1979 (n. pag.) and have subsequently been reprinted at higher quality, along with additional drafts, in *The Art of* The Lord of the Rings (77–87).

Mazarbul, at least, because it was partly represented in a supposedly "authentic" language of Middle-earth, Sindarin (*Art of* The Lord of the Rings 232–35).[19] Similar artifacts are Tolkien's facsimile of the contract between Thorin and Company and Bilbo Baggins (*Art of* the Hobbit 34–35) and Thror's Map, drawn by Tolkien and referred to in *The Hobbit* as if it were a genuine artifact—although here again, like the pages of the Book of Mazarbul, these documents cannot be genuine artifacts, because the runes transliterate English, and in the case of the map are not even the Dwarvish runes of *The Lord of the Rings* but rather authentic medieval Anglo-Saxon runes.[20]

Beyond this pictorial evidence of veracity, Tolkien offers textual attempts to authenticate his found manuscript as genuine in several places. Tolkien added further authenticating details about the Red Book of Westmarch to the second-edition prologue to *The Lord of the Rings*, describing two specific copies of the book and giving them quite an elaborate fictive history:

> The original Red Book has not been preserved, but many copies were made [...]. The most important copy [...] has a different history. It was kept at Great Smials, but it was written in Gondor, probably at the request of the great-grandson of Peregrin, and completed in S.R. 1592 (F.A. 172). Its southern scribe appended this note: Findegil, King's Writer, finished this work in IV 172. It is an exact copy in all details of the Thain's Book in Minas Tirith.[21] That

---

[19] I might also briefly mention the Tomb of Balin here. Like the King's Letter, Tolkien represents the inscription in both English and authentic Dwarvish. Transliterated, the runes read BALIN / FUNDINUL / UZBADKHAZADDŪMU / BALINSONOVFUNDINLORDOFMORIA. For Tolkien's commentary of the Khuzdul in the inscription, see Tolkien, "Words, Phrases and Passages" 47.

[20] Although Tolkien used genuine historical Anglo-Saxon runes transliterating English on the map, there is some tantalizing evidence to hint that Tolkien may already have had a translation conceit behind *The Hobbit* in his mind, a conceit that would become quite formal with *The Lord of the Rings*. In a letter to G. E. Selby written in late 1937, Tolkien claims that "Icelandic was in a foolish moment substituted for the proper language of [his] tales" (*Drawings, Watercolors, and Manuscripts* [4]). That in itself is scant enough, but there is a little more. In one draft of the map, which, notably, indicates that it was "Copied by B. Baggins [Bilbo Baggins]," Tolkien translated the moon-letters into Old English (*Art of* The Hobbit 51), and in another draft of the moon-letters, Tolkien translated them into Old Norse (*Art of* The Hobbit 55–56). These translations could have been idly made, Tolkien simply amusing himself, or they may suggest Tolkien was beginning to think of his text as the translation of a found manuscript. See also further thoughts on these texts at Fisher.

[21] There is another reference to the Thain's Book in *The Lord of the Rings*, just one other, in a note to Appendix F in which "a commentator of Gondor" explains how Frodo failed to recognize the Sindarin spoken in Lothlórien because of its Silvan accent (1127). This note does not appear in the first edition but was added

book was a copy, made at the request of King Elessar, of the Red Book of the Periannath, and was brought to him by the Thain Peregrin when he retired to Gondor in IV 64.

The Thain's Book was thus the first copy made of the Red Book and contained much that was later omitted or lost. In Minas Tirith it received much annotation, and many corrections, especially of names, words, and quotations in the Elvish languages [...]. But the chief importance of Findegil's copy is that it alone contains the whole of Bilbo's 'Translations from the Elvish'. These three volumes were found to be a work of great skill and learning in which, between 1403 and 1418, he had used all the sources available to him in Rivendell, both living and written. But since they were little used by Frodo, being almost entirely concerned with the Elder Days, no more is said of them here. (*LotR* Prologue.14–15)[22]

Also in *The Lord of the Rings*, Tolkien takes some pain to assure his readers that the map of the Shire is an accurate one. This note occurs only in the first edition foreword: "some maps are given, including one of the Shire that has been approved as reasonably correct by those Hobbits that still concern themselves with ancient history" (*Fellowship*, 1st ed 8). Here Tolkien, tongue in cheek, implies that there are still hobbits in the world and that he has consulted with them in drawing the map of their ancestral homeland.

Turning back to The Notion Club Papers, I promised to return to Tolkien's claim that the book was a second edition. Tolkien actually wrote a "Note to the Second Edition" of this unfinished text, a fictive introduction to a fictive manuscript! Here, he invents two additional academics, "Mr. W. W. Wormald of the School of Bibliopoly, and Mr. D. N. Borrow of the Institute of Occidental Languages" (*Sauron Defeated* 156), whom Tolkien depicts as so intrigued by the manuscript that they asked the editor for permission to scrutinize it. These two

---

to the second. It may be that a reader inquired about Frodo's failure to understand the speech of the Elves of Lothlórien, given Tolkien's comment in Appendix F that the Silvan tongue does not appear in the novel, or perhaps Tolkien noticed the discrepancy himself. In any case, the note attempts to reconcile the inconsistency by appealing to the authority of an invented manuscript of Middle-earth.

[22] We commonly equate Bilbo's "Translations from the Elvish" with *The Silmarillion*, but it's not quite so simple. Bilbo's translations are referred to by Tolkien as three volumes. But what three volumes? It could be that these three together comprise the published *Silmarillion*, more or less as we have it today, but that would be rather arbitrary. It seems perhaps more likely that Tolkien had in mind the three "Great Tales" to which Tolkien made reference many times: the Fall of Gondolin, the Children of Húrin, and Beren and Lúthien. If my surmise is correct, then other aspects of *The Silmarillion* such as the Ainulindalë and the Akallabêth fall outside Bilbo's translations, and the three standalone volumes edited by Christopher Tolkien in his last years might better fit the description.

then produced a joint report—again, also fictive—in which they examine the very paper on which it was written and conclude that the manuscript pages might actually be forty or fifty years older than assumed by Mr. Green, the editor of the first edition. Subtracting from the claimed publication date of 2012, this would place the origins of the fictive manuscript in roughly the same time period when Tolkien himself *actually* wrote it. And this would certainly explain why Mr. Green found no evidence the club existed in the 1980s. Of course, Mr. Green and his associates also find no record of the existence of any of its members in the 1940s either! And Mr. Green has his own theories about the origins of the paper. Amid all of this mock-scholarly debate, the astonishing thing is that all of this is made up entirely by Tolkien—as David Bratman puts it, "fictional wrappings upon wrappings, and the virtuoso use of verisimilitude" (email message). Offering a putative second edition at all is a detail in service of credibility; an extended note on the further examination of the manuscript all the more so, particularly in order to have a fictive second edition contradict the fictive first edition! And even the uncertainty and disagreement of Tolkien's invented academics serves the purpose of feigned authenticity. This is exactly how the investigation of *real* manuscripts works.

In addition to these points, Tolkien also made several attempts, though often abortive, to connect his fiction with the genuine history of England. Let me offer a few brief examples. Recall Eriol, the frame narrator of the Book of Lost Tales, Tolkien's earliest mythological writings. Eriol, it is suggested by Tolkien, was the father of two legendary figures of real English history: Hengest and Horsa, the Anglo-Saxon invaders who came to the British Isles in the 5th century AD. Tolkien also parodied Hengest and Horsa in the two hobbits, Marcho and Blanco, who set out from Bree and founded the Shire. Tolkien equated England itself in his early mythography with the mythical land of Luthany. To the island of Númenor Tolkien gave another name after its destruction, Atalantë, meaning the "downfallen," evoking the Greek myth of Atlantis—although Tolkien called the resemblance of the names only "a curious chance" (Tolkien *Letters* #257, p. 347). Avallónë, a city on the eastern coast of the Elves' island of Tol Eressëa, echoes the Arthurian island of Avalon. Most of these connections are merely adumbrated in fleeting drafts, but they suggest efforts on Tolkien's part to authenticate his stories as part of a chain of genuine legends of the primary world.

All of the forgoing discussion supports a general observation that found manuscripts buttress the believability of fantastic tales, but Tolkien may have had more personal reasons to prefer this technique as well. Tolkien was a professor at Oxford, where he taught medieval language and literature, mainly Old English, but also Gothic, Old Norse, Medieval Welsh, and related subjects. In addition to teaching, Tolkien wrote scholarly essays and developed editions of some important medieval texts. Since much of his professional labor involved medieval manuscripts, it should come as little surprise that his fiction would touch on this scribal tradition at several points. Tolkien's notes on the Red Book of Westmarch, the Thain's Book, Findegil's copy, not to mention editions within editions of The Notion Club Papers, echo the kind of work Tolkien and other medievalists routinely engaged in to unravel the history and provenance of medieval texts. The very name of the Red Book of Westmarch recalls a genuine Welsh manuscript of the late 14th century, the Red Book of Hergest.[23]

An example or two will suffice to show the similarities between Tolkien's work as a literary scholar and the mock-scholarly presentation of found manuscripts in his fiction. In his preface to M. B. Salu's modern English translation of the *Ancrene Wisse*, Tolkien writes:

> For her new translation Miss Salu has chosen the version which names itself *Ancrene Wisse*, or "Guide for Anchoresses". It is one of the oldest, possibly the oldest, surviving copy so far as the date of actual writing goes; though it is not the original, and presents a form that already shows the processes of editing and expansion to which this Rule, destined for long popularity, seems at once to have been subjected. It is, however, for a translator probably the best text to use, since it was made by a scribe who not only wrote a beautiful and lucid hand but seems also to have been perfectly at home with the language (the spelling, the grammar, and the vocabulary) with which he was dealing. (*Ancrene Riwle* v)

This ought to remind attentive readers of Tolkien's comments on the various manuscripts and copies of the Red Book of Westmarch. A few years later, Tolkien published his own edition of the *Ancrene Wisse* for the Early English Text Society, for which his colleague N. R. Ker provided an introduction that reads at many points rather like the discussion of the date, provenance, and even the paper of the Notion

---

[23] See also Flieger, who notes: "it seems clear that Tolkien's Red Book was intended to echo the great medieval manuscript books whose names sound like an Andrew Lang color series for the Middle Ages—The White Book of Rhydderch, the Black Book of Carmarthen, the Yellow Book of Lecan, and most important as his immediate color model, the real Red Book of Hergest" (285).

Club "written by" Professors Green, Wormald, and Borrow (but really by Tolkien). Such introductions usually describe, and often attempt to date, the pages, handwriting, and other characteristics of medieval texts. Another such example is Tolkien and E. V. Gordon's introduction to their edition of *Sir Gawain and the Green Knight*, which opens:

> The manuscript is a small quarto on vellum (7 x 5 in.) in the Cotton Collection in the British Museum—MS. Nero A. x. It contains three other poems, known as *Pearl*, *Purity* (or *Cleanness*), and *Patience*. They are all written in the same small sharp hand which has been dated about 1400. The ink has faded considerably, and some lines were blotted against the opposite page when the manuscript was written, so that it is not easy to read. The first transcribers deserve great credit for their care and accuracy [...]. (vii)

Numerous echoes of this description are heard later in Tolkien's fiction, from the description of Bilbo's and Frodo's handwriting in the Red Book of Westmarch and Ori's hand in the Book of Mazarbul to the fidelity with which the former was copied and preserved and the difficulties of reading the latter. Several of the relevant descriptions have been quoted above and need not be repeated here. Others of Tolkien's studies of language and literature read very much like the appendices he wrote for the *Lord of the Rings* along with various philological essays on the languages of Middle-earth that were published posthumously. Of these, perhaps two of the best examples are his essays, "Ancrene Wisse and Hali Meiðhad" and "Sigelwara land."

Part of Tolkien's desire to situate his own fictive Red Book within a larger manuscript tradition no doubt relates to his well-known desire to produce a mythology for England. Tolkien was "from early days grieved by the poverty of [his] own beloved country: it had no stories of its own (bound up with its tongue and soil), not of the quality that [he] sought, and found (as an ingredient) in legends of other lands" (*Letters* #131, p. 144). Tolkien's own myth-making sought to fill this void, and part of the goal was to produce something believable to fill it. By its very nature it should not be *outlandish*. Rather the reverse: for Tolkien, such myths should be *of* England, the land and its language. All the uses of found manuscripts we've talked about up to this point are in service of this goal. He wanted his tales to stand as the equals of the Arthurian legends and *Beowulf*, but more profoundly English than either. The Arthurian material originates in Welsh tales written down mainly by Britons and Normans (and later, French and Germans on the Continent); *Beowulf* is a Scandinavian tale written down by the English. Tolkien's stories are English tales written by an Englishman.

Farmer Giles of Ham contains, or contained in draft, some subtle references that help to make this point. In the first drafts of his mock-scholarly foreword, Tolkien quotes several lines from *Sir Gawain and the Green Knight* and implies that in one of them — "And oft bothe blysse and blunder" — the *Gawain*-poet might have been referring to Farmer Giles's blunderbuss. Tolkien wrote: "This is the only reference that has been discovered in other writers of early history [*real-world* writers, I might interject] to the legends of the Little Kingdom, and it must be admitted that it is far from certain" (*Farmer Giles* 106). Here, Tolkien bodies forth the very wish he expressed to Milton Waldman: that his tale of English antiquity might be "found (as an ingredient) in legends of other lands."

Also in the foreword to *Farmer Giles*, Wayne G. Hammond and Christina Scull find several oblique references to Geoffrey of Monmouth's 12th-century *Historia Regum Britanniae*, a pseudohistorical, one might say *feigned*, history of the Kings of Britain, and notably King Arthur. Geoffrey also claimed to be the editor and translator, but not the author, of his work, just as Tolkien would do centuries later (107). In his dedication of the work — the equivalent of Tolkien's foreword — Geoffrey writes that one

> Walter, archdeacon of Oxford, a man of great eloquence, and learned in foreign histories, offered me a very ancient book in the British tongue [...]. At his request, therefore, though I had not made fine language my study, by collecting florid expressions from other authors, yet contented with my own homely style, I undertook the translation of that book into Latin. (Geoffrey 89)[24]

Of Tolkien's sprawling and voluminous writings, the vast majority remained unpublished until after his death. First, readers got *The Silmarillion*, offering new vistas into the Elder Days. The *Unfinished Tales* followed, bringing with it a fuller picture of Númenor. Then the expansive twelve-volume *History of Middle-earth*, accompanied by many other works — *Roverandom, Mr. Bliss, The Legend of Sigurd and Gúdrun, The Fall of Arthur, The Story of Kullervo*, and the three Great Tales, *The Children of Húrin, Beren and Lúthien*, and *The Fall of Gondolin*. Tolkien's unpublished academic works continued to appear as well — *The Monsters and the Critics, The Old English Exodus, Finn and Hengest, Beowulf*, and most recently Tolkien's work on an edition of Chaucer for

---

[24] This is from an edition of 1900, an edition that would have been current during Tolkien's undergraduate days at Exeter College, originally edited about fifty years before Tolkien's time by a man I am happy to tell you was named Giles. No, not Farmer Giles, but John Allen Giles, a Fellow of Corpus Christi College, Oxford, and a scholar of Anglo-Saxon, as Tolkien would come to be.

the Clarendon Press, portions of which have just been published by Professor John Bowers. Tolkien's artwork came to a larger audience too—a little at first, and then much more, many examples of which have appeared at recent exhibitions in Oxford, New York, and Paris. And with all of this, it's rather astonishing that there is still material making its way to the public almost fifty years since Tolkien sailed into the West. Many of the works Tolkien left unpublished were brought to us through decades of labor by Tolkien's third son and literary executor, Christopher, who has himself now recently passed. But there is still more waiting for "expert treasure-hunters" in the Bodleian Library and elsewhere. It strikes me as a delightful irony that Tolkien would make references to a wealth of manuscripts, both lost and found, when he himself would leave behind such a trove of his own pages. And I can say from personal experience that grappling with Tolkien's difficult handwriting sometimes feels like transliterating the runes of a long-lost language. We continue to pore over these leaves, as Tolkien and his son Christopher did, in search of new stories, new commentaries, and new insights. To paraphrase a conversation between Frodo and Sam, the great tales never do end, not so long as we are still here to turn the page.

Works Cited

The Ancrene Riwle. Edited by M. B. Salu, Burns and and Oates, 1955.

Anderson, Douglas A. *The Annotated Hobbit*. Revised and expanded ed., Houghton Mifflin, 2002.

Bratman, David. "The Artistry of Omissions and Revisions in *The Lord of the Rings*." The Lord of the Rings, *1954–2004: Scholarship in Honor of Richard E. Blackwelder*, edited by Wayne G. Hammond and Christina Scull, Marquette UP, 2006.

——. Email to the author. 10 Sept. 2019.

Bowers, John M. *Tolkien's Lost Chaucer*. Oxford UP, 2019.

Bryan, Mike. *The Afterword: A Novel*. Pantheon Books, 2003.

Buchan, John. *Midwinter*. Grosset and Dunlap, 1923.

Christopher, Nicholas. *The Bestiary*. Random House, 2007.

Croft, Janet Brennan. "Doors into Elf-mounds: J. R. R. Tolkien's Introductions, Prefaces, and Forewords." *Tolkien Studies* 15 (2018), pp. 177–95.

Eco, Umberto. *The Name of the Rose*. Harcourt, 1983.

The English Text of the Ancrene Wisse. Edited by J. R. R. Tolkien, Early English Text Society, Oxford UP, 1962.

Fisher, Jason. "Tolkien's translation conceit—new evidence?" *Lingwë – Musings of a Fish,* 28 Nov. 2011, lingwe.blogspot.com/2011/11/tolkiens-translation-conceit-new.html.

Flieger, Verlyn. "Tolkien and the Idea of the Book." The Lord of the Rings, *1954–2004: Scholarship in Honor of Richard E. Blackwelder.* Edited by Wayne G. Hammond and Christina Scull, Marquette UP, 2006, pp. 283–99.

"Geoffrey of Monmouth's British History." *Six Old English Chronicles.* Edited by J. A. Giles, George Bell and Sons, 1900, pp. 87–292.

Haggard, H. Rider. *She: A History of Adventure.* Rev. ed., Longmans, Green, 1888.

Hammond, Wayne G. and Christina Scull. *The Art of* The Hobbit *by J. R. R. Tolkien.* HarperCollins, 2011.

———. *The Art of* The Lord of the Rings *by J. R. R. Tolkien.* Houghton Mifflin Harcourt, 2015.

———. *The Lord of the Rings: A Reader's Companion.* Houghton Mifflin, 2005.

Harkness, Deborah. *A Discovery of Witches.* Penguin, 2011.

Hooker, Mark. "Journey to Center of Middle-earth." *The Tolkienaeum: Essays on J. R. R. Tolkien and his Legendarium.* Llyfrawr, 2014, pp. 1–12.

———. "Reading John Buchan in Search of Tolkien." *Tolkien and the Study of His Sources: Critical Essays,* edited by Jason Fisher. McFarland, 2011, pp. 162–92.

J. R. R. Tolkien: The Hobbit; Drawings, Watercolors, and Manuscripts. Exhibition catalogue, Haggerty Art Museum, Marquette Univ., 1987.

Lem, Stanisław. *Memoirs Found in a Bathtub.* Seabury Press, 1973.

Márquez, Gabriel García. *One Hundred Years of Solitude.* Harper and Row, 1967.

Nabokov, Vladimir. *Lolita.* Olympia Press, 1955.

———. *Pale Fire.* G. P. Putnam's Sons, 1962.

Palahniuk, Chuck. *Lullaby.* Doubleday, 2002.

Poe, Edgar Allan. "MS. Found in a Bottle." *The Complete Tales and Poems of Edgar Allan Poe.* Modern Library, 1938, pp. 118–26.

———. *[The] Narrative of A[rthur] Gordon Pym [of Nantucket].* The Complete Tales and Poems of Edgar Allan Poe. Modern Library, 1938, pp. 748–883.

Rateliff, John D. *The History of* The Hobbit. One-volume ed., HarperCollins, 2011.

Shelley, Mary. *Frankenstein; or, the Modern Prometheus.* Hughes, Harding, Mavor and Jones, 1818.

Sir Gawain and the Green Knight. Edited by J. R. R. Tolkien and E. V. Gordon. Clarendon Press, 1925.

Thwaite, Anthony. "Hobbitry." *The Listener,* 22 Nov. 1962, p. 831.

Tolkien, J. R. R. *The Adventures of Tom Bombadil and Other Verses from the Red Book*. Edited by Christina Scull and Wayne G. Hammond, HarperCollins, 2014.

———. "Ancrene Wisse and Hali Meiðhad." *Essays and Studies by Members of the English Association, Oxford*, vol. 14, 1929, pp. [104]–26.

———. *Farmer Giles of Ham*. 50th Anniversary Edition, edited by Christina Scull and Wayne G. Hammond, Houghton Mifflin, 1999.

———. *The Fellowship of the Ring*. George Allen and Unwin, 1954.

———. *The Hobbit*. Revised edition, Houghton Mifflin, 1966.

———. "Leaf by Niggle." *Tree and Leaf, Mythopoeia, the Homecoming of Beorhtnoth, Beorhthelm's Son*. New ed., HarperCollins, 2001, pp. 91–118.

———. *The Letters of J. R. R. Tolkien*. Edited by Humphrey Carpenter. Houghton Mifflin, 1981.

———. *The Lord of the Rings*. 50th Anniversary Edition. Houghton Mifflin, 2004.

———. *The Peoples of Middle-earth*. Edited by Christopher Tolkien, Houghton Mifflin, 1996.

———. *Pictures by J. R. R. Tolkien*. Foreword and notes by Christopher Tolkien, Houghton Mifflin, 1979.

———. *The Return of the King*. George Allen and Unwin, 1955.

———. *The Return of the Shadow: The History of* The Lord of the Rings, *Part One*. Edited by Christopher Tolkien, Houghton Mifflin, 1988.

———. *Roverandom*. Houghton Mifflin, 1998.

———. *Sauron Defeated: The End of the Third Age (The History of* The Lord of the Rings, *Part Four); The Notion Club Papers and The Drowning of Anadûnê*. Edited by Christopher Tolkien, Houghton Mifflin, 1992.

———. *The Shaping of Middle-earth: The Quenta, the Ambarkanta and the Annals*. Edited by Christopher Tolkien. Houghton Mifflin, 1986.

———. "Sigelwara land." (I) *Medium Aevum*, Vol. 1, No. 3 (December 1932), pp. [183]–196; (II) *Medium Aevum*, Vol. 3, No. 2 (June 1934), pp. [95]–111.

———. *The Silmarillion*. Edited by Christopher Tolkien, Houghton Mifflin, 1977.

———. *Smith of Wootton Major*. Edited by Verlyn Flieger, extended edition, HarperCollins, 2005.

———. "Words, Phrases and Passages in Various Tongues in *The Lord of the Rings*." *Parma Eldalamberon*, edited by Christopher Gilson, iss. 17, 2007.

Verne, Jules. *Journey to the Center of the Earth*. Edited by Peter Cogman, translated by Frank Wynne, with an introduction by Jane Smiley, Penguin, 2009.

A Brief History of Libraries in Middle-earth: Manuscript and Book Repositories in Tolkien's Legendarium

David D. Oberhelman

A T THE END OF J. R. R. TOLKIEN'S *The Lord of the Rings*, the four heroic Hobbits return from their adventures and begin to chronicle their feats as well as other details of history and lore they have learned on their journeys throughout Middle-earth. Those who remain after the Ringbearers depart ultimately become librarians, custodians or curators dedicated to preserving those records in various collections for subsequent generations. The word "library" occurs only in the "Note on Shire Records" in the Prologue,[1] and it stands out as perhaps another one of those anachronisms in the Shire, such as umbrellas, the postal system, and the metaphorical "express train" of Bilbo's party. Yet if we take a broader view, it is clear that there are many scattered references to libraries, archives, manuscript repositories, and other collections for the preservation of literature, lore, and history not only in *The Lord of the Rings* but also throughout Tolkien's legendarium. These references are often tied to the relationship between oral culture and manuscript culture, and thus belong to the greater history of the preservation of cultural memory in Tolkien's universe.

Much has been written on the presence of oral culture and oral poetic traditions in Tolkien's works: Patrick Wynne and Carl Hostetter's technical analysis of Elven verse forms is one of the most detailed.[2] Other scholars such as Wayne G. Hammond and Verlyn Flieger have investigated the history of writing and manuscripts in Tolkien's universe in terms of how they relate to history of the book in Western European history.[3] Along the lines of those analyses, I

---

[1] Based on a consultation of Richard E. Blackwelder's *A Tolkien Thesaurus*, a detailed concordance to *The Lord of the Rings*.

[2] Their examination of the *Minlamad thent/estent* verse form includes a broad discussion of Tolkien's understanding of oral tradition and poetic practices as well as his efforts to incorporate oral traditions into his legendarium (Wynne and Hostetter 121–30).

[3] See Wayne G. Hammond's studies on book culture and paper manufacturing in the Shire ("Books, Literature, and Literacy in Middle-earth," and "Papermaking in the Shire") and Verlyn Flieger's analysis of the Red Book of Westmarch and the medieval manuscript tradition ("Tolkien and the Idea of the Book").

would like to examine how the history of libraries in the legendarium roughly echoes the history of such repositories in our own world from antiquity through the advent of the printing press in the 1450s. I will map out a chronology of libraries in Europe and then examine the parallel history of libraries in Middle-earth culminating in the private libraries of the Shire at the dawn of the Fourth Age.

The history of libraries in ancient and early modern civilization provides the template Tolkien used in forming his own history of writing from the First through the Fourth Ages of his subcreated universe. The advent of writing, according to the historian of language Walter Ong, led to the making of records, and the setting down of experience in a tangible format that had to be safeguarded and catalogued.[4] At this point libraries, houses of memory, were born. The first libraries appeared in Mesopotamia and Egypt from 3500 to 3000 BC, not long after the invention of the earliest scripts, cuneiform and hieroglyphics.[5] Hoarding the written knowledge of all nations and peoples became a sign of power, as demonstrated by institutions such as the great Assyrian library at Nineveh, the private collection of Assurbanipal founded around 700 BC; it was a prototype for later royal libraries and archives that amassed written knowledge in an era when the majority of the population still relied upon oral dissemination of information.

It was in the Classical Greek and Hellenistic period that the great libraries of the ancient world appeared to make the creative and intellectual output of their civilization available for scholarly consultation. The famous library at Alexandria, founded around 290 BC, functioned as a sign of the power of the Ptolemaic monarchs following Alexander the Great's conquest, but it also signaled the triumph of writing as a technology for saving the arts, sciences, and past of a culture and indeed of all cultures in antiquity. Although it was not the only great collection in this period, its approximately 70,000 titles and its famous scholar-librarians (such as the poet Callimachus) forever imprinted the image of the comprehensive library on the consciousness of the West,

---

[4] Ong's *Orality and Literacy: The Technologizing of the Word* provides the best introduction to the different theories of orality and literacy and maps out a theory for how oral and "chirographic" (writing-based) cultures are born out of the different means by which human consciousness experiences the world and preserves those experiences to transmit to others.

[5] For an overview of ancient libraries in Mesopotamia, Egypt, and Greece, see Lionel Casson, *Libraries in the Ancient World*. Casson outlines the development of libraries through Alexandria and the Roman Empire and their ties to manuscript practices in ancient civilizations. William A. Katz also provides a good historical survey of manuscript culture and rise of libraries in his edition of *Dahl's History of the Book*.

and most likely inspired Tolkien's image of the fabled storehouses of knowledge in his *legendarium*. Its destruction, which was a gradual process spanning the invasion of Caesar in 48 BC to approximately AD 641, is also the stuff of legend since the ancient wisdom and records it contained were forever lost, a pattern played out frequently as the Classical era gave way to the Dark Ages. Tolkien's universe follows a similar pattern, as I will explain, in which great library collections are lost during the transition from one age to the next.

After the fall of Rome, an era which had witnessed an explosion of private and even public libraries, monastic libraries emerged as outposts of literate culture. Ireland was a center for the preservation of manuscripts in the early medieval period.[6] Scriptoria and manuscript collections later became common features of European monasteries through the fourteenth century. It was after the 1000s that the epics and sagas were put down in writing even while they continued to be performed by minstrels or *scops* as they had been for centuries. Universities in cities such as Paris or Oxford also appeared with "publishing houses" or stationer's shops nearby to copy manuscripts for their collections.[7] With the invention of moveable type and the printing press in Germany around 1450, the nature of literacy and of libraries changed dramatically. More people could read, printers became book publishers, and the mass production of books meant even the new merchant classes could now own books and have their own personal libraries. Soon public libraries reappeared as books proliferated and spread to the masses.

Having sketched out this historic background of oral and manuscript cultures and the place of libraries in them, I will now turn to Tolkien's history to explore how he devised a parallel, equally complex chronology for the development of library collections in his invented world. This history begins with a culture based entirely upon orality or the immediacy of thought itself—the "culture" of the Valar. In the essay "Quendi and Eldar" Tolkien explains that the Valar, who

---

[6] Thomas Cahill's book *How the Irish Saved Civilization* offers a popular account of how the monastic institutions in Ireland preserved manuscripts of Western thought in an era when Continental civilization was at a low ebb and many manuscripts had been lost. The Irish preserved and transcribed scrolls which they saved in vellum wrappings; a Psalter from c. 800 was discovered in a bog in 2006. That Tolkien does not have an exact counterpart to the Irish monasteries in his fiction is not surprising, given his Anglo-Saxon focus.

[7] See Kenneth M. Setton, "From Medieval to Modern Library." Setton writes a detailed account of the rise of monastic libraries with the Benedictines (371–79).

took incarnate forms, would also have a language, though references to the Valian tongue were only preserved "by tradition of mouth" in "'the Sayings of Rúmil' [...], the ancient sage of Tirion" (*War of the Jewels* 391–98) that were salvaged long after in Beleriand. The treatise *Lhammas* notes that Valar do not need to record thought or preserve it in writing because theirs is a living memory: "for rich as are the minds of the Elves in memory, they are not as the Valar, who wrote not and do not forget" (*Lost Road* 173). Thus it is with the Elves, the first Children of Ilúvatar, that writing, and inevitably libraries, are born, for they must turn to writing to record their memory and consequently house those records.

The newly awakened Elves at Cuiviénen initially had a purely oral culture. The Quendi took to naming all that they encountered in the world, and, like the traditional oral cultures of our own ancient world, used song and verse to preserve their earliest memories of life amidst Melkor's beasts. But when the Caliquendi arrive in Valinor, they develop writing as well as storehouses to preserve it. According to the account in *The Book of Lost Tales, Part I*, "Aulë aided by the Gnomes [Noldor] contrived alphabets and scripts, and on the walls of Kôr [Tirion] were many dark tales written in pictured symbols, and runes of great beauty were drawn there too or carved upon stones" (141), and when Melkor infected them with unrest, "the Noldori ceased to sing, [...] for their hearts grew somewhat older as their lore deepened and the desires more swollen, and books of their wisdom multiplied as the leaves of the forest" (*Book of Lost Tales, Part I* 141). In this account of the Noldor's early literacy Tolkien conflates what in ancient Scandinavian culture were two distinct scripts: runes, used in inscription on stone and other hard materials, and letters (the Roman alphabet in our world), used on parchment.[8] Indeed, runes appear both in monumental inscriptions and in the books prior to the destruction of the Two Trees, and these two great "collections" of writing form the earliest libraries in Arda. The loremaster Rúmil—the Noldo who "first achieved fitting signs for the recording of speech and song" (*Silmarillion* 63) and is cited as the chronicler of the *Ainulindalë* and early historical accounts of the Elves in Valinor—inspired the formation of a manuscript culture which in turn led to the awakening of the concept of the library in the Blessed Realm.[9]

---

[8] Terje Spurkland gives a detailed study of Scandinavian runes and alphabetical writing as two systems of literacy (or literacy and "runacy") from 1150 to the 1400s.

[9] As Paul Kocher states, Rúmil's invention of the Tengwar indicates that "the Noldor had a tradition of interest in language and its written forms, of which there is not trace among either the Vanyar or the Teleri" in Aman (41–46). Daeron

In the accounts of the Elves in Beleriand, the most overt references to caches of books and to libraries occur in the descriptions of Turgon's hidden fortress city of Gondolin, which becomes perhaps the greatest of all the repositories or royal libraries across the sea. In "The Fall of Gondolin" Turgon alludes to what must be an assembled collection of writings in the isolated city when he greets Tuor with "Lo! Thy coming was set in our books of wisdom" (*Book of Lost Tales, Part II* 161), and in the essay "Quendi and Eldar," references to stores of manuscripts and books occur in the comments on Pengoloð, the writer of the Quenta Simarillion and perhaps the archetypal scholar-librarian of a fabled ancient collection. A member of Fëanor's school of the "Loremasters of Tongues" created to preserve written tradition, Pengoloð lived with Turgon's people until the end and "was one of the survivors of the destruction of Gondolin, from which he rescued a few ancient writings, and some of his own copies, compilations, and commentaries. It is due to this, and to his prodigious memory, that much of the knowledge of the Elder Days was preserved" (*Jewels* 396). He rescued both key texts from the official archives of Turgon and parts of his own private library collection and was thereby able to reconstruct the documentary record of Beleriand. At the Mouth of Sirion he collected papers concerning languages from the other surviving Elves, and thus ensured the survival of Elven lore and linguistic study into the later ages of Middle-earth.

The Edain also begin in a purely oral culture but then go on to create their own doomed library of Alexandria on Númenor. Evidence of the oral tradition among the Edain comes from the unused introductory note to the Narn i Chîn Húrin which attributes the original lay to Dírhavel, a Mannish poet of the time of Eärendil.[10] The note attributes the survival of this oral tale to the Old English poet Ælfwine whose minstrelsy figures in The Notion Club Papers and The Lost Road, connecting the Edain to the Anglo-Saxon oral verse tradition Tolkien studied in his academic work.[11] Following the War of Wrath when the

the minstrel and loremaster of Thingol serves as Rúmil's counterpart in Beleriand, however, when he invents his Runes, providing the Sindar with their own means to record oral tradition in a written form.

[10] Christopher Tolkien explains that the discussion of Dírhavel occurs in the various versions of an "introductory note" to the Narn i Chîn Húrin his father wrote but which never appeared in the account published in *The Unifinished Tales* (*War of the Jewels* 311).

[11] Verlyn Flieger comments that Ælfwine leaves his imprint on Tolkien's mythology in the form of the "book" he supposedly passes down to later generations, and thereby serves as a transmitter of texts like Bilbo and Frodo later do with their written accounts in the Red Book of Westmarch and the Elvish translations that comprise the Silmarillion legends ("Footsteps" 193).

Edain reach their cultural zenith on the island of Númenor, we learn that they have established great libraries of texts in Quenya. The *Akallabêth* records that loremasters "made letters and scrolls and books, and wrote in them many things of wisdom and wonder in the high tide of their realm, of which all is now forgot" (*Silm* 262). The Númenoreans thus continued the Elven tradition of loremaster-librarians who preserved the wisdom of their people and presumably had a great library in Armenelos. As occurred in the Classical era and later in the Renaissance, other specialized libraries appeared on the island to house the records of the Edain's great expeditions. They had a great navigational collection similar to the famed maritime research institute Portugal's Prince Henry the Navigator founded at Sagres: "It is said that Aldarion himself wrote records of all his journeys to Middle-earth, and they were long preserved at Rómenna, though all were afterwards lost" (*Unfinished Tales* 175). When the island sank, only those few "scrolls of lore written in scarlet and black" (*Silm* 276) that Elendil and his followers (the "Faithful") gathered onto the ships survived the devastation. Like the libraries of Gondolin, those of Númenor perished, though the loss of their holdings was perhaps even greater since the accumulated knowledge of Men and other marvels of the Edain disappeared forever.

It is from the rescued scrolls of Númenor that the royal libraries of Gondor and the Northern Kingdom are established. The "Description of Númenor" in the *Unfinished Tales* begins with a reference to the lost library collection and the comparatively smaller collection of remnants located in the Gondorian archives:

> The account of the Island of Númenor that here follows is derived from descriptions and simple maps that were long preserved in the archives of the Kings of Gondor. These represent indeed but a small part of all that was once written, for many natural histories and geographies were composed by learned men in Númenor; but these, like nearly all else of the arts and sciences of Númenor at its high tide, disappeared in the Downfall. (165)

The drowning of those Númenórean archives represents a great blow to Mannish culture, for much of the great scientific feats and collective wisdom of that island nation vanished in the cataclysm.

Indeed, the Third Age of Middle-earth in *The Lord of the Rings* resembles the early Middle Ages in terms of the small number of libraries or "academies" in the midst of a largely depopulated, primarily illiterate world. Gondor still has one of the greatest libraries, but its manuscripts are no longer being read, for as Faramir tells the Hobbits, "in our treasuries" there are "many things preserved: books and tablets writ on withered parchments, yea, and on stone, and on leaves of silver and of gold, in divers characters," yet "Some [of those characters] none can read; and for the rest, few ever unlock them" (*Lord of the Rings* IV.5.670). Gandalf notes that in Denethor's hoards lie "many records that few even of the lore-masters now can read, for their scripts and tongues have become dark to later men" (*Lord of the Rings* II.2.252); the archives and the ability to read the Quenya texts have fallen into disuse as the civilization of Gondor wanes at the end of Third Age and only few are learned enough to read them. The herb-master's useless knowledge in the "Houses of Healing" chapter testifies to the extent that the records of Gondorian lore no longer retain the wisdom of the past whereas oral tradition still keeps some of that wisdom alive.

Alongside the declining manuscript culture of Gondor with its unread records exists one of Tolkien's most idealized images of an oral culture, the kingdom of Rohan. Aragorn characterizes the Rohirrim as "wise but unlearned, writing no books but singing many songs, after the manner of the children of Men before the Dark Years" (*Lord of the Rings* III.2.430).[12] Martin Ball notes that Tolkien's portrayal of Rohan, which he modeled upon the oral culture of the Anglo-Saxon civilization he so admired, makes *The Lord of the Rings* a lament or "threnody to the lost culture of oral traditions" (par. 23). Yet their illiteracy stands in marked contrast to the literate manuscript culture of Gondor which is in decline. Just as the high-born Men of Westernesse are giving way to lesser men, so too is the cultural heritage preserved in scrolls and books receding as orality once more begins to take hold among Men in Middle-earth.

Elven civilization has also largely returned to its oral roots by the last years of the Third Age (there are no references to written collections in the great centers such as Mirkwood or Lothlórien), but there are still small reminders of the great manuscript cultures of the past. Rivendell and, perhaps to a lesser extent, the Grey Havens,[13] function as quasi-monastic or university libraries of Elven lore on the borders of the Wilderland, the last true outposts of learning to which the Wise travel in order to consult documents. Elrond established this refuge to gather the last of the Noldor in the northern half of Middle-earth and preserved their wisdom and lore, both oral and written, within his refuge. In the Hall of Fire the ancient songs, tales, and other

---

[12] The Entish catalogue of beings is another example of an oral poetic tradition that preserves the knowledge of a people.

[13] We know little about the manuscripts preserved in Lindon, but the *palantír* facing the Uttermost West, the greatest artifact of Elven design, remains as an object of veneration. The Grey Havens, then, could be considered the great museum of their culture whereas Rivendell is the last library of the Elves in Middle-earth.

oral traditions of the First and Second Ages are replayed, but Imladris also holds a large cache of maps, books, and manuscripts the Noldor have managed to retain after the destruction of Beleriand and Eregion in the Second Age. It is there that the lore books of the Elven past are still a part of living memory, unlike the seldom used scrolls and documents of Men stored in the archives of Minas Tirith.

Although the academic or intellectual centers in Minas Tirith and Rivendell still exist late in the Third Age, other great repositories have suffered far worse fates. It is ironic that the one library which the Fellowship enters turns out to be one that has been ravaged and stripped of its holdings save one lone volume. The brief overview of the Chamber of Mazarbul ("Records") in Khazad-dûm is the most specific physical description of a library in Tolkien's work, though like its great predecessors, it too is now characteristically in ruins: "There were many recesses cut in the rock of the walls, and in them were large iron-bound chests of wood. All had been broken and plundered; but beside the shattered lid of one there lay the remains of a book" (*Lord of the Rings* II.5.321). The Chamber of Records with its niches for scrolls and codices, common features in medieval monastic libraries and scriptoria, is now literally an empty tomb both for Balin and for the sole surviving written account of Dwarves in Moria.[14] As Tolkien learned from our own ancient history, the great libraries are the treasure houses of their civilizations, but yet are the most vulnerable when those civilizations fade.

In this context we witness the rise of the Hobbits as the ones who preserve civilization and become the most prolific producers of books and builders of libraries in Arda. We know from the reaction of the Breelanders to Frodo's story about writing a book and other statements that literacy is not widespread in the Shire, but nevertheless it is there that the beginnings of a book revolution are taking shape, one that in Europe was ushered in by the invention of moveable type. The anachronistic book culture of the Hobbits has been well documented. Hammond has written a detailed speculative account of the papermaking and book binding technologies in the Shire and has even

---

[14] Tolkien attached great significance to the idea that one book alone had survived the devastation of that great Dwarven collection. He even painted several facsimile images of leaves from the Book of Mazarbul, but cost of reproducing them meant that they were not included in published versions until the 50th Anniversary Editions HarperCollins and Houghton Mifflin released in 2004 featuring color plates in the Moria sequence. As the plates indicate, the book was written in Daeron's Runes like the inscription on Balin's tomb, indicating that the Dwarves, like the Noldor in Tirion, used the same script for both monuments and leaves of parchment.

proposed that Sharkey could have introduced the printing press to the Hobbits to mass produce his lists of Rules ("Books" 31–38). I would now like to focus more narrowly on the development of personal libraries that accompanies the burgeoning book culture of the Shire, the rise of middle-class book owners and personal library collections as opposed to the great royal or scholarly libraries of Elves, Men, and Dwarves.

Late in the Third Age and into the first century of the Fourth, there appear to be a number of not only family libraries connected to the important Hobbit clans, but also personal libraries of the rising "middle class." Bilbo Baggins is a bookish Hobbit whose collecting habits are part of his "queerness," but there is the suggestion that his fondness for collecting books is not unique in the Shire. Among the labels on the furnishings inside Bag End after his disappearance is this one: *"For the collection of HUGO BRACEGIRDLE, from a contributor,* on an (empty) book-case. Hugo was a great borrower of books, and worse than usual at returning them" (*Lord of the Rings* I.1.37). The idea that books are plentiful enough for one to lend to others, and the presence of bookcases in Bag End, an item of furniture that was not common in bourgeois European households of our own world until the 1700s,[15] suggests that personal libraries are not unheard-of even in the mostly oral, peasant social milieu of the Shire. Bilbo's translations from the Elvish, the putative origin of the "Silmarillion" accounts, place him squarely in the tradition of the librarian-scholars or loremasters of the past, but suggest that a new breed of bibliophile is being born.

The "Note on Shire Records," as I suggested at the beginning of this paper, illustrates the extent to which written records, books, and libraries proliferate in the Shire following the War of the Ring. As the note explains, "At the end of the Third Age the part played by the Hobbits in the great events that led to the inclusion of the Shire in the Reunited Kingdom awakened among them a more widespread interest in their own history; and many of their traditions, up to that time still mainly oral, were collected and written down" (*Lord of the Rings* Prologue.14). With these books came more libraries to house them, even

---

[15] English manor houses of the late 1600s and early 1700s generally included libraries with built-in or freestanding bookcases, but that was an architectural rarity in many colonial American dwellings from that period (Symonds 184). This suggests a relationship between literacy and bourgeois economic prosperity, and certainly a complex such as the Hill and Bag End would be a Hobbit equivalent of an English manor house. See also Marshall Brooks's *A Brief Illustrated History of the Bookshelf* for information on the evolution of bookshelves and cases from ancient libraries to the twentieth century.

specialized libraries. The three great family libraries at the Undertowers, Brandy Hall, and the Great Smials form the basis for a new book culture that closely resembles that of Europe after the printing press made books available, and antiquarian interests made the collecting of old manuscripts (especially after many of the monastic library collections in England were dispersed during Henry VIII's reign), a pastime among the gentry and the newly moneyed. The Red Book is passed down from Samwise to the Fairbairns, and kept in their collection. Pippin becomes a librarian whose manuscripts from Gondor allow him to write *The Tale of Years*, and Merry with his large library of historical documents, his writings on herblore, the calendars of different peoples in Middle-earth, and even language, appears to be a veritable Thomas Jefferson among the Shire-folk—loremaster and librarian for a new world.

Tolkien thus suggests that the Fourth Age of Middle-earth, that which followed the decline of literacy and documentation in the Third Age, represents a fundamental change in the way the past is recorded as books and libraries finally begin to become the warehouses of memory. Whereas earlier the great libraries of the Noldor or the heroic Dúnedain were vast compilations of all the knowledge of their peoples that rose and fell along with their cultures, the Fourth Age ushers in a more "democratic" form of collection made possible by the rise of literacy and written texts. Indeed, the modern library takes shape among the latter-day inhabitants of Eriador, leading us to conclude that Hobbits are the ones who saved the civilizations of Arda from ruin, and ultimately gave us the texts that comprise the legendarium.

Works Cited

Ball, Martin. "Cultural Values and Cultural Death in *The Lord of the Rings*." *Australian Humanities Review* 28, Jan. 2003. australianhumanitiesreview.org/2003/01/01/cultural-values-and-cultural-death-in-the-lord-of-the-rings.

Blackwelder, Richard E. *A Tolkien Thesaurus*. Garland, 1982.

Brooks, Marshall. *A Brief Illustrated History of the Bookshelf*. Birch Brook Press, 1999.

Cahill, Thomas. *How the Irish Saved Civilization: The Untold Story of Ireland's Heroic Role From the Fall of the Roman Empire to the Rise of Medieval Europe*. Anchor, 1996.

Casson, Lionel. *Libraries in the Ancient World*. Yale UP, 2001.

Flieger, Verlyn. "The Footsteps of Ælfwine." *Tolkien's Legendarium: Essays on The History of Middle-earth*, edited by Verlyn Flieger and Carl F. Hostetter, Greenwood, 2000, pp. 183–98.

——. "Tolkien and the Idea of the Book." *The Lord of the Rings, 1951–2004: Scholarship in Honor of Richard E. Blackwelder,* edited by Wayne G. Hammond and Christina Scull, Marquette UP, 2006, pp. 283–300.

Katz, William A. *Dahl's History of the Book.* 3rd English ed. Scarecrow, 1995.

Kocher, Paul. *A Reader's Guide to* The Silmarillion. Thames and Hudson, 1980.

Hammond, Wayne. "Books, Literature and Literacy in Middle-earth." *Mallorn: The Journal of the Tolkien Society,* vol. 26, 1989, pp. 35–38.

——. "Papermaking in the Shire." *Amon Hen,* vol. 94, November 1988, pp. 17–18.

Ong, Walter. *Orality and Literacy: The Technologizing of the Word.* Routledge, 2002.

Setton, Kenneth M. "From Medieval to Modern Library." *Proceedings of the American Philosophical Society,* vol. 104, no. 4, 1960, pp. 371–90.

Spurkland, Treje. "Literacy and 'Runacy' in Medieval Scandinavia." *Scandinavia, and Europe 800–1350: Contact, Conflict, and Coexistence,* edited by Jonathan Adams and Kathrine Holman, Brepols, 2004, pp. 333–44. Vol. 4 of *Medieval Texts and Cultures of Northern Europe.*

Symonds, R. W. "English Furniture and Colonial American Furniture — A Contrast." *The Burlington Magazine for Connoisseurs,* vol. 78, no. 459, 1941, pp. 182–187.

Tolkien, J. R. R. *The Book of Lost Tales, Part I.* Edited by Christopher Tolkien, Houghton Mifflin, 1984. Vol. 1 of *The History of Middle-earth.*

——. *The Book of Lost Tales, Part II.* Edited by Christopher Tolkien, Houghton Mifflin, 1984. Vol. 2 of *The History of Middle-earth.*

——. *The Lord of the Rings.* Edited by Wayne G. Hammond and Christina Scull, 50th Anniversary Edition, Houghton Mifflin, 2004 [2005]. Reader's companion separately cited.

——. *The Lost Road and Other Writings.* Edited by Christopher Tolkien, Houghton Mifflin, 1987. Vol. 5 of *The History of Middle-earth.*

——. *The Silmarillion.* Edited by Christopher Tolkien, 2nd ed., Houghton Mifflin, 2001.

——. *Unfinished Tales of Númenor and Middle-earth.* Edited by Christopher Tolkien, Houghton Mifflin, 1980.

——. *The War of the Jewels.* Edited by Christopher Tolkien, Houghton Mifflin, 1994. Vol. 11 of *The History of Middle-earth.*

Wynne, Patrick and Carl F. Hostetter. "Three Elvish Verse Modes: *Ann-thennath, Minlamad thent/estent,* and *Linnod.*" *Tolkien's Legendarium: Essays on The History of Middle-earth,* edited by Verlyn Flieger and Carl F. Hostetter, Greenwood, 2000, pp. 113–39.

Education (and Poetry Recital) in Middle-earth and in England

Nancy Martsch[1]

> *"Standing up, with his hands behind his back, as if he was at school, he [Sam] began to sing to an old tune."* (LotR I.12.206)

TO WHAT "SCHOOL" DOES Tolkien refer: Sam's, or his own?

In this essay I intend first to examine education (especially literacy and poetry recitation) in *The Hobbit* and *The Lord of the Rings*, then briefly to survey education in England (again with emphasis on poetry recitation), and finally to return to Tolkien and Middle-earth, to see if there may be any connections.

But why poetry recitation? Because so many characters in *The Hobbit* and *The Lord of the Rings* sing and recite poetry. In our world children recited poetry in school, too, especially when J. R. R. Tolkien was young. Indeed, from about 1870 until 1930, the memorization and recitation of poetry was compulsory in state-sponsored primary schools, in both England and the United States.[2] Although students in England's elite public schools and America's private schools may have focused on Latin and Greek, they also learned poems in English. Surely so common a practice must have affected people's experience of poetry. Might this be reflected in Tolkien's writing?

I'll begin with education (and literacy and poetry recital) in Middle-earth.[3] How widespread was literacy at the end of the Third Age, the time of *The Hobbit* and *The Lord of the Rings*? Let's start with the Hobbits. Tolkien describes Hobbits, the protagonists of his stories, in his Prologue to the Second Edition of *The Lord of the Rings*: "They do not and did not understand or like machines more complicated than a forge-bellows, a water-mill, or a hand-loom, though they were skilful with tools" and "A love of learning (other than genealogical lore) was far from general among them, but there remained still a few in the

---

[1] Presented at Mythcon 49, July 21, 2018, Atlanta, GA.

[2] Information about education (and poetry recitation) is derived from *Heart Beats: Everyday Life and the Memorized Poem* by Catherine Robson, Princeton UP, 2012. Robson gives a history of education (with poetry recitation) in England and the United States, followed by several case studies. Her book was the inspiration for this paper.

[3] See also essays by David D. Oberhelman and Janet Brennan Croft in this volume for additional perspectives on literacy and writing in Middle-earth. –Eds.

older families who studied their own books" (*LotR* Prologue.1–3). Of the Messenger Service: "By no means all Hobbits were lettered, but those who were wrote constantly to all their friends" (10). When the Gaffer was holding forth at The Ivy Bush, he said of his son Sam, "Mr. Bilbo has learned him his letters—meaning no harm, mark you, and I hope no harm will come of it" (I.1.24). This implies that that the Gaffer was not "lettered," Tolkien's term for literate. Like England, the Shire had a class system: the Bagginses were wealthy middle-class, or gentry, Tooks and Brandybucks aristocracy, the Gaffer and Sam working class. And, like 19th-century England, the upper and middle classes were literate, but some members of the working class were not.

Returning to the Prologue, in the "Note on the Shire Records" (11–16), we are told that after the Travelers returned Hobbits took a greater interest in their own history, "and many of their traditions, up to that time still mainly oral, were collected and written down." "By the end of the first century of the Fourth Age" there were libraries "at Undertowers, at Great Smials, and at Brandy Hall." Merry and Pippin visited the South: Merry wrote and collected information about Rohan, Pippin and his successors "collected many manuscripts written by scribes of Gondor." The Red Book of Westmarch was originally written by hand by Bilbo, Frodo, and others (VI.9.1027). When Pippin went to Gondor for the last time, he took with him a complete copy of the Red Book (including Bilbo's Translations from the Elvish and the Hobbit genealogies), from which (with annotations and additions), a copy was made by Findegil, King's Writer, and finished in F.A. 172 (Prologue.14). Other less complete copies were made in the Shire for the descendants of Sam's children.[4]

All this talk of copying and manuscripts implies that books were copied by hand. Certainly, there is no mention of printing in the published texts of *The Hobbit* and *The Lord of the Rings*. But Tolkien never explicitly states how books were reproduced.

However, not all the peoples of Middle-earth were lettered. The Rohirrim were "wise but unlearned, writing no books but singing many songs" as did Men in the past (III.2.430). This was probably also true of the Ents and of Sméagol's family long ago.[5] As for the Orcs, whether or not they were "lettered" in the formal sense, some of them

---

[4] See also Fisher in this volume on The Red Book. —Eds.

[5] Entish was never even written down, for "even the lore-masters of the Eldar had not attempted to represent [it] in writing […] for no others could learn it" (Appendix F.1131).

used "foul symbols" among themselves—and Azog had branded his name "in Dwarf-runes" upon the severed head of Thrór (IV.7.702, Appendix A.1073).[6]

What of books themselves? *The Hobbit* and *The Lord of the Rings* take place in the northwest of Middle-earth at the end of the Third Age. While there may have been other repositories of books and manuscripts, the two great libraries in our stories were at Rivendell and Minas Tirith. Rivendell was known for lore and maps (II.3.277, 283), and Elrond himself had set down the history of the Ring (II.2.242). The archives at Minas Tirith held much antique material, including "scrolls and books," and "books and tablets writ on withered parchments, [...] and on stone, and on leaves of silver and gold," some in characters and tongues "none can now read" (II.2.252, IV.5.670).

Where does poetry fit in all this? In a society where books are rare, knowledge is often transmitted orally—and poetry is easy to remember. Middle-earth had many forms of poetry, from "Rhymes of Lore" and gnomish sayings, to formal lays recounting the deeds of heroes and of lovers, to cheerful songs and improvised rhymes.[7] Throughout *The Lord of the Rings*, and to a lesser extent *The Hobbit*, there are many references to songs, stories and tales; to tales told at the fireside, to children's tales, story-telling, and to stories told to the young. Gandalf speaks of the "Rhymes of Lore" (III.11.597). And Treebeard remembers "the old lists that I learned when I was young [...] *Learn now the lore of Living Creatures!*" (III.4.464).

Poetry could take the form of formal compositions, such as lays. Aragorn recognized the lines Sam recited about Gil-galad: "It is part of the lay that is called *The Fall of Gil-galad*, which is in an ancient tongue. Bilbo must have translated it" (I.11.186). Minstrels composed and sang lays for the celebration at the Field of Cormallen and for Théoden's funeral. The Lay of Nimrodel seems to have been well-known. It was composed in the tongue of the Woodland Elves, and translated into the Westron Speech; Legolas sang the verses in Westron while the Company was encamped on the border of Lórien, which were heard by the Elven guards (II.6.331–341, 342). During the siege of Minas Tirith, when Gandalf and Prince Imrahil went about encouraging the troops,

---

[6] Azog boasts "But if his family wish to know who is now king here, the name is written on his face. I wrote it! I killed him! I am the master!" (Appendix A.1073). My thanks to an audience member at Mythcon for this reference.

[7] For an analysis of song improvisation in Middle-earth, and the methods Tolkien used to create songs, see Martsch: "Middle-earth Improv: Song Writing and Improvisation in Tolkien's Works."

men would take heart "And then one would sing amid the gloom some staves of the Lay of Nimrodel, or other songs of the Vale of Anduin" (V.4.824). So it would appear that (at least for Men and Elves), certain compositions (such as the Lay of Nimrodel) were a part of knowledge and formal education, widely translated, and learned like Homer, Virgil, and Shakespeare in Tolkien's day. It is likely that the four Hobbits heard some of these well-known lays at Rivendell.

But there were other, less formal, forms of learning. Faramir and Théoden each mentioned tales of their families' histories, told to them by their fathers (IV.5.670, V.3.797). And when Gandalf came to research in the archives at Minas Tirith, Faramir studied under him (IV.5.671).

Hobbits weren't as fond of story-telling as were Elves, but they had lots of songs. Frodo was asked for a song at the Prancing Pony Inn in Bree, and then asked to sing it again, so his audience could learn it. Tom Bombadil spent a whole day telling stories to his Hobbit visitors. And in the Pass of Cirith Ungol Sam had a vision of a hoped-for future: "Still, I wonder if we shall ever be put into songs or tales. [...] I mean: put into words, you know, told by the fireside, or read out of a great big book with red and black letters, years and years afterwards" (IV.8.712).

Although we have many examples of the transmission of knowledge, from books and speech, through poetry and tales, in formal and informal settings, there is no evidence that Middle-earth had schools in our sense. No classrooms or schools where children were sent to be educated, or colleges, symposia, or centers of instruction.

I propose therefore that in the Middle-earth of *The Hobbit* and *The Lord of the Rings* education consisted primarily of parents or elders teaching their children. Perhaps in large families children were taught in a group, or perhaps in noble families certain retainers would instruct the sons and daughters. Perhaps the children may have been required to recite what they had learned, as Treebeard implied. A person aspiring to specialized knowledge, such as a loremaster or minstrel, might study under a master, like an apprentice, somewhat as Faramir did with Gandalf. And an individual seeking knowledge might search the archives, or live in a place of learning, like Gandalf in Minas Tirith or Bilbo at Rivendell. But there is no evidence that Middle-earth had schools in our sense of the word.

And yet...Let us return to Shire, to observe Bilbo's Birthday Party. Bilbo sent out handwritten invitations, including a "magnificent" invitation card for the Sackville-Bagginses "written in golden ink" (I.1.28). The Messenger Service was inundated with invitations and replies. After the Party Bilbo "folded up and wrapped in tissue-paper his embroidered silk waistcoat [...]. From a locked drawer, smelling of moth-balls, he took out an old cloak and hood" (I.1.31). In "a large bulky envelope" he put the Ring "'And my will and all the other documents too'" (35).

Bilbo wrote labels for his bequests: *For DORA BAGGINS in memory of a LONG correspondence* [...] on a large waste-paper basket." She was Bilbo's aunt, who had offered much unsolicited advice. "*For MILO BURROWS, hoping it will be useful* [...] on a gold pen and ink-bottle. Milo never answered letters." "*For the collection of HUGO BRACEGIRDLE, from a contributor*; on an (empty) book-case" (I.1.37).

And when the Travelers returned to the Shire and stayed at the Sherriff house by the Brandywine Bridge, they found "In the upper rooms [...] on every wall there was a notice and a list of Rules. Pippin tore them down" (VI.8.1000).

In *The Hobbit* we read that "[Bilbo] loved maps, and in his hall there hung a large one of the Country Round with all his favourite walks marked on it in red ink" (I.26). With regard to the Dwarves' contract, Gandalf instructed Bilbo "'If you had dusted the mantelpiece, you would have found this just under the clock,' [...] handing Bilbo a note (written, of course, on his own note-paper)" (II.32). Two wall clocks are shown in Tolkien's illustration of "The Hall at Bag-End," one of which has a pendulum and weights.

This abundance of paper—cardstock, tissue paper, books, maps, notices, waste-paper baskets and bookshelves—this is not the material assemblage of a society in which books are rare and copied by hand.[8] And some of this—the mothballs, gold pen, pendulum clock—is not the material assemblage of hand-loom and forge-bellows society, either. In fact it sounds very much like the countryside of late Victorian England, right down to the abundance of food in *The Hobbit*. Tolkien even says as much in a letter: "[The Shire] is in fact more or less a Warwickshire village of about the period of the Diamond Jubilee [1897]" (*Letters* 230). Nor can we ascribe this to invention by the Red Book's translator, because these elements are integral parts of the stories. This Shire is a fantasy England, with 3-foot-tall Englishmen with furry feet.[9]

---

[8] For what it's worth, Frederick Warrillow, the father of Tolkien's wife Edith Bratt, was a "'coloured paper dealer, printer, stationer & [general] paper dealer.'" Her mother Frances Bratt inherited the business upon his death, when Edith was two years old (*Guide* 1304).

[9] This observation is not original. This situation came about because Tolkien wrote *The Hobbit* first. Bilbo leaves the English Shire, has adventures in a quasi-medieval Middle-earth, and returns to the Shire. But when Tolkien wrote *The Lord*

So we really have two Shires: the one described by Tolkien in his Prologue, and the one depicted in the text, laid one over the other. The former has hand-copied manuscripts, the latter has lots of paper and books, seemingly without printing. However, if the Shire can be a fantasy England, we can look to the real England for possible educational influences.

What follows will be a very brief, very simple survey of education in England (and to a lesser extent, the United States), derived largely from *Heart Beats: Everyday Life and the Memorized Poem* by Catherine Robson.

In Middle-earth, writing was developed by the Elves. In our world writing grew out of trade and organized religion. Literacy was already well established in the Mediterranean when Jesus was born. His followers wrote down his story, which was then translated into the vernacular; in the West, this was Latin. Over time Latin ceased to be the vernacular, but remained the language of the Church. A knowledge of Latin enabled learned men (and women) to read the writing of Rome. Education, whether by tutors, in schools, or in universities, was generally associated with the Roman Catholic Church and with Latin. In the late Middle Ages the English grammar school was a privately funded school (originally free, later fee-based) which taught Latin.

When King Henry VIII broke with Rome and dissolved the monasteries, the educational system was reorganized, but Latin remained language of learning. In 1552 Edward VI, son of Henry VIII, founded King Edward's School as a grammar school in Birmingham. This would become Tolkien's school.

England has had a wide variety of schools, with many technical definitions regarding sponsorship, charter, organization, etc. Broadly speaking, the public school was a subset of the grammar school, so-called because it was open to the public, not a religious or local school; and generally a boarding school. The first schools of this type were for boys: girls' schools came much later.

In 1900, when Tolkien started at King Edward's, public and grammar schools were gender segregated. Boys usually started around age 8–10 and remained in school until age 16–18, which corresponds to contemporary American grades 3–4 through 12 and perhaps the first year or two of college. (Tolkien was 19 when he left—

---

of the Rings as a sequel to *The Hobbit*, he retained the format (leave, have adventures, return) but expanded the quasi-medieval Middle-earth to incorporate the Shire; with the result that the Shire became a technological anomaly in its midst.

he stayed an extra year in order to get his scholarship to Oxford.) King Edward's had Forms or Classes rather than grades: a boy started at 13th class and worked up to 1st. The emphasis was on mastery of Latin and Greek, which was an entrance requirement for Oxford University and for a civil service job. Boys learned and recited passages in Latin and Greek (and in English, too). Corporal punishment was common—beating with a rod or switch on the bare buttocks or whacking with a ruler. I don't know if corporal punishment was still practiced at King Edward's when Tolkien was a student or not (it had been in the past), but it was a standard practice in England at the time.

There were other types of schools: religious schools (Tolkien attended a Roman Catholic school for a time), specialized schools (Edith Bratt went to a music school), and so forth. But the public and grammar schools were the bastion of the upper and middle classes, and their Latin-oriented curriculum served to separate their students from the lower classes. (And also the men from the women. While some girls' schools emphasized the Classics, others were more like American finishing schools, teaching a young woman how to be a lady. Frequently the men attended grammar schools while the women did not.) Since school, especially a boarding school, occupied so much of a young person's life, it was very important. English biographies always name the school a man attended.

But what of the working classes? What kinds of schooling did they receive (aside from apprenticeship to trades)? Again a brief survey. With the rise of Protestantism (and printing), the Bible was translated into the vernacular, which in England meant English. Protestants felt that literacy was needed in order to read the Bible. The Pilgrims and Puritans who settled New England believed that the Bible was the Word of God, so everyone, master and servant, man and woman, had to learn to read in order to save their souls. They established schools to teach their children—and the teaching was primarily in English.

There was much variation in American education, especially in different parts of the country and for different ethnic groups, but eventually this concept prevailed: education in English for everyone. Although Latin-based and private schools did exist, the United States never placed such a heavy emphasis on mastery of the Classics as did England. The emphasis was on local, later state-sponsored ("public") primary schools and education in English.

English popular education is often dated from the Sunday School movement in the 1780s, with its free schools for the lower classes founded by various church and charitable groups (Robson 46). If originally for boys, schools eventually became co-ed, and they offered instruction in English.

From about the 1700s even into the 1900s, teaching for both upper and lower classes emphasized rote learning. The student memorized the lesson and parroted it back word-perfect to his teacher or parent. Textbooks were scarce, and children of different ages shared a classroom together. And poetry is especially suited for recitation and rote learning (Robson 40), as well as for moral instruction, learning the multiplication table, etc.

The publication of textbooks, called "Readers," gained momentum in the United States in the 1830s, a little later in England (54–55). Americans may think of the *McGuffey's Readers* but there were many others. Readers included poetry for recitation. And there were Speakers for just that. A child's position in school was based on his place in the Reader. The grade system started in 1860s, though it took a while to spread (64–65). Under the grade system the government sponsor could dictate the curriculum, including which textbooks to use. Although recitation had long been a common practice, from around 1870 onwards it became a compulsory part of the curriculum. In American state-sponsored primary schools recitation, called "elocution," was held on Friday afternoon (66). The American primary (elementary) school went from grades 1–6 (12 years old), the English primary education ended at age 13 (139). And in both England and the United States the curriculum was more demanding for boys than for girls.

In the United States, state-sponsored secondary (high) schools became common in late 1800s-early 1900s (68–69). But in England, while state-sponsored secondary schools existed, the preference was for state-sponsored scholarships to fee-based grammar schools (14). In the 1900s primary schools had a regular "scholarship track." King Edward's boasted of its tradesmen's sons and primary scholarship recipients as students. After Tolkien had to drop out when his mother converted to Catholicism, he and his brother Hilary got scholarships to King Edward's. Later Tolkien got a scholarship to Oxford University.

But many lower-class English students had no education beyond age 13—that was when they left school to go to work; in the factory, in the service, in the fields (148). Thus England's class system was maintained by its dual educational curricula. Still, though their education might be brief, in theory they would forever bear within their hearts the gems of English poetry which they had memorized in school!

So, what types of "literature" were English and American school children required to memorize? Often this was poetry, in ballad meter or some other easy-to-remember rhythmic form (Robson 114–15). The child would start with something simple, like "Twinkle, twinkle little star."[10] An 8-year-old was expected to learn a 40-line poem, such as "The boy stood on the burning deck." Gray's "Elegy Written in a Country Churchyard" (32 verses, 128 lines) was popular in the higher grades. In the 6th and 7th grades a young person learned 150 lines— speeches, or passages from Shakespeare and Milton (61 ff.). As for the subject matter, some were nature poems, especially the ones for younger children. Others were narrative poems, often quite lurid, with emphasis on death and sacrifice; further, at least in the United States, the child didn't just recite the poem, he'd emote the poem as well, with appropriate theatrical gestures.

The nationalistic movements of the later 1800s encouraged the use of patriotic themes, especially sacrifice for country. American children would learn Lincoln's Gettysburg Address or Patrick Henry's "Liberty or Death" speech. English children learned patriotic English subjects. Robson notes that "children in British mass education were far more likely to find themselves reciting poems about bravery in the face of defeat than verses celebrating victory" (89). We can find an example of this in *The Hobbit*, when, during the Battle of the Five Armies as defeat seemed likely (before the arrival of the Eagles), Bilbo thought "I have heard songs of many battles, and I have always understood that defeat may be glorious. It seems very uncomfortable, not to say distressing. I wish I was well out of it" (XVII.240). Tom Shippey, who also attended King Edward's School, remarked on this passage in *J. R. R. Tolkien: Author of the Century*, where he noted the words of the King Edward's School Song: "Oftentimes defeat is splendid, / Victory may still be shame, / Luck is good, the prize is pleasant, / But the glory's in the game" (44). One can see where Tolkien got the idea.

How were the poems for recital selected? Some, especially the ones for the younger children, were composed by the textbook writers. But magazines and newspapers were the Internet of the 19th century, and they printed poetry. Sometimes a poem would "go viral" and be picked up by the textbook writers. Once embedded in the curriculum a poem became immortal. As was the case with "The boy stood on the burning

---

[10] It is both a poem and a song. Tolkien wrote "Eadig Beo Þu!" to this tune in his and his colleagues' *Songs for the Philologists* (*Guide* 1244).

deck"—the title is "Casabianca," and it's by Felicia Hemans. Hemans was a best-selling poet of the 19th century, but she is forgotten today.

Poetry recital in schools declined in the 20th century. Robson cites changing educational theories, less rote memorization, more emphasis on understanding the poem and on the individual child, the disillusionment following World War I (after which patriotic verses rang rather hollow), and the rise of Modernism in the 1920s (22–23).[11] I think population increase may have been another factor, as this led to there being fewer one-room schools. The English educational system was revised in 1944, which put an end to scholarships to grammar schools and also to compulsory recitation. Recitation died out more slowly in the United States (8–9, 80).

Robson notes that when one recites poetry aloud, as opposed to silent reading, one feels the rhythm ("heart beats") and music of the words—which is lost today (96, 112).[12] She also thinks that the disrepute into which rhymed poetry has fallen today (and with it an ignorance of poetic structure) is a reaction against the erstwhile practice of reciting simple, sentimental, rhymed poems in elementary school (113, 117). Today rhyme survives in nursery rhymes, humorous poetry, and song lyrics; and narrative poetry in country music. But not in Serious Poetry.

But in its heyday the commonly recited poems would have been known by almost everyone, quoted by politicians and preachers, recited by parents to children, and frequently parodied.

Did Tolkien know any of these poems? There is evidence that he did. We can find scattered references to the standard poems (and to educational practices) in Tolkien's writing and art.

Although Tolkien wrote of English poetry that his "chief contacts with poetry were when one was made to try and translate it into Latin"

---

[11] The Moderns execrated Victorian poetry: "The age commonly called Victorian came to an end about 1885. It was an age distinguished by many true idealists and many false ideals […]. Its poetry was, in the main, not universal but parochial; its romanticism was gilt and tinsel; its realism was as cheap as its showy glass pendants, red plush, parlor chromos and antimacassars" (4). This by Louis Untermeyer, in his Preface to *Modern British Poetry: A Critical Anthology*, 1925. My father owned this book. One can see how with this attitude "The boy stood on the burning deck" wouldn't fare very well.

[12] I think this may be true: I have noticed a "tin ear" in fan poems. I find myself mentally rearranging the words for a better scan and wonder why the writer could not hear them. Tolkien learned the basic structure of poetry, and his poems have a strong, sure rhythm. Some settings of Tolkien's poetry to music seem to miss the rhythm completely.

(*Letters* 213) this doesn't mean he did not recognize the standards. Tolkien was well educated. His father Arthur Tolkien, uncles Wilfred Tolkien, Thomas Mitton, and Roland Suffield, aunt Jane Neave, and Mabel Suffield's cousin Mark Oliver all went to King Edward's Schools; and perhaps other relatives went to other grammar schools (Scull and Hammond *Guide* 601; Burns, "Schooldays" 28). But his wife Edith did not. Nor did all of his friends and relatives, parishioners at church, administrative staff at University, families of his students, servants, soldiers, people met while travelling, etc., many of whom would have had primary-school educations. One can speculate that any or all of these people may have quoted lines from or recited entire poems at one time or another. It is my belief that certain descriptions in *The Lord of the Rings*, such as Sam's recital or the soldiers at Minas Tirith singing staves of the Lay of Nimrodel, are modeled on Tolkien's own experiences.

To give an example: King Edward's School had poetry recital prizes, competition for which was compulsory for boys in the lower classes; "commonly poems by Milton, Gray, Tennyson and Macaulay" (Burns, "Battle" 15). For the competition in 1906 Tolkien's brother Hilary had to learn part of "The Battle of the Lake Regillus," from Thomas Babington Macaulay's *Lays of Ancient Rome*. Tolkien could have heard him practicing it (Scull and Hammond 110–11).

Tolkien wrote "The Battle of the Eastern Fields," a poem about a rugby game, as a parody of "The Battle of the Lake Regillus," with a stanza from Macaulay's "Horatius." It was published in the King Edward's School *Chronicle* in March 1911. Excerpts from "Horatius" (also known as "Horatius at the Bridge") were also recited. It is a very long poem: Winston Churchill received a prize while at Eton for reciting it in its entirety. "Horatius" casts his shadow over *The Lord of the Rings*, as, for instance, when Boromir at the Council of Elrond describes the fight at Osgiliath: how the dark forces attacked from the East; how his company held the bridge until it could be torn down behind them, and only four—he and his brother and two others—escaped by swimming (II.2.245). This closely parallels Macaulay's fictionalized account and the Roman history upon which it is based. Burns notes that William H. Stoddard saw "Horatius" in Gandalf's stand against the balrog upon the bridge of Khazad-dûm ("Battle" 15). Tolkien knew his Macaulay and Roman history quite well.

We have another example of Tolkien's use of a poetic standard, this one from a non-Classical source. In April 1904, when Mabel Tolkien was in the hospital, Tolkien stayed with his aunt Jane Suffield's fiancé Edwin Neave. Tolkien drew a picture of Edwin and himself in bed titled "They slept in beauty side by side." This is a paraphrase of Felicia Hemans's— yes, *that* Felicia Hemans—poem "The Graves of a Household," about four siblings: "They grew in beauty, side by side, / They fill'd one home with glee; — / Their graves are sever'd, far and wide, / By mount, and stream, and sea" (Hammond and Scull, *Artist* 10, 12–13; *Guide* 842).

There may be another example, though this might be just coincidental. It's Alfred Lord Tennyson's poem "Crossing the Bar": "Sunset and evening star, / And one clear call for me! / And may there be no moaning at the bar, / When I put out to sea."[13] This imagery— the ship, sunset, star—is prominent in Tolkien's poem "Bilbo's Last Song." Another of Tolkien's poems, "The Last Ship," shares the ship and sailing imagery, but not the sunset or star. Of course this could simply be a case of both poets drawing on similar themes—sailing into the sunset is an obvious analogy of death (or in Tolkien's case, seeking the Undying Lands). Still, "Crossing the Bar" was a commonly recited poem at the time.

And in the recently-published *Music in Tolkien's Work and Beyond* (2019), Jörg Fündling suggests that the English patriotic poem "The English Flag" by Rudyard Kipling (1891) may have provided a pattern for Tolkien's Lament for Boromir ("Through Rohan over fen and field," III.1.411–18), through its call-and-response format, invocation of the four winds (three in Tolkien's published poem but four in the first drafts), and similarities in rhyme structure (111–31).

Can we find any other examples of English education in *The Hobbit* and *The Lord of the Rings*? A few. Students stood when reciting poetry, usually in front of the class. Gimli stands up to chant the "Song of Durin" in the darkness of Moria (II.4.315). Sam is twice described as "Standing up, with his hands behind his back, as if he was at school" (I.12.206, singing the Troll Song) and "Sam stood up, putting his hands behind his back (as he always did when 'speaking poetry')" (IV.3.646, reciting "Oliphaunt"). For a readership of Tolkien's day this posture might also reflect Sam's working-class origin, lost on modern readers. The only other use of the word "school" is also by Sam; at Parth Galen, when speculating on Frodo's decision: "Of course he's had a bit of schooling, so to speak—we all have—since we left home" (II.10.403). I found two other educational references: the first, before the Battle of the Hornburg, when Gimli and Éomer declare a truce regarding their dispute over the Lady of the Golden Wood. Éomer remarks: "I have not

---

[13] My mother recited this. She learned it from her mother, who went to school in Ireland in the late 1800s.

had time to learn gentle speech under your rod, as you promised" (III.6.524). As Éomer had previously referred to Gimli's *axe*, this appears to be a reference to the use of a rod for corporal punishment in school. A student could be whipped for a poor recital (Robson 112). And the second, outside the throne room of Gondor, when an exasperated Gandalf says to Pippin: "though it might have been better, if you had learned something of it [history of Gondor], when you were still birds-nesting and playing truant in the woods of the Shire" (V.1.754). But these are all school analogies—perhaps inserted by Tolkien the translator?— none of which point to a school system in Middle-earth.

I think the greatest connection with English education is this: poetry was popular in early 20th century. Educated young men wrote serious poetry. When Tolkien's friend G. B. Smith was killed in World War I, his friends honored his memory by publishing a book of Smith's poems. Can you imagine a group of junior officers honoring a fallen comrade this way in World War II? Or Vietnam? Or Afghanistan? No. Much poetry was written after the First World War: by Siegfried Sassoon, Rupert Brooke, Roy Campbell, T. S. Eliot. These were the generation who grew up reciting poetry, in grammar and in primary schools. The World War II generation, for the most part, did not.

I think that poetry recitation and interest in poetry reinforced each other.

Tolkien interpolated many poems into *The Hobbit* and *The Lord of the Rings*. As early as 1914 he wrote to his fiancée Edith Bratt that he was trying to turn one of the stories of the *Kalevala* "into a short story somewhat on the lines of Morris' romances with chunks of poetry in between" (*Letters* 7). William Morris was in turn inspired by Germanic myths and Norse Sagas, some of which contain interpolated poetry. But Morris was by no means the only prose writer to insert poems into his work. George MacDonald, whose work Tolkien read, often included poetry in his stories. As did others.

But characters spout poetry and songs all the time in *The Hobbit* and *The Lord of the Rings*. This just might have been influenced by the world in which Tolkien grew up. And so to answer the question, to what school does Tolkien refer, Sam's or his own, I would say "his own"—the schools of England.

Works Cited

Burns, Maggie. "The Battle of the Eastern Field." *Mallorn*, no. 46, Autumn 2008, pp. 15–22.

——. "John Ronald's Schooldays." *Mallorn,* no. 45, Spring 2008, pp. 27–31.

Fündling, Jörg. "'Go forth, for it is there!': A Imperialist Battle Cry behind the Lament for Boromir?" *Music in Tolkien's Work and Beyond,* edited by Julian Eilmann and Friedhelm Schneidewind, Walking Tree, 2019, pp. 111–31.

Hammond, Wayne G., and Christina Scull. *J. R. R. Tolkien: Artist & Illustrator.* Houghton Mifflin, 1995.

Martsch, Nancy. "Middle-earth Improv: Song Writing and Improvisation in Tolkien's Works." *Music in Tolkien's Work and Beyond,* edited by Julian Eilmann and Friedhelm Schneidewind, Walking Tree, 2019, pp. 59–76.

Robson, Catherine. *Heart Beats: Everyday Life and the Memorized Poem.* Princeton UP, 2012.

Scull, Christina, and Wayne G. Hammond. *The J. R. R. Tolkien Companion and Guide: Reader's Guide.* Revised and expanded ed., HarperCollins, 2017.

Shippey, Tom. *J. R. R. Tolkien: Author of the Century.* Houghton Mifflin, 2001.

Stoddard, William H. "Horatius at Khazad-dûm." *Franson Publications,* July 2003, www.troynovant.com/Stoddard/Tolkien/Horatius-at-Khazad-dum.html.

Tolkien, J. R. R. *The Hobbit.* 50th Anniversary Edition, Unwin Hyman, 1987.

——. *The Letters of J. R. R. Tolkien.* Edited by Humphrey Carpenter, Houghton Mifflin, 2000.

——. *The Lord of the Rings.* 50th Anniversary Edition, Houghton Mifflin, 2004.

Untermeyer, Louis, ed. *Modern British Poetry: A Critical Anthology,* Revised and enlarged ed., Harcourt, Brace and Co., 1925.

Part 4: Other Individual Authors and Sources

L-Space: Libraries and Liminality, A Place of Magic

Elise Caemasache McKenna

L IBRARIES ARE MAGICAL PLACES. They contain vast amounts of knowledge, shelved through arcane systems of retrieval, housed on multiple floors, in single or connected sets of buildings. One of the more magical libraries in fantasy literature was created by Sir Terry Pratchett in his 41-novel Discworld series. The Library is located on the grounds of Unseen University (UU). The UU's library is described as "a low, brooding building with high narrow barred windows and a glass dome high above its centre" (Pratchett and Briggs 228). This seems general enough and about as standard as expected of libraries at universities, but it can be applied to certain older state and county libraries as well. UU Library's foreboding exterior makes the entrance into it all the more solemn, as if entering a sacred place. It is like crossing a threshold into the unknown.

All my life I have loved libraries, and luckily for several summers while I was growing up, a particular library became my haven as we uncharacteristically lived in one place for a while. I remember leaving the noise of the streets to cross the threshold into an immensely large but muted environment, redolent of the smells of old rugs and wood polish. The walls were wood-paneled and the carpeting on the floors and stairs had a maroon diamond pattern. The landing was straight ahead and two staircases turned left and right off of it. This library was colder than the freezer section at a grocer's, and I always brought a cardigan to wrap about me, as I searched for the fiction section and a dozen or so books to read while I was there.

One of my favorite authors early on was Zilpha Keatley Snyder. In *The Velvet Room*, Snyder describes a time when Robin, the protagonist, is brought to the local library by her father:

> Just looking at the outside of the library made Robin lose herself for a minute, remembering the feel of libraries. There was that special smell made up of paper, ink, and dust; the busy hush; the endless luxury of thousands of unread books. (Snyder 64)

Libraries were a place away from home—a carpeted landscape where I could curl up alone in an armchair and lose myself within the safety of a quietly monitored place. Libraries were the only place where I could go on myriad adventures, travel to other countries, increase my virtual experiences, and tap into arcane knowledge—all within a cubby hole on the third floor of a five-story brick building. The building housed all books for ease of access, whereas I could only take on loan a few books at a time, and really only bring one when climbing a tree and nestling in the branches to read, as space and dwindling light thwarted aught else. And there is a certain power, an awe that is felt, that is part of the atmosphere of a library. Simply said, the gathering of all of the books on all of the different subjects in one space is powerful.

Terry Pratchett seems to have thought the same thing. In an interview relating his early experience, he said "I wanted to read everything, I wanted to know everything. [...] I taught myself more in the library than school taught me" ("Sir Terry Pratchett" 00:01:26–00:01:36). Pratchett credits the power of the library and its vast repository to awaken in him the voracious desire to read everything. "More history, more interesting history, more just about everything" ("Sir Terry Pratchett" 00:01:50), Pratchett continues. He clearly answered the call to adventure that the library cast out.

One of the transformative aspects of the library is that we can expand on what we would only ordinarily be able to perceive through our limited sensory experience in the real world. It is true that "we have a need for fantasy, to escape our everyday world and travel to another for a time, a world where we are not limited by our five senses" (Ma). That we can experience other worlds through the language of books is an example of the transcendent power of libraries, but only if we dare to enter and partake of its offerings.

In Joseph Campbell's hero's journey, "The Crossing of the First Threshold" is part of the departure into the unknown. I'd take this idea a step further and apply Campbell's description of "the zone of magnified power" (64) to libraries. This zone, for Campbell, is fraught with "darkness, the unknown, and danger" (64), "yet for anyone with competence and courage danger fades" (68). The unknown here applies to libraries as they are "free fields for projections of unconscious content" (65). Most importantly, for the person crossing the threshold, libraries hold the unknown, as the person has yet to know what this zone of magnified power has to offer. With the foreboding exterior of the library, it takes some courage to enter, and no small amount of competence to not get lost once inside.

Terry Pratchett understood the significance of libraries when he created L-Space. While L-Space stands for Library Space, it is also Liminal Space in the sense that the brick-and-mortar building called a library is a mutable area and walking through its doors is the equivalent of crossing a threshold. Not surprisingly, Pratchett gave this description in the *Discworld Companion*:

> **Libraries, nature of.**
>
> Even big collections of ordinary books distort space and time, as can readily be proved by anyone who has been around a really old-fashioned second-hand bookshop, one of those that has more staircases than storeys and those rows of shelves that end in little doors that are surely too small for a full sized human to enter.
>
> The relevant equation is Knowledge = Power = Energy = Matter = Mass; a good bookshop is just a genteel black hole that knows how to read. Mass distorts space into polyfractal L-space, in which Everywhere is also Everywhere Else.
>
> All libraries everywhere are connected in L-space by the bookwormholes created by the strong space-time distortions found in any large collection of books. Only a very few librarians learn the secret, and there are inflexible rules about making use of the fact—because it amounts to time travel. (Pratchett and Briggs 228)

This is definitely a "zone of magnified power" because there is more knowledge in a library than there is in a person, as shown in Pratchett's equation: Knowledge = Power = Energy = Matter = Mass. But what does this mean for us? It means that we have created a solid area of collected and condensed literature that has a profound effect on all who move into and back out of that area. It is magical in the sense that those who do cross a library's threshold are transformed. They become more than they were. They enter as people in search of something and they become heroes, scientists, professors, astronauts, farmers—all manner of people. They are more than the simple folk who wander outside this zone, never daring to accept its "call to adventure" or to cross into "a zone unknown" (Campbell 48).

Unseen University's library is a part of L-Space, but so is every bookstore and place where a large collection of books can be found. In his description, Pratchett creates the archetype of L-Space as a thing unto itself—a place of infinite possibilities, much like the contents of the books that reside there. L-Space branches out from the university setting and into other book places. L-Space is what unites all repositories of books, making it a virtual place as well as a place tied to brick and mortar. In the *Discworld Companion*, the L-Space theory entry concludes that "the [UU] Library contains every book everywhere, including ones that never actually got written" (Pratchett and Briggs 229). This description continues with a way of organizing what type of book is put in which spot of the Library, no less humorously, of course. Like the images in an Escher painting with floors as walls and impossible staircases, the contents of the library distort perspective. There is a 1,000-

piece puzzle of UU's Library which almost does justice to that infinite space; the image is chaotic and unbelievably packed with all manner of items magical and non-magical.

Pratchett said that L-Space "has opened gateways to all other libraries" (Pratchett, Pratchett, and Briggs 126). Remind anyone of inter-library loan, perhaps? While I worked at Eden-Webster Library in St. Louis, my job was to keep track of the special collection: digitize the card catalogue, add brief descriptions, and process the loan and return of said materials. At my fingertips, I had access to all the knowledge. I was a threshold guardian, *à la* Campbell. The gateways have keepers, and I was now one of them. My responsibilities aligned perfectly, but I found that my perspective on the sacrosanctity of libraries relaxed a bit. Before then, I treated the library space as a medieval temple, a place where only those who were worthy could enter and receive its gifts. Every book and item was to be kept pristine, and I felt, like the Librarian of UU, that they were best left as nature intended, on a shelf, undisturbed. Now, I wanted desperately to share that place and promote its innermost treasures to everyone.

Libraries have been considered a 'third place' where 'first place' is home and 'second place' is work (Morehart). It is my opinion that libraries fill that function of third place much like a church, where people can come to worship and commune in the sacredness of books and microfiche. When I attended the University of North Dakota, my focus was the deep, dark of the library stacks in the basement. My grail? All thirty-seven volumes of Pliny the Elder's *Naturalis Historia* or *Natural History*. These books were relegated to the safest place for them at the University, not unlike the more dangerous magical books at UU, which were chained, hidden behind bars, and otherwise placed in maximum security. If you've read anything about either collection, similarities can be humorously drawn.

For me, libraries were a home away from home and a refuge, but for libraries to survive, they may need to become third places—neither work nor home, but communal. As the years have passed, it has been strange to me to see libraries evolve into third places by adding spaces like cafés, playgrounds, or other social meeting places for the express purpose of meeting, not intellectual edification. I agree with Martin's belief that "libraries should be a place every child can explore, finding knowledge beyond what they can glean from their homes and schools." However, as libraries continue to evolve, can they continue to be liminal spaces? When L-Space becomes adjunct to cafés like a Barnes & Noble, does it change the effect? Is there a threshold to cross? If I had left the noise of the street and entered a place of communal noise, I am not sure I would have felt like I had crossed a threshold into a 'zone of magnified power' because there was not a perceivable difference in the atmosphere. Part of that power lies in the silence—the one rule of 'shhhh,' as it were. Even Pratchett says, "It's generally very quiet in the Unseen University library" (Pratchett, Pratchett, and Briggs 146), even if there are a few noises of shuffling or a cough or sneeze indicating presence. I fear that as libraries continue to evolve into third places, they are losing some of their magic. It is not possible to lose yourself in the stacks, while the hustle and bustle of commerce intrudes.

There is a legend of the Lost Reading Room at UU. As a child, the lost reading room was a place that I searched for at any library—that ultra-sequestered place where I could truly be alone in a public space. I was lucky enough to find a sequestered reading room while at school in England, complete with large armchair and velvet drapery that blocked out light and muted sound. The feel of timelessness, antiquity, and weight lent a gravitas to the space. As a student at University of Florida, I worked in the special collections of the children's library on the second floor, known as the Baldwin Library, contained within the George A. Smathers Libraries. The only way in was to take a class in kiddie lit, which I did, or to be a work-study student, which I was afterwards. The collection was tucked deep inside the Library East. Inside was a mass of boxes and shelves in all manner of disarray. It felt like L-Space's closet.

At Unseen University, "[b]y law and tradition [it] is open to the public, although they are not allowed as far as the magical shelves" (Pratchett, Pratchett, and Briggs 320). As with the Baldwin, the magical shelves were not accessed by the general public. In fact, many of the donations were in such delicate condition that gloves were needed to sort through fragments of late seventeenth- and eighteenth-century chapbooks, historical letters, and out-of-print children's books. As a treasure, these items held more weight in the contents of their leaflets than in their physical bulk—defying the laws of physics just as books in L-Space do.

Another aspect of the distortion associated with L-Space is that time and the nature of things are mutable therein. When researching, I find that time inside a library passes oddly, particularly in spaces where I cannot glimpse outside lights or the sun to give me a sense of time. Pratchett noted that at Unseen U, "the Library did not obey the normal rules of space and time" and "you could wander for days among the distant shelves" (Pratchett, Pratchett, and Briggs 69). Part of the beauty of libraries is the fact that so much information is housed there, and the thrill of the hunt for what you need is compelling. Pratchett again remarks that "somewhere beyond the common shelves lies an entire library universe, peopled by creatures that have evolved [...] such as the kickstool crab and the wild thesaurus" (Pratchett and Briggs 230). What is amazing is that while I grew up loving the erudite nature of being a patron of libraries, the libraries, themselves, have transformed into a place for everyone.

In "Freedom to Live," Campbell says, "the hero is the champion of things becoming, not of things become, because he is" (209). The hero in that sense acts to change—him/herself, society, or possibly the world. Through the liminal power of L-Space, we can become that hero. Since crossing the first threshold, the hero has changed, and now that he/she is crossing back—the world outside the library is not the same. When first and second places drag us away from third place, we return, changed enough to have the freedom to live. We cannot stay in liminality forever, but we can affect the world outside of L-Space by bringing the wealth of knowledge and experience acquired back with us into our primary world. Some of that knowledge must, at the end of the journey, also change L-Space, for it is not immune, and as an entity, must survive by any means. I hope that the magic of L-Space can continue to positively influence future crossers of the threshold, as it evolves both from without and within.

Works Cited

Campbell, Joseph. *The Hero With a Thousand Faces*. 3rd ed., New World Library, 2008.

Ma, Kevin. "The Realm of Turtles: Why We Read Novels in the Electronic Age, As Demonstrated by Pratchett's *Reaper Man*." *The L-Space Web*, 2002, www.lspace.org/books/analysis/kevin-ma.html.

Martin, Kendra. "Public Libraries Evolve as the 'Third Space.'" *Kendra Martin*, 27 Mar. 2012, kendramartin.ca/2012/03/public-libraries-third-space.

Morehart, Phil. "'Moving Beyond the 'Third Place': IFLA forum examines library designs that embrace the community." *American Libraries Magazine*, 17 Aug. 2016, americanlibrariesmagazine.org/blogs/the-scoop/library-design-moving-beyond-third-place.

Peterson, Christopher. "Happy Places: Third Places." *Psychology Today*, 1 Dec. 2009, www.psychologytoday.com/us/blog/the-good-life/200912/happy-places-third-places.

Pratchett, Terry and Stephen Briggs. *Turtle Recall: The Discworld Companion…So Far*. HarperCollins, 2012.

Pratchett, Terry, Lyn Pratchett, and Stephen Briggs. *Terry Pratchett: The Wit & Wisdom of Discworld*. HarperCollins, 2007.

"Sir Terry Pratchett on Libraries." *HarperTeen*, 19 Dec. 2012, *YouTube*, youtu.be/pBQWp-DqdAI.

Snyder, Zilpha Keatley. *The Velvet Room*. Scholastic Books, 1975.

"What is this L-Space thing." *The L-Space Web*, 2019, www.lspace.org/about/whatis-lspace.html.

Fforde's BookWorld as Meta-Library

David L. Emerson

JASPER FFORDE'S SERIES OF SURREAL comic adventure fantasies featuring the character of Thursday Next, literary detective, centers around the concept that books contain inner realities of their own, and that these inner worlds are connected in a coherent universe, called the BookWorld, which Thursday and certain other characters can enter and traverse at will.

The first novel in the series, *The Eyre Affair* (2001),[1] eases into this concept, as Thursday, in her capacity as an operative of a branch of law enforcement that deals with crimes against literature, enters into, and ends up changing the plot of, *Jane Eyre*. In this first book, a few other works are referred to as having been entered by characters from the "real world," but the coherent universe is not explicitly defined until the second novel, *Lost in a Good Book* (2002), in which Thursday encounters the BookWorld as a whole and begins her secondary career as a member of the BookWorld's police force, Jurisfiction. The BookWorld reaches its peak of description in the third volume of the series, *The Well of Lost Plots* (2003), in which (unlike the first two) most of the action takes place entirely within the BookWorld. As the fourth book, *Something Rotten* (2004), is more concerned with events in the "real world," further explication of the nature and structure of the BookWorld next appears in the fifth, *Thursday Next: First Among Sequels* (2008).[2]

The slowly developing emergence of the BookWorld concept is partly due to the fact that Fforde originally meant for *The Eyre Affair* to be a stand-alone novel, but his publisher insisted on a series ("*Lost in a Good Book* Special Features"). It seems that Fforde's concepts developed in the course of writing, rather than being extensively worked out in advance. This, in addition to the author's self-professed indifference to the slavish consistency that many "serious" fantasy writers strive for in creating secondary worlds, results in some inconsistencies in the concept and structure of the BookWorld, as we shall see later.

---

[1] Dates given here are of first British publication. Works cited at the end of this paper are the U.S. paperback editions, which often were published slightly later.

[2] This title is sometimes given as *Thursday Next in First among Sequels*, sometimes as *Thursday Next—First Among Sequels*, sometimes merely *First Among Sequels*, no doubt causing frustration and anxiety for catalogers and indexers.

But the main point is that the series as a whole is about books — not just some books themselves, but all our concepts around the general topic of "book," including what happens within them, how they are written, published, and remaindered, what genres they belong to, how those genres relate to each other, how the concepts embedded in the written words make their way into readers' minds, and much more. As Rebecca-Anne Do Rozario points out, "The series' focus upon a parallel BookWorld [...] promotes an awareness of, and engagement with, bibliography as a narrative concern" (213).

The BookWorld seems[3] to be composed of two layers: the Great Library, and the books themselves. The Great Library contains the books, and the books contain their contents, which in the case of fiction would be the stories therein, complete with characters, settings, and action. Thursday's first adventures into fiction, in *The Eyre Affair*, were entries into books themselves, most notably the novel *Jane Eyre*. But *Lost in a Good Book* is where she discovers that all books exist in the BookWorld as a whole, and her main point of entry is to first get to the Great Library.

The Great Library, as one might guess from the name, resembles an actual library. She described her first visit there: "I was in a long, dark, wood-paneled corridor lined with bookshelves that reached from the richly carpeted floor to the vaulted ceiling. [...] On all of the walls, end after end, shelf after shelf, were *books*. Hundreds, thousands, millions of books" (*Lost in a Good Book* [LGB] 174–75, emphasis in original). However, this description is more accurately only Thursday's view of it. At a later point she says, "The library was as nebulous as the books it contained; its form was decided not only by the base description but by my *interpretation* of what a Great Library might look like" (*First Among Sequels* [FAS] 52, emphasis in original).

This Library, we are led to believe, contains all books ever written in English. However, due to Fforde's admitted inconsistency, it is sometimes implied that it is only published books, or even just officially published books. A plot point later on relies on a fictional character not being locatable because he was in a self-published book ("vanity press") and thus not on the shelves of the Great Library.

The Library has twenty-six floors, one for each letter of the English alphabet, so it is strongly implied that the organization is alphabetical, presumably by author's last name, as most fiction is

---

[3] At least before 2011's *One of Our Thursdays Is Missing*, in which Fforde changed the apparent physical nature of the BookWorld.

shelved in real-world libraries. Below the main section, there are also twenty-six subbasement floors, referred to as The Well of Lost Plots, which contain books "under construction," which supposedly means in the process of being written, or at least being thought of, by authors in the real world. Again, it's never made clear exactly how this works; Fforde seems more interested in creating concrete manifestations of abstract concepts for humorous effect, than in rigorously building a coherent secondary world.

He describes some of the less-populated upper floors, such as Q and X, as having otherwise unused space being given over to administrative functions of the BookWorld, such as the Council of Genres, the BookWorld's legislative body, about which more later.

The Great Library that Thursday encounters, which seems to her like a great tower, is merely the library of all books in English. There are other Great Libraries that she can see from the observation windows.

> Not more than five miles distant, just visible in the aerial haze, was another tower like ours, and beyond that, another—and over to my right, six more. We were just one towering library of hundreds— or perhaps thousands. [...] 'The nearest one to us is German,' said Miss Havisham, 'beyond that French and Spanish. Arabic is just beyond them—and that one over there is Welsh.' (*The Well of Lost Plots* [WLP] 258)

There is some indication that there is communication between the Great Libraries, but whether there is travel between them is not known.

The books in the Great Library are "*alive*, each one a small universe unto itself" as Thursday says (FAS 59, emphasis in original); the characters they contain act and react like living beings, the locations they describe are concrete and can be visited. From the Library, Thursday can enter one of these living books at will, merely by picking it up and reading it. Once inside, the book becomes more like the set for a movie or stage play, the characters more like actors playing their parts, and the written narrative is their script. Once the narrative moves on to other scenes, the "actors" exhibit free will and possibly different personalities from the characters they're playing. Sets no longer in the narrative can be re-purposed, such as the Dashwood family estate, Norland Park (from *Sense and Sensibility*), being used as the offices of Jurisfiction during the parts of the Jane Austen novel that have moved on to other locales.

Each book (and in fact, each *edition* of each book) exists as its own territory, but some movement between books can occur. In the course of such movement, Thursday sees that books are grouped into genres. Thursday explains: "Although each book exists on its own and is adrift in the intragenre space known as the Nothing, the books belonging to the various genres clump together for mutual protection, free trade of ideas and easy movement of characters" (FAS 55). Looking out into the Nothing from a portal in one book, she and another character see other books in the distance, "adrift in the firmament and each one burning [...] with the warm glow of being read and appreciated" (FAS 79).

This spatial representation of books and genres is given a graphical depiction in *First Among Sequels* in a series of full-page textless illustrations (340–43), where Thursday has to leap into space from book to book in a scene reminiscent of Dave Bowman's space jump in the film *2001: A Space Odyssey*. Here, clumps of books are pictured as rough spheres, more akin to stellar globular clusters than solid planets. These illustrations, by Bill Mudron and Dylan Meconis, met the author's enthusiastic approval (FAS 363) and are thus to be considered a more or less accurate portrayal of what the BookWorld genre constellations look like—at least to Thursday's subjective interpretation.

The genres in the BookWorld apparently have fixed locations determined by the Council of Genres, as the borders between them are sometimes subject of some debate. For example, Thursday explains one such issue: "Some idiot placed [Racy Novel] somewhat recklessly between Ecclesiastical and Feminist, with the tiny principality of Erotica to the far north and a buffer zone with Comedy to the south comprising the subcrossover genre of Bedroom Farce/Bawdy Romp" (FAS 55).

Other indications of the propinquity of some genres to others are scattered throughout the series:

- "[A] particularly bad [word] storm in '34 swept through Horror and rained detritus on Drama for weeks, the most notable result being the grisly spontaneous-combustion sequence in Dickens's *Bleak House*." (WLP 364)
- "[A] cloud of mis-punctuation arose in Horror, circled twice and then developed into a pretty stiff breeze of split infinitives and jumbled words before traveling through Fantasy into Romance. [...] ...it's...probable they will strengthen and then careen off on a destructive course towards Drama." (WLP 366)
- "Thriller was placed next door to Crime, which itself is bordered by Human Drama—a fine demonstration of inspired genreography for the very best mutual improvement of both." (FAS 55)
- "If we wanted to go from Maritime to Frontier quickly and easily, we wouldn't jump direct but go through Western." (FAS 283)
- "Longfellow is at the other end of the BookWorld [...]." (FAS 288)

Even geographical relationships between books within genres are sometimes described:

- Discussing routes into the works of Edgar Allan Poe: "We know you can get from 'Thingum Bob' into 'The Black Cat' by way of an unstable verb in the third paragraph, and from 'Black Cat' into 'The Fall of the House of Usher' by the simple expedient of hiring a horse from the Nicaean stables [...]." (LGB 185–86)
- Describing a taxicab route in the Maritime genre: "We'll hang a left after the HMS *Sutherland* and move through *The African Queen* to join the cross-Maritime thoroughfare at *The Old Man and the Sea*. Once there we'll double back through *The Sea Wolf* and come out at *Moby-Dick*, which neatly sidesteps *Treasure Island*, as it's usually jammed at this hour." (FAS 310)
- Using navigational aids: "Don't forget the ISBN numbers either—they weren't introduced *just* for cataloguing, now were they? [...] New technology is here to be used, guys. Anyone who wants to attend a training course on how ISBN numbers relate to transbook travel [...]." (LGB 290–91)

Even though certain other modes of writing, such as poetry, anecdotes, and knitting patterns, are mentioned here and there, Fforde never really addresses the distinction between fiction and nonfiction, so it's never clear exactly whether nonfiction has its own genres or where they are located relative to the fiction genres.

Within the fiction genres, there are subgenres: at the Council of Genres, "'The main genres are seated at the front,' whispered Miss Havisham. 'The subgenres are seated behind and make up a voting group that can be carried forward to the elected head of each genre, although they do have a veto. Behind the subgenres are elected representatives from the Congress of Derivatives...'" (WLP 259). And apparently the designations of subgenres are up for discussion as well: "'The Thriller delegate [is] arguing against Detective having a genre all of its own—at present Detective is under Crime, but if they break away, the genres at Thriller will want to split themselves three ways into Adventure, Spy and Thriller'" (*ibid*).

Even though Thursday maintains that she could "draw from memory a genre map of the BookWorld" (FAS 161), the clues from the above passages are nowhere near complete enough for the reader to do the same. However, we should be able to form a general impression of the size, number, and variety of genres in the BookWorld.[4]

---

[4] A further complication in the visual conception of the BookWorld is that in the sixth book of the series, *One of Our Thursdays Is Missing* (OOTIM), Fforde has the BookWorld reshaped, so that it resembles an archipelago rather than a galaxy. In the remade BookWorld, Fiction is an island in the Text Sea, as are "Artistic Criticism [...] Psychology, Philately, and Software Manuals" (OOTIM 13). This also allowed Fforde to create a map for the frontispiece, as is the fashion in so many fantasy novels with invented worlds. Fforde said on his website, "This

We know that in the BookWorld, Fiction, at least, is divided into genres, and most if not all genres have subgenres. The number of genres that can be inferred by a general reader is both more and less than the number in the real world. More, because the fiction sections in most public libraries may have separate shelves for a few genres, but usually not more than four or five. Less, because the Library of Congress lists thousands of genre classifications; even limiting the selection to printed fiction books, it's still quite a large number (Genre).

To compare the structure of the BookWorld with current real-world library systems depends on which systems we're looking at. For example, if the genres in BookWorld were comparable to all the possible fiction genre entries in the Library of Congress Subject Headings, the Council of Genres would be an enormous body, probably too large to meet in one room. Fforde's description of main genres at the front, subgenres behind them, and smaller divisions further back seems more like the Dewey Decimal System, which is based on a hierarchy of subject and sub-headings. With such a hierarchical seating arrangement, it's possible that the Council could encompass such a large and comprehensive categorization system, but it would still be considerably larger than what's implied in the above-mentioned scene from *The Well of Lost Plots*.

Looking from the other side, is the BookWorld's organization at all appropriate for real-world libraries? A normal public library will usually shelve what they consider "general" fiction in one large section, with separate sections for, say, Mysteries, Romance, Western, and Science Fiction (which usually includes fantasy, without differentiation). Some libraries might have additional sections, depending on the needs of the community, for example, shelves of "Urban Fiction" in predominantly African-American neighborhoods. But Mysteries are not usually subdivided into Detective, Crime, Spy, etc. In fact, the general fiction section may stack thrillers and family dramas alongside classics, "chick lit," and bestsellers. If a public library were to organize their novels to the degree of granularity reflected in the BookWorld's genreography, it might make it much more difficult

---

new, improved Bookworld [sic] makes it so much easier to navigate. Instead of all the books being stuck within a central library that you have to enter by reading, all the various genres are on 'Fiction Island,' itself one of hundreds of island in the Bookworld. If you want to visit a certain book, you simply go by train to the correct genre, and knock on the front door. It adds a sense of geopolitical fun to the proceedings, too" (Special features). However, the remade, map-worthy version of the BookWorld is beyond the scope of the present paper.

for patrons to find what they're looking for without relying heavily on the catalog. On the other hand, if a reader is browsing for a particular subgenre, having, say, all the British cozy mysteries together without having to skip past hard-boiled detective might be easier on them in the long run. But it would also remove the serendipity of browsing the stacks and coming across something that simply looks interesting.

A similar situation applies to bookstores, where the patron is expecting to buy rather than to borrow. Smaller bookstores, usually independent and owner-managed, may be as organized or disorganized as the owner pleases, since they would almost always know where to steer a customer who is looking for something in particular. Bookstores specializing in a particular genre might want to separate subgenres, such as a mystery bookstore having sections for cozies, noir, true crime, etc. And larger bookstores may want to provide more granularity in their fiction genre choices than libraries. For example, they may have a separate section for "classics," i.e., fiction more than 100 years old. And they would usually display current best-sellers together in an area near the front of the store, or possibly near the registers (if those are not the same location).

However, the more granularity is used in sorting by physical location, the more pressing becomes the problem of items that combine genres, like *Pride and Prejudice and Zombies*, or the Thursday Next books themselves—where do *they* go? Like libraries, larger stores, especially national chains, cannot depend on every employee knowing about every book in the place, so even if the stock is organized in an intuitively obvious manner, there must be a robust indexing and locating system available to employees so that they can assist customers.

Archives, on the other hand, usually having stacks closed to the public, need only have means for their custodians to locate materials at will, like catalogs and finding aids. Items for archiving can be placed anywhere, in any system (such as by date of arrival, or physical size, or format), just as long as the archivists have the ability to retrieve them promptly and easily.

Home libraries present a different aspect to this. The organization and placement of books is entirely up to the resident who owns them, and can be as idiosyncratic as the owner. There would be nothing to prevent a person from separating their science fiction and fantasy, for instance, or clumping mysteries by subgenre. One might mix everything together, but alphabetical by author, and within a particular author's work the books could be alphabetical by title, or in publishing order, or (in the case of ongoing series) by internal chronology, or completely randomly. Someone might want to have a shelf for their favorite and most beloved books, so it would not be out of place to see *Anne of Green Gables* next to *Lord of the Rings* next to Hesse's *Siddhartha* next to Chandler's *The Big Sleep*. Nor would media have to be separate—if one wants to mix their DVDs in with their books, there's no reason not to. The point is, the system must make sense for the owner, but does not need to make sense for anyone else.

So creating a home library modeled along the lines of the genre configurations of the BookWorld might not be everybody's cup of tea, but it could be done. I would not be surprised if some Jasper Fforde uber-fan has already done so.

Works Cited

Do Rozario, Rebecca-Anne. "Fforde's Book Upgrades: Downloaded Errata and Metafictional Cancellation." *Script & Print, Bulletin of the Bibliographical Society of Australia & New Zealand*, vol. 32, no. 4, 2009. pp. 212–18.

Fforde, Jasper. *The Eyre Affair*. Penguin, 2002.

——. *Lost in a Good Book*. Penguin, 2004.

——. "*Lost in a Good Book* Special Features: 'Making of' Wordamentary." March 2003, www.jasperfforde.com/lostmusing2.html#full.

——. *One of Our Thursdays Is Missing*. Penguin, 2011.

——. *Something Rotten*. Penguin, 2005.

——. "Special Features." www.jasperfforde.com/featurestn6.html.

——. *Thursday Next in First Among Sequels*. Penguin, 2008.

——. *The Well of Lost Plots*. Penguin, 2004.

Library of Congress. "Genre." www.loc.gov/aba/publications/FreeLCGFT/GENRE.pdf.

Libraries as a Fulcrum of Change: Eric Flint's *Ring of Fire: 1632*

Susan Adams-Johnson and Anna Holloway

I N 2000, BAEN BOOKS PUBLISHED *1632*, a sci-fi/alternative history novel by Eric Flint. The premise of *1632* is that in April 2000, a six-mile sphere centered on Grantville, West Virginia (a fictional town based on the actual town of Mannington, WV), was displaced in time and space by a mysterious alien civilization (Flint *1632* 1–3) to Thuringia in the Germanies in May 1631—the midst of the Thirty Years' War. This effectively begins a new timeline, and essentially a new universe, as the displaced West Virginians begin to interact with the world as it was in 1631. Called 'the Ring of Fire' by the Grantville residents, the displacement event triggers the butterfly effect[1] so that the further in time one progresses from the occurrence, the more likely historical and everyday events will diverge from the recorded history of the prior world—the history that the readers "know." The novel is an excellent example of the fusion of the alternative history and science fiction genres, and it has spawned a series—almost a network—of novels, stories, and games placed in the alternate 1632 timeline. According to the official website, Flint's original opus "has spawned more than 25 books, over 70 issues of a magazine, more than fifteen annual conventions, and works by over 130 authors" (*Welcome to 1632*).

In the first books and stories of the series, the "up-timers" (displaced late 20th-century Americans) quickly come to realize that their books, recorded media, tools, homes and personal items, and even personal knowledge and oral traditions, are critically important sources of information that have become artifacts in their own right (Brown and Davis-Brown 19–20). After electing a leader, the Grantville inhabitants agree essentially to start the American Revolution early, introducing a 20th-century American political context to the socio-political stew of war-torn Europe. Many of the leaders of 17th-century principalities are informed and inspired by

---

[1] Developed from chaos theory, Geoff Boeing noted that the butterfly effect is the subtle dependency on initial circumstances in which a minor alteration in one state of a deterministic nonlinear systemic structure may cause large alterations in a future state. In other words, seemingly inconsequential actions can cause significant responses and changes over the long haul.

the technology and knowledge of the future, while others are seduced by the potential power that "changing their future" might give them. The presence of that knowledge in their midst spawns a new set of socio-political dilemmas to confront the known historical figures and the up-timers now living among them.

After writing the first novel, Flint took the interesting step of opening his universe to other authors, which resulted in the collection of stories published as *Ring of Fire* in 2004. He specified that the resources (besides limited fuel supplies, various machine shops, and auto repair shops) that would make the journey through time and space included: (1) computers and the kind of software which might be available in April of the year 2000, (2) books, magazines, newspapers, and pamphlets available in small-town public libraries, school libraries and small personal libraries, and (3) a high school with vo-tech capabilities (Boatright "How It All Started").

It may be useful at this point to offer a definition of "library" that explains the breadth of what Grantville offers to the populations of 17th-century Europe. In *The Librarian's Book of Lists*, George Eberhart defines a library as follows:

> A library is a collection of resources in a variety of formats that is (1) organized by information professionals or other experts who (2) provide convenient physical, digital, bibliographic, or intellectual access and (3) offer targeted services and programs (4) with the mission of educating, informing, or entertaining a variety of audiences (5) and the goal of stimulating individual learning and advancing society as a whole. (1)

This very broad definition, which encompasses all sorts of materials, describes the collections of resources that accompany Grantville from 2000 to the 17th century.

By contrast, the Society of American Archivists defines archives as primarily a collection of documents associated with or received by an institution of some sort (e.g., a family, a school, a business, an artist) that is curated around the life and/or work of that institution. It is the common association that makes a collection an archive, rather than the individual elements, which tend to be primarily documentary.

> Within the professional literature, archives are characterized by an organic nature, growing out of the process of creating and receiving records in the course of the routine activities of the creator (its provenance). In this sense, archivists have differentiated archives from artificial collections. ("Archives")

To a professional archivist, a museum or library collection is an artificial collection (created by artifice), rather than an archive, created by an association with an individual or institution (Rayward 209; Rinehart). However, legitimate contributions to an archive may differ over time, and those differences can affect the nature and use of the archive; change becomes a function of shifting boundaries (Cook, "From Information to Knowledge" 35; Manoff 10). Thus the archive both reflects and inspires change in the culture it represents and serves; metaphorically, it acts as a fulcrum of those changes for those studying and observing the culture.

The collections of the town of Grantville, by virtue of their association with the uniquely displaced town, constitute archives of collections. Some of these collections, having been assembled intentionally, are artificial collections (e.g., libraries) and some are archives (collected by or associated with an individual or institution for institutional purposes), thus they constitute together the Grantville archives.

Within the series, Flint establishes a post-custodial approach to the use of the various materials, including library books and other forms of print, various media formats, and a wide range of technology. A post-custodial approach to archival material establishes the concept that archives are to be managed, maintained, and preserved but are there to be used (Cook, "From Information to Knowledge" 35 and "Electronic Records, Paper Minds" 399; Schwartz and Cook 1–3). Finding these resources available to them, the 17th-century leaders who are engaged in the Thirty Years War, one of one of the most devastating conflicts in human history (Wilson 787), make various attempts at using the materials from the libraries of the displaced Americans. Flint manages this conflict of desired use versus post-custodial care by giving the Americans a leader who understands not only the value of information and the risk of letting 20th-century technology loose in the 1600s, but also one who understands the real danger of suppressing and limiting access to information, education, and imagination (Flint *1632* 72–76; Weber and Flint 194).

Mike Stearns, the initial protagonist of the series, is the president of the coal miners' union local prior to the Ring of Fire event. He is a former prize fighter, has several years of National Guard service, and spent three years of college in a history major that focused on early American History. He becomes the elected leader of Grantville, and later the first President of the new United States of Europe, as they face their first crisis that includes fighting off mercenaries and dealing with the onslaught of refugees from the Thirty Years War.

Stearns insists that the new government they create must include a version of the American Constitution, including the Bill of Rights, so that there are also strong unions, a free press, free enterprise, freedom of religion, civil rights, and freedom of information. Stearns's voice is prevalent throughout the series; it is not a stretch to the understanding that Mike Stearns's opinions may be a reflection of Flint's personal views, especially on freedom of information. The very concept of freedom of information is one of the most revolutionary ideas to the 17th-century characters (sometimes referred to as "down-timers"), and its implementation involves the core practices of post-custodial archival management, maintenance, and use.

Throughout the series many aspects of archival maintenance and use come up for evaluation and decision. Are print and recorded materials to be kept only for the use of the transplanted characters, or are they available to the larger population of Europe? Do the everyday objects that travel through time and space become hallowed artifacts needing care and protection even from their up-time owners, or do they become some form of paradigm or prototype? How does one integrate records (e.g., taxes, birth and death) from the 20th century and the 17th century as the population moves forward in a past time? Perhaps the most important question is, how do these archives from the future begin to change the political and cultural landscape of the 17th century—and therefore of the centuries that follow?

While Flint has established a post-custodial approach to the use of the various public, school, and personal libraries and technology, in the context of the Thirty Years War, the characters who enact this policy often have other agendas. Flint's socio-political design for Grantville allows for the sale of privately held print materials—except for some engineering and gun manuals—never actually identified in Flint's books (Boatright "Dead Horses"). One Grantviller, whose son collected many books as an escape from his abusive home life, begins to sell the books to spies of the Cardinal Richelieu, igniting a blaze of espionage and assassination as the Cardinal tries to eliminate his enemies before they become dangerous. When presented with a prediction of his future demise at the hands of Cromwell's armies, Charles I of England begins to take the same approach. This leads the main characters in Grantville's leadership to consider that "history books would rapidly become one of the most prized objects for espionage. Technical books, yes; blueprints, yes anything which would enable the United States opponents to steal some of the incredible new technology. But...*high school history books*?" (Weber and Flint 6–7)

The print, recorded media, and other aspects of daily 20th-century life for the transplanted Americans become a repository of stored memories; these materials become an aspect of collective memory by providing artifacts of their heritage (Jacobsen, Punzalan, and Hedstrom 220) and a historical consciousness of their past in the 20th century (Taylor 119). As they reinvent their way of life under 17th-century limitations, the libraries, archives, and personal belongings become resources for their changes in technology and lifestyle.

While the Grantville electric plant has made the journey to the 1600s, maintaining the plant and replacing needed parts is a major issue. Therefore, recognizing the limitations on producing electricity, the up-timers decide to rely mostly on 19th-century technology with a 20th-century understanding of theories and methodologies (Bergstralh 282–88; Flint *1632* 82–83, 371–72; Jones 189). They build a mechanical printing press which is more advanced than the 17th-century examples (Flint *1632* 250–51). This makes their print production faster and smoother, but the availability of paper becomes an issue. The lack of 20th-century toilet paper is a chronic complaint, for example (Howard). In the course of their alliance with one side or another in the war, the (re)development of ironclad sailing ships is applied to canal boats, and they (re)create a U.S. Navy that is primarily designed for riverine and shallow sea combat (Weber and Flint 32–45; Weber 5–62). The up-time guns have a significantly higher rate of fire than any of the 17th-century firearms, which gives the Americans an extreme advantage on the battlefield (Flint *1632* 301–02). This in turn gives Mike Stearns an advantage in the area of political negotiations.

The print materials, which are the most familiar and comfortable to the 17th-century Europeans, become an especially important element of change in the new temporal environment. In addition to the buying, selling, and lending of books, the buying and selling of copies—the up-timers are rationing the use of the school and municipal copiers, and some copies are made by hand with errors deliberately added—becomes another part of how different players, through forms of espionage, manage the changes that occur in Europe as a result of having the archive of Grantville dropped into history.

Newer technology changes the course not only of the Thirty Years War but of the lives of the populations. Sanitation is introduced—over the objections of many of the locals—to limit the spread of disease (Flint *1632* 179–82, 255). Modern types of antibiotics are introduced allowing actual cures (Gottlieb 333). However, the archive of new technologies does not make the most significant differences. The presence of a free and accessible library—*the availability of information*—changes the world in marked and meaningful ways.

One example of the change created by information is demonstrated in the imprisonment of John Milton, a young man not yet blind and not yet famous, by Charles I of England. (Charles has seen up-time histories that indicate Milton's future influence in Charles's overthrow.) While captive, Milton is given access to a volume of his own later writing:

> For three weeks, [Milton] paced back and forth in his cell, reading in his own voice words that were familiar. His "collected works." Some of the poems written in college he considered sophomoric. He remembered writing those but never imagined they would be reprinted three centuries later.
>
> There was a selection of criticisms that accompanied his writings. When the embargo of paper and writing was lifted, he finally had access to the library his father and brother accumulated during his incarceration. The library of materials was impressive. The books from Grantville were meticulously reprinted, then smuggled with great risk to England. Milton's writings were outlawed on the pain of death, by order of the king.
>
> He especially enjoyed his essay on censorship "Areopagitica" in light of the present situation. (Huston 90)

Milton must then consider whether to write some version of what history says he has written or to write instead from the new perspective that the presence of those writings provides. This is one version of the kind of changes that the "library" that is Grantville brings to the 17th-century world. The ready availability of the books in the Grantville libraries, and the dispersal of the books to others—non-Grantvillers—as artifacts of heritage and verification of Grantville's origins, stands as an illustration of the complex interface of archives and cultures (Hedstrom 26).

Flint's concept of his alternative history dovetails with Jean-Francis Lyotard's appraisal that complexification is a feature of modern society (Lyotard 44–45). Anthony Miccoli notes that complexification resists the natural propensity for any system to come to a place of rest. Complexification results when any system experiences an inflow of information and vigorously attempts to adapt that information so that society is further developed (Miccoli 74). The addition of Grantville to the Thirty Years War complexifies, and necessarily changes, every aspect of the war and the lives of the people in it.

Custody of archives also goes through complexification. Flint's characters wade through a series of choices of how to preserve old information and skills and then utilize new information and hybridize skills and technology. They must resolve the "complexification of ownership, possession, guardianship and control" (Upward 199). In *1633*, Weber and Flint begin to tackle this issue of whether freedom of information should be extended to the enemies of Grantville and their political allies (Flint "Portraits" 9–13).

As noted earlier, Flint, through the character of Mike Stearns, established a post-custodial overarching model toward archives for this series; in other words, print materials are maintained in the town's libraries but the original materials are available for use by almost everyone. In *1633*, the sequel co-written by David Weber and Eric Flint, Mike Stearns explains:

> Every old maid in the country—most of 'em pot-bellied men—will set up a howl and a shriek for every book in sight to be put under lock and key. Before you know it, it'll be harder to get into a library than Fort Knox. Leaving aside the damage to real civil liberties, that'll cause ten times worse damage to our own technical development than any amount of spying could do. I mean, face it. Do you *really* want to see all the books published in the old universe declared 'items of national security'? (194)

Flint and his co-authors realize that the print and recorded materials that came through time and space are not only archives of the past but are also artifacts that change the future. In his 1996 article, Frank Upward made the point that possession has two aspects: physical and constructed. The possession of records, the actual ownership, and the custody/control may be held by several entities (Upward 199). Custody of the archives and collective memory are elements of a social construct (Schwartz and Cook 3) that can shape social experience (Mifflin 227–28).

Possession of copies—in whole or part—of the Americans' history books and encyclopedias allows the existing political structure to shift throughout the series. Gustav II Adolf, King of Sweden, avoids his historically recorded death in November 1632 and, in Flint's universe, continues to lead the Swedish-Germanic alliance, changing the balance of the war (Flint *1632* 496; Weber and Flint 83). In the novel *1633*, Charles I of England causes Oliver Cromwell and others of his potential killers to be placed in the Tower of London or executed to prevent them from taking power and beheading him (Viehl 220, Weber and Flint 83–88, 93–94). Richelieu negotiates the division of the North American Continent with the British and Spain so that France has control of the former British colonies such as Jamestown and New Amsterdam—the future New York (Sakalaucks and Sakalaucks). The Austro-Hungarian Empire, still in development in the 1632 we know, splits in Flint's world between the Hapsburgs and Wallenstein, creating a new Bohemian kingdom (Flint "The Wallenstein Gambit" 401).

1634: The Bavarian Crisis sets up Spain's loss of the Spanish Netherlands and initiates an independent Holland (Flint and DeMarce). The plot of *1634: The Baltic War* causes Denmark and Sweden to ally under the leadership of Gustav II Adolf, creating a powerful northern kingdom (Flint and Weber). Clearly a favorite of Flint's, Gustav II Adolf is a strong presence throughout the series, opening the "what if?" doors to speculative history. It also opens the door to a form of social justice activism, as shown in the authors' approach to various forms of ethnic or religious hate crimes (Flint "The Wallenstein Gambit" 401; DeMarce 175–76, 178).

Among the earliest rescued refugees in *1632* is a father and daughter who are Sephardic Jews, Balthazar and Rebecca Abrabanel. Rebecca is the love interest for Mike Stearns and also develops into a formidable figure throughout the series. When the Abrabanels are rescued, they are hosted by Grantville's only Jewish residents, Morris and Judith Roth. During the period that they stay with the Roths, they are introduced to the history of the Holocaust:

> Morris leaned forward, planting his elbows on his knees. "You read the book I gave you? The one on the Holocaust?"
> Balthazar winced and spread his hand as if to ward off demons. "As much of it as I could bear. Which was not much."
> Morris took a deep breath. "The world we came from was no paradise Dr. Abrabanel. Not for Jews, not for any one. But if there were devils aplenty, there were also those who dealt with them." (Flint, *1632* 123)

By introducing Dr. Abrabanel to the record of the Holocaust, Morris Roth begins to share custody of the memory of the extermination of most of Europe's Jewish population in the 20th century. Access to the information in the Roth's library, as well as other libraries in Grantville, viewed collectively as an archive from an alternate past, inspires the Abrabanels and the Roths—as well as other characters—to use the libraries and collections as resources to change the devastating (at this point, potential) history of anti-Semitic massacres. The characters of the series begin a sequence of events that they hope will set in motion ways for the politics of Europe to realign so that many, if not all, pogroms and holocausts may be avoided.

As the up-timer Americans become more of a military, financial, and political presence in Europe, Morris Roth works on methods to prevent the Ukrainian Khmelnytskyi pogroms of 1648–1657 that murdered between 40,000–100,000 Jewish individuals (Tatz 146; Weiss 193). These horrific events—the worst massacre of Jews prior to World War II—are now in

Roth's future and might therefore be avoided. He shares that information with Mike Sterns who agrees that the pogrom must be prevented.

In "The Wallenstein Gambit," a novella published in the volume *Ring of Fire*, Stearns and Roth make a deal with Albrecht Wenzel Eusebius von Wallenstein, who has access to the Grantville history books and encyclopedias, to avoid the massacre. Wallenstein, an enemy in the novels *1632* and *1633*, becomes an ally.

> Stearns said [...] abruptly: "You've asked me four times to think of a way to stop the coming massacres of the Jews in the Ukraine. Probably the worst pogrom in Jewish history before the Holocaust, you told me. This is the best I can manage, Morris. I can't do it, but Wallenstein…maybe. But it's a hell of a gamble—and frankly, one which has a lot more parameters than simply the Jewish problem in eastern Europe."
>
> Morris's mind was finally starting to work clearly again. "To put it mildly. Am I right in assuming that Wallenstein came here secretly to propose an alliance? He'll break from the Austrian Habsburgs and take Bohemia out of Ferdinand's empire?"
>
> [...].
>
> [Stearns replied] "We've got fifteen years, theoretically—assuming the butterfly effect doesn't scramble so-called 'future history' the way it usually does." (Flint, "The Wallenstein Gambit" 401)

In choosing to engage with Wallenstein to aid the Ukrainian Jews, Stearns and Roth provide to their former enemy all of the print material that they can find on the Khmelnytskyi Pogroms to discuss strategies and implement tactics that could avert the disasters. In this way, they treat the archived materials as specific tools of social change—even as they realize that the modes and potential effectiveness of that change are out of their control.

All of the above scenarios illustrate that Flint and his co-authors exhibit an understanding that preserving the elements of the archives as artifacts—books, records, items—is not sufficient. It matters to preserve and understand the patterns that the archives represent and to disseminate these patterns to instruct and alter a horrific future. This is a key aspect of post-custodial guardianship: not only to maintain the actual documents, but to extract meaning and make that widely available via access to the archive and the archivists. In this way, the archives and their libraries actively participate as a fulcrum of change.

Works Cited

"Archives." *Glossary*, Society of American Archivists, 2019, www2.archivists.org/glossary/terms/a/archives.

Boatright, Rick. "Dead Horses." 1632: *Eric Flint's Ring of Fire*, 2017, 1632.org/1632-tech/dead-horses/#Censorship.

——. "How It All Started." 1632: *Eric Flint's Ring of Fire*, 6 Apr. 2015, 1632.org/how_it_started.

Bergstralh, Karen. "The Impact of Mechanization on German Farms." *Grantville Gazette III: Sequals to* 1632, edited by Eric Flint, Baen, 2006, pp. 277–92.

Boeing, Geoff. "Visual Analysis of Nonlinear Dynamical Systems: Chaos, Fractals, Self-Similarity and the Limits of Prediction." *Systems*, vol. 4, no. 4, 2016. www.mdpi.com/2071-8954/4/4/37/htm.

Brown, Richard Harvey, and Beth Davis-Brown. "The Making of Memory: The Politics of Archives, Libraries and Museums in the Construction of National Consciousness." *History of the Human Sciences*, vol. 11, no. 4, 1998, pp. 17–32. doi.org/10.1177/095269519801100402.

Cook, Terry. "From Information to Knowledge: An Intellectual Paradigm for Archives." *Archivaria*, vol. 19, ser. 1984–85, Winter 1984, pp. 28–49.

——. "Electronic Records, Paper Minds: The Revolution in Information Management and Archives in the Post-Custodial and Post-Modernist Era." *Archives & Social Studies: A Journal of Interdisciplinary Research*, vol. 1, no. 0, 2007, pp. 399–443.

De Marce, Virginia. "Motherhood and Apple Pie, While You're at It." *1634: The Ram Rebellion*, edited by Eric Flint and Virginia DeMarce, Baen, 2006, pp. 175–79.

Eberhart, George. *The Librarian's Book of Lists*. American Library Association, 2010.

Flint, Eric. *1632*. Baen, 2000.

——. *Ring of Fire*. Baen, 2004.

——. "Portraits." *Ring of Fire*, edited by Eric Flint, Baen, 2004, pp. 5–15.

——. "The Wallenstein Gambit." *Ring of Fire*, edited by Eric Flint, Baen, 2004, pp. 397–518.

Flint, Eric, and David Weber. *1634: the Baltic War*. Baen, 2008.

Flint, Eric, and Virginia DeMarce. *The Bavarian Crisis*. Baen, 2009.

Gottlieb, Bob. "They've Got Bread Mold, So Why Can't They Make Penicillin?" *Grantville Gazette: Sequels to* 1632, edited by Eric Flint, Baen, 2004, pp. 319–34.

Hedstrom, Margaret. "Archives, Memory, and Interfaces with the Past." *Archival Science*, vol. 2, iss. 1–2, 2002, pp. 21–43.

Howard, Terry. "The Future Is Where You Started." *Grantville Gazette*, vols. I–XXIV, orion.crucis.net/Eric-Flint/gazette31/1011250076___4.htm.

Huston, Mark. "Milton's Choice." *Ring of Fire III*, edited by Eric Flint, Baen, 2011, pp. 77–95.

Jacobsen, Trond, Ricardo L. Punzalan, and Margaret L. Hedstrom. "Invoking 'collective memory': mapping the emergence of a concept in archival science." *Archival Science*, vol. 13, no. 2–3, 2013, pp. 217–51.

Jones, Loren K. "Power to the People." *Ring of Fire*, edited by Eric Flint, Baen, 2004, pp. 175–93.

Lyotard, Jean-Francis. *The Inhuman: Reflections on Time*. Translated by Geoffery Bennington and Rachel Bowlby, Polity Press, 1991.

Manoff, Marlene. "Theories of the Archive from Across the Disciplines." *Portal: Libraries and the Academy*, vol. 4, no. 1, 2004, pp. 9–25, doi.org/10.1353/pla.2004.0015.

Miccoli, Anthony. *Posthuman Suffering and the Technological Embrace*. Lexington Books, 2010.

Mifflin, Jeffrey. "'Metaphors for Life Itself': Historical Photograph Albums, Archives, and the Shape of Experience and Memory." *The American Archivist*, vol. 75, no. 1, 2012, pp. 225–40.

Rayward, W. Boyd. "Electronic Information and the Functional Integration of Libraries, Museums, and Archives." *History and Electronic Artefacts*, edited by Edward Higgs, Clarendon Press, 1998, pp. 207–26.

Rinehart, Richard. "MOAC—A Report on Integrating Museum and Archive Access in the Online Archive of California." *D-Lib Magazine*, vol. 9, no. 1, 2003, doi.org/10.1045/january2003-rinehart.

Sakalaucks, Herbert, and William Sakalaucks. "Northwest Passage, Part Four." *Grantville Gazette 29*, edited by Paula Goodlett, orion.crucis.net/Eric-Flint/gazette29/1011250074___7.htm.

Schwartz, Joan M., and Terry Cook. "Archives, Records, and Power: The Making of Modern Memory." *Archival Science*, vol. 2, iss. 1–2, 2002, 1–19.

Tatz, Colin Martin. *With Intent to Destroy: Reflections on Genocide*. Verso Books, 2003.

Taylor, Hugh A. "The Collective Memory: Archives and Libraries as Heritage." *Archivaria*, vol. 15, Winter 1982–1983, pp. 118–30, archivaria.ca/index.php/archivaria/article/view/10975.

Upward, Frank. "Structuring the Records Continuum—Part One: Post-custodial Principles and Properties." *Archives & Manuscripts*, vol. 24, no. 2, 1996, pp. 197–222.

Viehl, S. L. "A Matter of Consultation." *Ring of Fire*, edited by Eric Flint, Baen, 2004, pp. 195–220.

Weber, David. "In the Navy." *Ring of Fire,* edited by Eric Flint, Baen, 2004, pp. 55–62.

Weber, David, and Eric Flint. *1633.* Baen, 2002.

Weiss, Mosheh. *A Brief History of the Jewish People.* Rowman and Littlefield, 2004.

"Welcome to 1632." *1632.org.*

Wilson, Peter H. *Europe's Tragedy: A New History of the Thirty Years War.* Penguin, 2011.

"My kind of librarian or your kind of librarian?": Information Seeking Behavior in *Supernatural*

Liorah Golomb

MIDWAY THROUGH SEASON 8 of the long-running CW show *Supernatural* (2005–2020), brothers Sam and Dean Winchester, monster hunters and the show's main characters, learn that hunting is not their only "family business."[1] It turns out they are also legacies of a defunct secret society called the Men of Letters. The Men of Letters were responsible for finding, collecting, and organizing information on supernatural beings of all kinds. Essentially, they were the librarians or archivists of all available knowledge concerning angels, demons, spirits, and monstrous beings. (Libraries and archives, archivists and librarians are frequently confused in *Supernatural*, but I will not belabor the point here. For an excellent discussion, see Karen Buckley, cited below.)

The Men of Letters collection resides in a hidden bunker which houses "every object, scroll, spell ever collected for thousands of years under one roof" ("As Time Goes By," 8.12).[2] The bunker becomes Sam and Dean's home and workplace, affording them ready access to this remarkable body of knowledge on the supernatural. At first Dean is dismissive, telling Sam "not to go all geek on this stuff…don't think [the Men of Letters] knew some big secrets that we don't know." But Sam understands its value: "I think we might have something here—something that could help us, help humanity" ("Everybody Hates Hitler," 8.13).

The importance of researching, of acquiring knowledge as an essential component of the monster hunter's toolkit, is introduced long before the Winchesters move into the Men of Letters' bunker. In the pilot episode of *Supernatural*, a scene in a Jericho, California public

---

[1] One of the most iconic lines in the show comes from the second episode of the series, "Wendigo." Referring to their father John and the journal he left behind, Dean tells Sam, "I think he wants us to pick up where he left off. You know, saving people, hunting things. The family business."

[2] Throughout this essay, episodes of *Supernatural* are designated by season, episode number within that season, and episode title. For episode synopses, transcripts, original air dates, writers, directors, cast and crew, I refer the reader to supernaturalwiki.com. It is inarguably the best online source for all things *Supernatural*.

library shows the brothers at a computer terminal looking for a case lead in the local newspaper. Dean, the older brother, is at the keyboard and having no success with his search terms. Sam pushes him out of the way, changes one word in the search, and up pops the relevant news item. This small gesture reflects the way the brothers are frequently portrayed throughout the series: Sam, who was an upperclassman at Stanford when he was pulled back into hunting by his brother, is the expert researcher…and his expertise includes using a microform reader, as we see in 1.18, "Something Wicked." Dean appreciates the necessity of understanding their prey but mostly wants to get to the monster killing. The bulk of figuring out which monster is doing the brain sucking, shapeshifting, possessing, savage clawing, or just plain eating of people falls to Sam.

"The Girl Next Door" (7.03) shows how far back Sam's role as the designated researcher goes. In flashback we see a 15-year-old Sammy on the phone with Dean. He has been helping Dean and their father identify a monster they are hunting. We hear only Sam's side of the conversation:

> SAM. Yeah, so, from what I can tell, it's something called a Kitsune. Not much. They…look human…till they sprout out claws and stab you behind your ear to get to your brain. I don't—I don't know yet. Yes, Dean, I realize killing 'em's important. Maybe if Uncle Bobby sent a book in English. I am! No, no, don't—don't put him on the phone. Hi, Dad. Yes, sir. I realize people are dying. Yeah, I'm on my way to the library right now.

Sam is burdened with the responsibility of keeping both his family and the public at large safe, not with fists or weapons (though he is skilled with those as well), but with his ability to find information. The public library to which Sam is headed, by the way, is in Lincoln, Nebraska. Sam finds the book he needs, which is notable because the characters in *Supernatural* nearly always find the books they need, no matter how small the library.

Sam's research skills help define his character and distinguish him from his brother—and sometimes, from other hunters. In "Metamorphosis" (4.04), for example, Sam and Dean join up with Travis for a rugaru hunt. The rugaru is a creature that starts off indistinguishable from a human, but at a certain age transforms into a human-flesh eating monster. Travis has a broken arm and needs the Winchesters to kill the as-yet untransformed creature by the only known method: fire. But Sam has some concerns.

> SAM [*to Travis*]. Not wasting any time, are you?
> TRAVIS. None to waste. The guy hulks out, we won't be finding bodies, just remains.

SAM. What if he doesn't hulk out? I did a little homework. Uh, I've been checking out the lore on rugarus.

TRAVIS. What, my 30 years of experience not good enough for you?

SAM. What? No. No, I—I—I just wanted to be prepared. I mean, not that you didn't.

DEAN. Sam loves research. He does. He keeps it under his mattress right next to his KY. It's a sickness.

Returning to the pilot episode (1.01), after finding their news item and chasing down the monster, the brothers check in to a motel where, it turns out, their father had also stayed. John Winchester's research covers the walls: an assortment of newspaper clippings, missing person flyers, a timeline of the murders, and notes and illustrations from the lore on various devils and witches. There is a lot more to the study of monster hunting than typing keywords at a library computer.

One reason that research is so important in *Supernatural* is that it was important to Eric Kripke, the show's creator and its showrunner for the first five years. As related by Executive Producer Robert Singer, "Eric [Kripke] was very specific about what he thought the show should be. Eric originally would say, 'You have to have Google-able monsters or Google-able urban legends'" (*Entertainment Weekly: The Ultimate Guide to Supernatural* 52). This was an early talking point for the actors as well. In an interview with Ellen DeGeneres that aired a week before *Supernatural* debuted, Jared Padalecki (Sam) said "What's great about the show…is that our show is about true urban legends…true folklore, and it's stuff that you can look up in Google and see Wendigo or Bloody Mary or the Hook Man legend. […] We're not just kind of making up stories…the writers are researching and Googling" (Padalecki).

Dean's forte is getting people to give him information through the use of his charm, good looks, and confident ability to lie. But when it comes to buckling down with a book—particularly those arcane volumes of occult lore—he typically approaches them grudgingly or out of sheer necessity. In "Shadow" (1.16) Dean charms a woman at the police department into giving him the complete records of two victims. Notably, in this episode Dean identifies a sigil. Sam asks how Dean figured out the sigil. Dean responds, "Give me some credit, man. You don't have a corner on paper chasing around here." But it turns out Dean has not chased any paper; he called another hunter.

When Sam and Dean separate to work different cases in "Scarecrow" (1.11), they have a phone conversation about the pagan god Dean is hunting. Sam tells Dean that when he figures out which god Dean is up against he'll be able to figure out how to kill it. Dean agrees. "I know," he tells his brother. "I'm actually on my way to a local community college. I've got an appointment with a professor. You know, since I don't have my trusty sidekick geek boy to do all the research."

In "The Monster at the End of this Book" (4.18) Sam and Dean resolve to do the exact opposite of what they normally would, trying to avoid a fate that has literally been written for them:

> DEAN. It's opposite day. It says that we, uh, we get into a fight. So, no fighting. No research for you...
> SAM. No bacon cheeseburger for you.

The most amusing example of Dean's aversion to hitting the books and Sam's reluctance to have fun occurs in "Changing Channels" (5.08), in which Sam and Dean are forced to take part in a series of television genre shows. The episode opens with Sam entering a set done up to look like the kitchen of a 1970s sitcom. Sam asks his brother whether he's done his research yet. Dean replies, "Oh, yeah. All kind of research. All night." Sam seems impressed until a scantily-clad young woman enters the set and says, "Oh Dean...We have some more research to do."

The information keepers used by the Winchesters can be sorted into three groups: the "civilian" world of libraries, records offices, and archives; the hunter world of arcane and occult literature, journaled experience, and passed-down wisdom; and the world of museum curators, local history buffs, and college professors. This last category contains people who are experts in their fields but have only an academic knowledge of their subjects; they have the rare books or cursed objects but don't actually believe in the supernatural creatures they study. As such, they are both civilians and cognoscenti.

In one of several instances where one or both Winchesters visit a college posing as students, Dean meets with a professor of Islamic studies in "What Is and What Should Never Be" (2.20). Their exchange is typical of the civilian-cognoscenti. Dean has asked the professor about Djinn:

> PROFESSOR. Well, a lot of Muslims believed the Djinn are very real. And they're mentioned in the Koran—
> DEAN. Yeah, yeah, yeah, yeah. I know. Get to the wish part.
> PROFESSOR. What about it?
> DEAN. Do you think they could really do it?
> PROFESSOR. Um...Uh, no. No, I don't think they can "really do it." You understand these are mythic creatures?

Hunters have their own libraries and their own guardians of knowledge. What Young Sam learned about Kitsune was no doubt entered in his father's journal. The brothers find their father John's journal (but not their father) in the pilot, and as we learn in the following episode, it is "Dad's single most valuable possession— everything he knows about every evil thing is in here" ("Wendigo,"

1.2). John Winchester's journal, a leather-bound book filled with notes, telegrams, sketches, newspaper clippings, and the characteristics, habits, and dietary preferences of all kinds of monsters, was a knowledge base upon which Sam and Dean relied for much of the early seasons of *Supernatural*. Nor was John the only hunter to keep a journal. As we learn in "Frontierland" (6.18), Sam and Dean's maternal grandfather, Samuel Campbell, had an underground library that included several volumes of hunters' journals, including one from Samuel Colt, the gunsmith. Information Sam and Dean find in Colt's journal help them defeat the monster of the week.

At the center of this information hub is the seasoned hunter Bobby Singer—the "Uncle Bobby" young Sam refers to in "The Girl Next Door." Bobby's collection of books on demons, monsters, pagan gods, and mythical creatures (who turn out to be not mythical after all), is perhaps second only to that in the Men of Letters bunker. But unlike the Men of Letters, Bobby has first-hand hunting experience and a wide network of contacts. He was a crucial source of information for Sam, Dean, and other hunters, as evidenced in the episode "Weekend at Bobby's" (6.04). In this episode we get a glimpse into Bobby Singer's busy life as a researcher, fake validator of hunters' fake identities, and hunter in his own right. Although he is in the middle of his own investigation and fielding calls from other hunters, when Dean calls to get "an ID ASAP" on a clawed creature that rips open its victims, Bobby surrounds himself with books and gets to work on the Winchesters' case. When hours of page-turning don't turn up anything from his own collection, he heads to the Sioux Falls University Library, only to find it closed...so Bobby breaks in and grabs the volume he needs.

Some suspension of disbelief is often required when it comes to watching the Winchesters do their research. One might have an easier time believing in ghosts and ghouls than in the possibility that even the smallest town's public library or community college seem always to have accurate books on the lore of assorted supernatural creatures. When we see Sam at the reader in "Something Wicked this Way Comes," he is finding newspaper articles related to their monster in different cities, years apart, going back to the 1890s...all on the same reel of microfilm. To be sure, there is very little relationship between the process of gathering information in the real world and in the world of *Supernatural*. As Karen Buckley notes, "in one episode alone ["Hook Man"] [Sam and Dean] access prison records, birth and death records, church ledgers, and cemetery and land records—all in a library setting" (98).

Of course, Sam and Dean also have access to the internet. As skilled researchers the brothers need to be able to determine the reliability of the sites they find on the web. Sam is seldom without his laptop, typing into Search the Web!, his search engine of choice. (With one regretable exception, *Supernatural* has resisted product placement, instead creating its own brands of beer, convenience stores, ubiquitous family restaurant chains, etc.) In "Hell House" (1.17), Sam and Dean are looking into a case about a possible malevolent spirit tied to an abandoned house. As they drive, Sam briefs Dean about the case. Dean thinks the "supernatural" incidents might be just pranks.

> SAM. Maybe, but I read a couple of the kids' firsthand accounts. They seemed pretty sincere.
> DEAN. Where'd you read these accounts?
> SAM. Well, I knew we were going to be passing through Texas. So, umm, last night, I surfed some local paranormal websites. And I found one.
> DEAN. And what's it called?
> SAM. HellHoundsLair.com.
> DEAN. Lemme guess, streaming live out of Mom's basement.
> SAM. Yeah, probably.
> DEAN. Yeah. Most of those websites wouldn't know a ghost if it bit 'em in the persqueeter.

Firewalls, encryption, and privacy policies do not seem to present much of an obstacle to Sam, Dean, and other hunters. Even before learning a few tricks from master hacker Charlie Bradbury, a recurring character introduced in season 7, Sam is able to look for tax records and addresses online ("The Monster at the End of this Book," 4.18) and somehow pull up medical records ("Heartache," 8.03). Their grandfather Samuel Campbell is able to access a home security company's client records despite very limited computing experience ("Two and a Half Men," 6.02). As is the case when considering Sam's other research skills, it's best not to expect a fictional world to follow reality's rules.

"Everybody Hates Hitler" (8.13) begins in the library of the newly discovered Men of Letters bunker and then immediately cuts to a scene in an academic library, where Rabbi Bass, a frequent patron judging by his interactions with the librarian, asks to see a particular manuscript. He is brought to a small interior room where he dons his white cotton gloves as a staff member brings him the box containing the item. Never mind that the "manuscript" is a ledger and that the Rabbi is permitted to take it out of the "special reference section." Knowing he is about to be killed, the Rabbi calls his grandson and has him write down a series of numbers and letters…which Sam immediately recognizes as a Library of Congress call number! And he knows it refers to ornithology, even though his major was pre-law. Sam's uncanny familiarity with the LC classification system leads him and Dean to where the Rabbi has hidden the ledger.

Despite playing a bit fast and loose with the normal practices of archival collections and Sam's dubious ability to remember call numbers more than eight years after leaving university, library design in *Supernatural* can be very realistic. For the episode "Book of the Damned" (10.18), set designer Jerry Wanek took great pains to build an accurate small library, albeit pre-computerized catalog era. There are several stacks of books, a card catalog, a dictionary on a stand, books with Dewey numbers, a reading table, and even another room visible through partly glass doors. In a video posted by actor Misha Collins (Castiel) in advance of the episode, Wanek explains,

> Because we couldn't find a library cool enough to shoot in the flavor of our lovely *Supernatural*, we built one. This library contains more than 20,000 books, all bought from resale, and each one has to be labelled and put into the proper category [...] and then the bookshelves also were all custom built [...]. This set will be exactly one day's worth of shooting and we spent seven days to build it. ("Getting literate on the set of Supernatural")

What's more, the set appears on screen for a total of around five minutes and is largely destroyed in two seconds. Sadly, the reason for constructing this library was to have a place where Metatron could hide something from Castiel; as Metatron says, "Nobody goes to libraries anymore. It's the safest place in the world" ("The Book of the Damned," 10.18).

Metatron's comment aside, as a series, *Supernatural* displays the proper reverence towards libraries and archives. Librarians and archivists, not so much. The title of this essay comes from episode 6.17, "My Heart Will Go On." History has been changed by the angel Balthazar, and Sam and Dean are on the hunt for Fate, who is trying to set things right. Sam spots her: a petite blonde woman in glasses, button-down shirt, and tweedy blazer carrying a leather-bound book with embossed cover and gilt-edged pages.

> DEAN. What'd she look like?
> SAM. Kind of like a librarian.
> DEAN. Your kind of librarian or my kind of librarian?
> SAM. Well, she was wearing clothes, if that's what you mean.

Sam and Dean are referencing two common female librarian stereotypes: the prim, proper cardigan-clad, shushing spinster on the one hand, and on the other, the one who takes off her glasses, lets down her hair, and turns into the librarian of sexual fantasy.

Supernatural's writers cling to unflattering stereotypes of librarians and library staff for much of the show's run. The librarian in "Everybody Hates Hitler" is a man so uptight and self-righteous that the Rabbi tells him, in Yiddish, that he hopes he's paid well to keep that stick up his *tuchas*. Young Sam is shushed by a large cardigan-clad, hair-bunned, date-stamp wielding librarian in "The Girl Next Door." Also wearing a cardigan, sensible shoes, and her hair in a bun is the public librarian Marjorie Willis in "Repo Man" (7.15), who Lucifer notes is an "indoor gardening enthusiast" in a way that suggests "lonely spinster." Sam believes she is the next victim of the killer they are hunting, so when a young man in a black leather jacket follows Marjorie into the stacks, Sam investigates. Instead of finding Marjorie in danger, though, he finds her making out with the young man while panting "Right here in my discontinued periodicals. Oh. Oh, that's it." Marjorie starts out as the stereotypical bookish librarian but turns into the pornographic librarian trope. Even when the librarian is young, attractive, and knowledgeable as is the one in "Southern Comfort" (8.06), she's still sporting a cardigan and an air of sobriety. Finally, in season 14, air date November 29, 2018, Harper, a beautiful librarian, is in her early 20s, smiling, and cardigan-free ("Optimism," 14.06). She is clearly not lonely and is the object of at least three men's desire. She is neither Sam nor Dean's kind of librarian. She is central to the plot and not there merely to provide a visual gag. Unfortunately, she is also the monster of the week.

The air date of "Optimism" may be significant in that, in a show running for 15 years, writers, directors, and show runners change; times change, and with them, in an ideal world, stereotypes fade away. The amount of time Sam and Dean spend researching in libraries (apart from the one in the Men of Letters bunker), seems also to have declined over the years, as might be expected. For one thing, much more information is available on the internet now than when *Supernatural* began, in 2005. But there is another possibility for the decline in the Winchesters' use of libraries. Recall that Eric Kripke, *Supernatural's* creator, wanted the show's monsters to come from urban legends and lore. But, as Robert Singer noted, "We quickly realized we were going to run out of good urban legends in a hurry" (Highfill). Angels were introduced to the show in its fourth season, and with them story arcs revolving around Heaven, Hell, and Purgatory—or what the fandom calls "angel-demon drama." Often the writers created or reimagined interesting foes for Sam and Dean to fight, but there was much greater reliance on witches, vampires, and werewolves.

Ending where we began, in Sam and Dean's inherited bunker, score one for the librarians. In "Slumber Party" (9.04), the character Dorothy dismisses the Men of Letters as glorified librarians. Charlie Bradbury responds, "Hey, these guys may have been sexist, but like all librarians, they were wicked smart, too."[3]

Works Cited

"As Time Goes By." *Supernatural*, created by Eric Kripke, season 8, episode 12, CW Television Network, 30 Jan. 2013.

"Book of the Damned." *Supernatural*, created by Eric Kripke, season 10, episode 18, CW Television Network, 15 Apr. 2015.

Buckley, Karen. "'The Truth Is in the Red Files': An Overview of Archives in Popular Culture." *Archivaria*, vol. 66, no. 0, 2008, pp. 95–123.

"Changing Channels." *Supernatural*, created by Eric Kripke, season 5, episode 8, CW Television Network, 5 Nov. 2009.

Entertainment Weekly: The Ultimate Guide to Supernatural. Time Inc. Books, 2017.

"Everybody Hates Hitler." *Supernatural*, created by Eric Kripke, season 8, episode 13, CW Television Network, 6 Feb. 2013.

"Frontierland." *Supernatural*, created by Eric Kripke, season 6, episode 18, CW Television Network, 22 Apr. 2011.

"The Girl Next Door." *Supernatural*, created by Eric Kripke, season 7, episode 3, CW Television Network, 7 Oct. 2011.

"Heartache." *Supernatural*, created by Eric Kripke, season 8, episode 3, CW Television Network, 17 Oct. 2012.

"Hell House." *Supernatural*, created by Eric Kripke, season 1, episode 17, WB Television Network, 30 Mar. 2006.

Highfill, Samantha. "*Supernatural*: Boss Robert Singer Talks Ditched Jumanji-Style Episode." *EW*, 16 Sept. 2016, ew.com/article/2016/09/16/supernatural-robert-singer-jumanji-style-episode.

"Hook Man." *Supernatural*, created by Eric Kripke, season 1, episode 7, WB Television Network, 25 Oct. 2005.

"Metamorphosis." *Supernatural*, created by Eric Kripke, season 4, episode 4, CW Television Network, 9 Oct. 2008.

---

[3] I refer the reader curious about the episodes referenced within to supernaturalwiki.com. There can be found complete information about the cast, writers, directors and original air dates of each episode, as well as a summary and transcript. At the time of this writing, all seasons of *Supernatural* are available to be streamed on Netflix.

"The Monster at the End of this Book." *Supernatural,* created by Eric Kripke, season 4, episode 18, CW Television Network, 2 Apr. 2009.

"My Heart Will Go On." *Supernatural,* created by Eric Kripke, season 6, episode 17, CW Television Network, 15 Apr. 2011.

"Optimism." *Supernatural,* created by Eric Kripke, season 14, episode 6, CW Television Network, 15 Nov. 2018.

Padalecki, Jared, guest. *The Ellen DeGeneres Show,* season 3, episode 20, 30 Sept. 2005, YouTube, youtu.be/-SfTj0Cahx8.

"[Pilot]." *Supernatural,* created by Eric Kripke, season 1, episode 1, WB Television Network, 13 Sept. 2005.

"Repo Man." *Supernatural,* created by Eric Kripke, season 7, episode 15, CW Television Network, 17 Feb. 2012.

"Scarecrow." *Supernatural,* created by Eric Kripke, season 1, episode 11, WB Television Network, 1 Jan. 2006.

"Shadow." *Supernatural,* created by Eric Kripke, season 1, episode 16, WB Television Network, 28 Feb. 2006.

"Slumber Party." *Supernatural,* created by Eric Kripke, season 9, episode 4, CW Television Network, 29 Oct. 2013.

"Something Wicked." *Supernatural,* created by Eric Kripke, season 1, episode 18, WB Television Network, 6 Apr. 2006.

"Southern Comfort." *Supernatural,* created by Eric Kripke, season 8, episode 6, CW Television Network, 7 Nov. 2012.

"Two and a Half Men." *Supernatural,* created by Eric Kripke, season 6, episode 2, CW Television Network, 1 Oct. 2010.

"Getting literate on the set of *Supernatural.*" YouTube, uploaded by Misha Collins, 24 Feb. 2015, youtu.be/PYK8Z0f9ct0.

"Weekend at Bobby's." *Supernatural,* created by Eric Kripke, season 6, episode 4, CW Television Network, 15 Oct. 2010.

"Wendigo." *Supernatural,* created by Eric Kripke, season 1, episode 2, WB Television Network, 20 Sept. 2005.

"What Is and What Should Never Be." *Supernatural,* created by Eric Kripke, season 2, episode 20, CW Television Network, 3 May 2007.

Curriculum Vitae

Last updated September 2016

David Dean Oberhelman
W. P. Wood Professor of Library Service
306 Edmon Low Library
Oklahoma State University Library
Stillwater, OK 74078
Tel.: (405) 741–9773 | Fax: (405) 741–7579
E-mail: d.oberhelman@okstate.edu

Education
University of Pittsburgh: M.L.I.S., Library and Information Science, 1997.

University of California, Irvine: Ph.D., English w/Emphasis in Critical Theory, 1993. Dissertation: *Mad Encounters: British Psychological Medicine and the Novel, 1840–1870*; Advisor: J. Hillis Miller.

University of California, Irvine: M.A., English, 1989.

Rice University: B.A., English, 1987 (*Summa Cum Laude*).

Employment
Oklahoma State University Library—Research and Learning Services, Academic Librarian Liaison Group, 2015–Present.; Humanities-Social Sciences Division, 1997–2014.

W. P. Wood Professor of Library Service, 2013–Present; Professor, 2010–Present; Associate Professor, 2002–2010 (w/ tenure conferred, 2002); Assistant Professor, 1997–2002.

Academic Liaison for English (British/American Literature, Linguistics, TESL, Rhetoric & Composition, Professional Writing, & Film/Screen Studies), Foreign Languages & Literature, History, Music, & Theatre.

Instruction Services Functional Specialist Group, 2015–Present.

Lead Instructor/Coordinator for Library Science (LBSC) 1011 credit course, 1999–2015.

Texas Tech University—Department of English

Visiting Assistant Professor of English, 1993–1995.

University of California, Irvine—Department of English and Comparative Literature

Teaching Assistant/Associate, 1988–1993.

Regents' Irvine Fellowship Graduate Assistant, 1987–1990.

Publications
Book

Oberhelman, David. *Dickens in Bedlam: Madness and Restraint in his Fiction*. Fredericton, New Brunswick: York Press, 1995.

Edited Book

The Intersection of Fantasy and Native America: From H. P. Lovecraft to Leslie Marmon Silko. Amy H. Sturgis and David D. Oberhelman, eds. Altadena, CA: The Mythopoeic Press, 2009.

Book Chapters & Contributions

Oberhelman, David D., Andrew Wadoski, and Sarah Coates. "Okstate Shakespeare: Bringing Special Collections and Digital Humanities into the Undergraduate Classroom." In *Collaborating for Impact: Special Collections and Liaison Librarian Partnerships.* Eds. Kristen Totleben and Lori Birrell. Chicago: Association of College and Research Libraries, 2016.

Oberhelman, David D. "Distant Reading, Computational Stylistics, and Corpus Linguistics: The Critical Theory of Digital Humanities for Literature Subject Librarians." In *Digital Humanities and Libraries: Challenges & Opportunities for Subject Librarians.* Eds. Laura Braunstein, Liorah Golomb, and Arianne Hartsell-Gundy. Chicago: Association of College and Research Libraries, 2015. 53–66. [Refereed chapter]

Oberhelman, David D. "From Iberian to Ibran and Catholic to Quintarian: Lois McMaster Bujold's Alternate History of the Spanish Reconquest in the Chalion Series." *Lois McMaster Bujold: Essays on a Modern Master of Science Fiction and Fantasy.* Ed. Janet Brennan Croft. Jefferson, NC: McFarland, 2013. 159–71.

Oberhelman, David D. "'Out of the Unknown Past into the Unknown Future': Information Technology and Degradation in H. G. Wells's *The Time Machine.*" *Presentations of the 2010 Upstate Steampunk Extravaganza and Meetup.* Ed. Gypsey Elaine Teague. Newcastle, UK: Cambridge Scholars Publishing, 2011. 33–44.

Oberhelman, David D. "'Coming to America': Fantasy and Native America Explored, an Introduction." *The Intersection of Fantasy and Native America: From H. P. Lovecraft to Leslie Marmon Silko.* Eds. Amy H. Sturgis and David D. Oberhelman. Altadena, CA: The Mythopoeic Press, 2009. iii–vii.

Oberhelman, David D. "A Brief History of Libraries in Middle-earth: Manuscript and Book Repositories in Tolkien's Legendarium." *Truths Breathed Through Silver: The Inklings' Moral and Mythopoeic Legacy.* Ed. Jonathan B. Himes. Newcastle, UK: Cambridge Scholars Publishing, 2008. 81–92. [Peer-Reviewed Book Article]

Oberhelman, David D. "Angband," "Class in Tolkien's Work," "Hierarchy," "J. M. Barrie," "Justice/Injustice," "Marxist Readings of Tolkien," "Oral Tradition," "Philippa Boyens," "Possessiveness," "Textual History: Errors and Emendations," "Towers," and "Valinor." *J. R. R. Tolkien Encyclopedia: Scholarship and Critical Assessment.* Ed. Michael D. C. Drout. New York: Routledge, 2007.

Peer-Reviewed Literary Journal Articles

Oberhelman, David. "Trollope's Insanity Defense: Narrative Alienation in *He Knew He Was Right*." *SEL: Studies in English Literature, 1500–1900* 35 (1995): 789–806.

Oberhelman, David. "*Waverley*, Genealogy, History: Scott's Romance of Fathers and Sons." *Nineteenth-Century Contexts* 15 (1991): 29–47. Reprinted in *Nineteenth-Century Literature Criticism*, v. 110. Detroit: Gale, 2002. 285–92.

Oberhelman, David. "An Encounter at Sais: The Masks of Melville and Nietzsche." *Lamar Journal of the Humanities* 8 (1987): 17–31.

Invited & Other Library Journal Articles

Oberhelman, David D. "Lights, Catalogs, Archives!: A Selected Annotated List of Web Resources for Film and Television Studies." *Reference Reviews* 28.1 (2014): 2–5.

Oberhelman, David D. "Alexandria, the World Brain, and the Universal Digital Library: Beyond the Google Books Settlement." *Reference Reviews* 25.8 (2011).

Oberhelman, David D. "Rekindling Reference?: E-Book Readers and Reference Collections." *Reference Reviews* 25.1 (2011): 5–7.

Oberhelman, David D. "Coming to Terms with Web 2.0." *Reference Reviews* 21.7 (2007): 5–6.

Oberhelman, David D. "Search Interfaces Revisited: The End of Native Interfaces?" *Reference Reviews* 21.5 (2007): 6–7.

Oberhelman, David D. "Reference Service and Resources in the Age of Instant Messaging" *Reference Reviews* 21.2 (2007): 7–8.

Oberhelman, David D. "OCLC Report on College Student Perceptions." *Reference Reviews* 20.8 (2006): 3.

Oberhelman, David D. "The Time Machine: Federated Searching Today and Tomorrow." *Reference Reviews* 20.3 (2006): 6–8.

Oberhelman, David D. "Google Scholar." *Reference Reviews* 19.8 (2005): 3–4.

Oberhelman, David D. "On Navigating Labyrinths and Webs: Print and the Internet as Institutions of Research." *Against the Grain* 14.6 (December/January 2002–2003): 24–27.

Newsletter Articles

Oberhelman, David D. "THATCamp Comes to the OSU Library." *Oklahoma Librarian* 66 (3) 2016: 63.

Oberhelman, David D. and Marcus Richter. "Cultural Heritage and Social Technology" [Report on Embedded Cultural Communities Program at ALA 2014.] *College & Research Library News* 75.8 (September 2014): 456–57.
http://crln.acrl.org/content/75/8/449.full.pdf+html

Oberhelman, David D. "The Literary Text and the Library in the Digital Age." [ALA 2013 Conference Program Report] *College & Research Libraries News* 74.8 (September 2013): 443–44.

Oberhelman, David D. "Notes on the MLA Libraries and Research in Languages and Literatures' 2013 Panel: 'How Many Copies is Enough? Too Many? Libraries and Shared Monograph Archives'." *Biblio-Notes* #61 (Spring 2013): 12–14. http://www.ala.org/acrl/sites/ala.org.acrl/files/content/aboutacrl/directoryofleadership/sections/les/biblionotes51/biblionotes61.pdf

Oberhelman, David D. "Hands-on from Chaucer to Prufrock: The 2009 LES Field Trip to the University of Chicago." *Biblio-Notes* #54 (Fall 2009): 3–4. http://www.ala.org/ala/mgrps/divs/acrl/about/sections/les/biblionotes51/BiblioNotes54.pdf

Oberhelman, David D. "Stillwater Libraries Remember the Dust Bowl and the WPA." *Oklahoma Librarian* 59.2 (March/April 2009): 9.

Oberhelman, David D., Barbara Miller, and Helen Clements. "Need Library-Oriented In-Service Training at Your High School *Oklahoma Librarian* 57.4 (July/August 2007): 33.

Oberhelman, David D. "Leading the Way" (Report on 2001 OLA Leadership Retreat). *Oklahoma Librarian* 51.4 (2001): 40–41.

Oberhelman, David D. Ethics Committee Report. *Oklahoma Librarian* 48.5 (September/Oct. 1998): 52.

Book Reviews

Enciclopedia del Románico en Cataluña [Encyclopedia of the Romanesque in Catalonia], *RREA (Reference Reviews Europe Annual)* 21/22 (2016). [Forthcoming]

The Latin American Story Finder. Ed. Sharon Barcan Elswit. *Oklahoma Librarian* 65.6 (2015).

Dicionário de etnologia angolana [Ethnographic Dictionary of Angola]. *RREA (Reference Reviews Europe Annual)* 19/20 (2015). [Forthcoming]

Diccionario histórico de la traducción en Hispanoamérica [Historical Dictionary of Translation in Hispanic America]. *RREA (Reference Reviews Europe Annual)* 19/20 (2015). [Forthcoming]

Virtually Embedded: The Librarian in an Online Environment. Reference & User Services Quarterly 58.1 (Summer 2014): 58–59.

The University of Chicago Spanish-English Dictionary (6th Ed.). *Reference Reviews* 28.3 (2014): 33.

Jasanoff, Sheila. *Science and Reason. Government Information Quarterly* 31.2 (2014): 347.

Diccionario ilustrado de símbolos del nacionalismo vasco [Dictionary of Symbols of Basque Nationalism]. *RREA (Reference Reviews Europe Annual)* 17 (2013) [2014].

Dicionário do cinema português, 1895–1961 [*Dictionary of Portuguese Cinema, 1895–1961*]. *RREA (Reference ReviewsEurope Annual)* 17 (2013) [2014]. [Forthcoming]

Woodward, Jeanette. *The Library Transformed: E-Books, Expertise, and Evolution. Internet Reference Services Quarterly* 18.2 (2013): 173–74.

Davis, Anita Price. *The Margaret Mitchell Encyclopedia*. *Reference Reviews* 27.8 (2013): 23–24.

Encyclopedia of the Environment in American Literature. *Reference Reviews* 27.7 (2013): 34.

Murphy, Joe. *Location-Aware Services and QR Codes for Libraries*. *Internet Reference Services Quarterly* 18.1 (2013).

Diccionario del cine iberoamericano: España, Portugal, y América [*Dictionary of Iberoamerican Cinema: Spain, Portugal, and America*]. *RREA (Reference Reviews Europe Annual)* 16 (2011) [2013]: 117–18.

Diccionario crítico de directoras de cine europeas [*Critical Dictionary of Female Directors of European Cinema*]. *RREA (Reference Reviews Europe Annual)* 16 (2011) [2013]: 111–13.

Justice, Daniel Heath. *The Way of Thorn and Thunder*. *Studies in American Indian Literatures (SAIL)* 25.3 (2013): 118–20. [Invited]

Olsen, Cory. *Exploring J. R. R. Tolkien's The Hobbit*. *Mythprint: The Monthly Bulletin of the Mythopoeic Society*. 49.9/#362 (September 2012): 10.

Terrance, Vincent. *Encyclopedia of Television Shows, 1925–2010* (2nd Ed). *Reference Reviews* 26.6 (2012): 52–53.

Chen, Fanfan and Thomas Honegger, eds. *Good Dragons are Rare: An Inquiry into Literary Dragons East and West*. *Mythlore: A Journal of J. R. R. Tolkien, C. S. Lewis, Charles Williams, and Mythopoeic Literature* 30:3/4 (2012): 137–39.

Matthews, Patricia O'Brien. *Fang-tastic Fiction: Twenty-first Century Paranormal Reads*. *Oklahoma Librarian*. 62.2 (March/April 2012): 52. http://publications.oklibs.org/ index.php/oklibrarian/article/view/167/164

Hisack, Thomas H. *Disney Voice Actors: A Biographical Dictionary*. *Reference Reviews* 26.2 (2012): 46.

Sullivan, C. W. III. *Heinlein's Juvenile Novels: A Cultural Dictionary*. *Reference Reviews* 26.2 (2012): 31.

Ferreras, Juan Ignacio. *La novela en España: Católogo de novelas y novelistas*. [*The Novel in Spain: Catalog of Novels and Novelists*]. *RREA (Reference Reviews Europe Annual)* 15 (2009 [2012]): 113–15.

Enciclopedia da música em Portugal no século XX [*Encyclopedia of Music in Portugal in the 20th Century*]. *RREA (Reference Reviews Europe Annual)* 15 (2009 [2012]): 135–37.

Enciclopedia del español en los Estados Unidos [*Encyclopedia of Spanish in the United States*]. *RREA (Reference Reviews Europe Annual)* 15 (2009 [2012]): 99–100.

Latham, Bethany. *Elizabeth I on Film and Television*. *Reference Reviews* 26.1 (2012): 44.

Foster, Allan. *Sherlock Holmes and Conan Doyle Locations: A Visitor's Guide*. *Reference Reviews* 25.6 (2011): 33–34.

McVicker, Mary F. *Women Composers of Classical Music*. *Reference Reviews* 25.5 (2011): 54–55.

Before (During) After: Louisiana Photographers' Visual Reaction to Hurricane Katrina." Oklahoma Librarian. 61.2 (March/April 2011): 42.

Diccionario fraseológico del Siglo de Oro: Fraseología o estilística castellana [Phraseological Dictionary of the (Seventeenth-Century) Golden Age: Spanish Phraseology or Stylistics]. RREA (Reference Reviews Europe Annual) 14 (2008 [2011]): 78–79. http://rre.casalini.it/2008/bc-08.htm

The Chicago Manual of Style, 16th Ed./*The Chicago Manual of Style Online. Reference Reviews* 25.1 (2011): 8.

Prinzi, Travis. *Harry Potter & Imagination: The Way Between Two Worlds. Mythlore: A Journal of J. R. R. Tolkien, C. S. Lewis, Charles Williams, and Mythopoeic Literature* #111/112. 29.1/2 (Fall/Winter 2010): 186–89.

Gale, Robert L. *Truman Capote Encyclopedia. Reference Reviews* 24.8 (2010): 36.

Morgan, Phyllis S. *N. Scott Momaday: Remembering Ancestors, Earth, and Traditions: A Bio-Bibliography. Oklahoma Librarian* 60.6 (November/December 2010): 47.

Warren, Bill. *Keep Watching the Skies!: American Science Fiction Movies of the Fifties. 21st-Century Edition. Reference Reviews* 24.7 (2010): 50–51.

Tolkien, Hilary. *Black & White Ogre Country: The Lost Tales of Hilary Tolkien. Mythprint: The Monthly Bulletin of the Mythopoeic Society* 47.9 (2010): 8.

Adams, Jerome R. *Liberators and Patriots of Latin America,* 2nd ed. *Reference Reviews* 24.6 (2010): 52–53.

Wilhite, Jeffrey R. *A Chronology of Librarianship, 1960–2000. Oklahoma Librarian* 60.3 (2010): 23.

Gray, William. *Death in Fantasy: Essays on Philip Pullman, C. S. Lewis, George MacDonald, and R. L. Stevenson. Mythlore: A Journal of J. R. R. Tolkien, C. S. Lewis, Charles Williams, and Mythopoeic Literature* #109/110. 28.1/2 (Spring/Summer 2010): 198–99.

Zemboy, James. *The Detective Novels of Agatha Christie. Reference Reviews* 23.7 (2009). 24–25.

Quay, Sarah E. and Gabrielle Watling, eds. *Cultural History of Reading." Oklahoma Librarian* 59.4 (2009): 29.

Keaney, Michael F. *British Film Noir Guide. Reference Reviews* 23.2 (2009): 43.

Eason, Cassandra. *Fabulous Creatures, Mythical Monsters, and Animal Power Symbols. Oklahoma Librarian* 58.4 (July/August 2008): 22.

Wiegand, Shirley A. and Wayne A. Wiegand. *Books on Trial: Red Scare in the Heartland." Oklahoma Librarian* 58.1 (January/February 2008): 4.

Lowitt, Ricard. *American Outback: The Oklahoma Panhandle in the Twentieth Century. Oklahoma Librarian* 58.3 (May/June 2008): 22.

Turner, Allan, ed. *The Silmarillion — Thirty Years On. Mythprint: The Monthly Bulletin of the Mythopoeic Society* 45.4 (2008): 5.

Glyer, Diana. *The Company They Keep: C. S. Lewis and J. R. R. Tolkien as Writers in Community. Mythprint: The Monthly Bulletin of the Mythopoeic Society* 44.5 (May 2007): 3–4.

Scull, Christina and Wayne G. Hammond. *J. R. R. Tolkien Companion and Guide.*

Mythlore: A Journal of J. R. R. Tolkien, C. S. Lewis, Charles Williams, and Mythopoeic Literature #97/98. 25.3/4 (Spring/Summer 2007): 183–85.

Gothic Literature: A Literary Companion. Reference Reviews 21.2 (2007): 27–28.

Encyclopedia of the Enlightenment (Revised Edition). *Reference Reviews* 19.2 (2005): 49.

Historical Dictionary of Science Fiction Literature. Reference Reviews 19.1 (2005): 36–37.

Reference Guide to Science Fiction, Fantasy, and Horror (2nd Ed.). *Reference Reviews* 17.5 (2003): 43–44.

Database/Web Resource Reviews

Confidential Print: Latin America, 1833–1969 [Adam Matthew]. *Reference Reviews* 27.6 (2013): 47–48.

Early American Imprints Series II: Supplement from the Library Company of Philadelphia [Readex-Newsbank]. *Reference Reviews* 26.8 (2012): 10.

Romanticism Redefined [Alexander Street Press]. *Reference Reviews* 26.7 (2012): 41–42.

Moving Image Source. *Reference Reviews* 26.6 (2012): 54–55.

Arte Público Hispanic Historical Collection: Series 1 [EBSCOhost]. *Reference Reviews* 25.8 (2011): 52–53.

Quijote Interactivo [Interactive Quixote]. *Reference Reviews* 25.5 (2011): 33.

The American West: Sources from the Everett D. Graff Collection of Western Americana at the Newberry Library, Chicago [Adam Matthew Digital]. *Reference Reviews* 24.5 (2010): 67–68.

Victorian Popular Culture. *Reference Reviews* 24.2 (2010): 66–67.

Electronic Enlightenment. *Reference Reviews* 23.6 (2009): 14.

Cambridge Companions Complete Collections. *Reference Reviews* 22.5 (2008): 7–8.

The Literary Encyclopedia. *Reference Reviews* 22.3 (2008): 126.

Google Book Search. *Reference Reviews* 22.3 (2008): 103.

Past Masters: Romantic Era [Intelex]. *Reference Reviews* 21.8 (2007): 385.

Digital Roman Forum. *Reference Reviews* 21.7 (2007): 350.

Biography Index: Past & Present. *Reference Reviews* 21.2 (2007): 60.

Film Literature Index Online. *Reference Reviews* 20.8 (2006): 44–45.

Early American Imprints II: Shaw-Shoemaker. *Reference Reviews* 19.7 (2005): 10–11.

Latino Literature (LALI) [Alexander Street Press]. *Reference Reviews* 19.2 (2005): 36.

Liddell-Scott-Jones Greek-English Lexicon. *Reference Reviews* 18.5 (2004): 30–31.

Internet Library of Early Journals. *Reference Reviews* 18.3 (2004): 8–9.

Consulta [Gale Group]. *Reference Reviews* 18.1 (2004): 6.

Times Digital Archive, 1785–1985 (Gale Group). *Reference Reviews* 17.1 (2003): 43–44.

Wright American Fiction Collection. *Reference Reviews* 16.7 (2002): 22.

Annual Egyptological Bibliography. *Reference Reviews* 15.7 (2001): 49.

Stanford Encyclopedia of Philosophy. *Reference Reviews* 15.6 (2001): 9.

Universal Survey of Languages. *Electronic Resources Review* 4.10 (2000): 130–31. Web. *EmeraldInsight.*

New Grove Dictionary of Opera Online. *Electronic Resources Review* 4.5 (2000): 38–39. Web. *EmeraldInsight.*

English Server Drama Collection. *Electronic Resources Review* 4.1–2 (2000): 3–4.

Éclat! The Essential Comparative Literature and Theory Site. *Electronic Resources Review* 3.11 (1999): 127–28.

Victorian Web. *Electronic Resources Review* 3.6 (1999): 68–69.

University of Michigan Humanities Text Initiative American Verse Project. *Electronic Resources Review* 3.4 (1999).

Project Open Book. *Electronic Resources Review* 2.12 (1998).

The Comprehensive Shakespeare Dictionary. *Electronic Resources Review* 2.9 (1998).

The Pompeii Forum Project. *Electronic Resources Review* 2.7 (1998). Web. *EmeraldInsight.*

Text Encoding Initiative. *Electronic Resources Review* 2.7 (1998). Web. *EmeraldInsight.*

Archives and Museum Informatics. *Electronic Resources Review* 2.5 (1998). Web. *EmeraldInsight.*

The WebMuseum, Paris. *Electronic Resources Review* 2.4 (1998). Web. *EmeraldInsight.*

The Vergil Project. *Electronic Resources Review* 2.3 (1998). Web. *EmeraldInsight.*

Editorships & Editorial Service

Book Prospectus Reviewer for Modern Language Association 2016.

Peer Reviewer for Chandos Publishing/Elsevier (book proposal), 2016.

Peer Reviewer for *Reference Reviews*, 2015–Present.

Referee for *Mythlore: A Journal of J. R. R. Tolkien, C. S. Lewis, Charles Williams, and Mythopoeic Literature*, 2011–Present.

Editorial Advisory Board Member for *Reference Reviews* (Emerald Publishing, Ltd.), 2012–Present.

North American Regional Editor of *Reference Reviews*, 2004–2012.

Secretary [Manager] of the Mythopoeic Press, 2006–2010; Member, Mythopoeic Press Advisory

Board, 2011–Present. [See *Mythopoeic Society* activities]

Papers & Presentations

International- & National-Level Library Presentations

Moderator, "Topics in European Studies." Paper Session at ACRL Western European Studies Section Research & Planning Meeting. American Library Association Annual Conference, Orlando, FL, June 25, 2016.

Convener/Moderator, Modern Language Association (MLA) International Bibliography in Academic Libraries Discussion Group Meeting. Discussion and Panel Session at the American Library Association Annual Conference, Orlando, FL, June 25, 2016.

Panel Organizer/Co-Presider, "The Evolving Scholarly Record." Panel Discussion Session at the Modern Language Association Convention, Austin, TX, January 9, 2016.

Moderator, "Topics in European Studies." Paper Session at ACRL Western European Studies Section Research & Planning Meeting. American Library Association Annual Conference, San Francisco, CA, June 27, 2015.

Convener/Moderator, Modern Language Association (MLA) International Bibliography in Academic Libraries Discussion Group Meeting. Discussion and Panel Session at the American Library Association Midwinter Meeting, Chicago, IL, January 30, 2015.

Panel Organizer/Presider/Respondent, "Libraries, Archives, and Public Memory." Paper Session at the Modern Language Association Convention, Vancouver, BC, Canada, January 8, 2015.

Convener/Moderator, Modern Language Association (MLA) International Bibliography in Academic Libraries Discussion Group Meeting. Discussion and Panel Session at the American Library Association Midwinter Meeting, Philadelphia, PA, January 25, 2014.

Panel Organizer/Presider, "How Many Copies is Enough, Too Many? Libraries and Shared Monograph Archives." Panel Session at the Modern Language Association Convention, Boston, MA, January 4, 2013.

Presentation on LibGuides for Shakespeare and the History of Printing for Association of College & Research Libraries Literatures in English Section Online Membership Forum, December 5, 2011.

"A Noteworthy Partnership: Library-Music Department Programming Collaborations at Oklahoma State University." Presentation at the National Popular Culture Association/American Culture Association & Southwest/Texas Popular Culture Association/ American Culture Association Joint Conference, San Antonio, TX, April 21, 2011.

"Talking Theory: Deconstruction." Panel Presentation on Literary Theory for Literature Librarians, Association of College & Research Libraries Literatures in English Section Membership Forum, American Library Association Annual Conference, Anaheim, CA, June 28, 2008.

"National Library Camp." Presentation with Sharon Saulmon on the OLA Information Matrix Camp by invitation of American Library Association President Loriene Roy. American Library Association Annual Conference, Anaheim, CA, June 28, 2008.

Poster: "They're Not in Kansas Anymore: Information Literacy Programming for High School Faculty to Help Students Transition to College." Presentation with Helen Clements and Barbara Miller. American Library Association Annual Conference, Anaheim, CA, June 28, 2008.

Poster: "Reforging the Canon: Collection Development and Assessment in English at Oklahoma State University," American Library Association Annual Conference, Chicago, IL, July 9, 2000.

Poster: "Chalk on the Sidewalk and Other Marketing Strategies for a One Credit Hour Library Skills Class." Presentation with Peggy M. Wolfe. American Library Association Annual Conference, New Orleans, LA, June 28, 1999.

Poster: "The New LIBSC 1011: Retooling a One Credit-Hour Library Skills Course for the New Millennium." Presentation with Peggy M. Wolfe. American Library Association Annual Conference, Washington, DC, June 28, 1998.

"Wouldn't You Rather Be in the Library?: Teaching Library Research Skills in the Information Age." Presentation at National Student Success Conference, Kansas City, MO, April 1, 1998.

International- & National-Level Literary/Humanities Papers & Presentations

Mythopoeic Fantasy and Scholarship Award Discussion (Moderator) and Presentation. 47th Mythopoeic Society Conference, San Antonio, TX, August 7, 2016.

Mythopoeic Fantasy and Scholarship Award Presentation. 46th Mythopoeic Society Conference Colorado Springs, CO, August 2, 2015.

"'On second thought, let's not go to Camelot. It is a silly place': Myth, Politics, and Parody in *Monty Python and the Holy Grail*." 46th Mythopoeic Society Conference, Colorado Springs, CO, August 2, 2015.

"The Body, Deformity, and Divinity in Bujold's Vorkosigan and Chalion Series." Paper at *Biology and Manners: The Worlds of Lois*

McMaster Bujold Conference. Anglia Ruskin University, Cambridge, United Kingdom, August 20, 2014.

Chair, *Religion* Paper Panel at *Biology and Manners: The Worlds of Lois McMaster Bujold* Conference. Anglia Ruskin University, Cambridge, United Kingdom, August 20, 2014.

Mythopoeic Fantasy and Scholarship Award Presentation. 45th Mythopoeic Society Conference (Mythcon 45), Wheaton College, Norton, MA, August 10, 2014.

Mythopoeic Fantasy and Scholarship Award Presentation. 44th Mythopoeic Society Conference (Mythcon 44), Michigan State University, East Lansing, MI, July 14, 2013.

Panel Participant, "The Mythopoeic Wilderness" [Nature and Wilderness in Fantasy Fiction]. Panel Discussion at the 44th Mythopoeic Society Conference (Mythcon 44), Michigan State University, East Lansing, MI, July 14, 2013.

"Westmansweed to Old Toby: The Economic and Cultural Herblore of Pipe-weed in Tolkien's *The Lord of the Rings*." Paper at 44th Mythopoeic Society Conference (Mythcon 44), Michigan State University, East Lansing, MI, July 13, 2013.

Mythopoeic Fantasy and Scholarship Awards Presentation. 43rd Mythopoeic Society Conference (Mythcon 43), University of California, Berkeley, CA, August 5, 2012.

"From Iberian to Ibran and Catholic to Quintarian: Lois McMaster Bujold's Alternate History of the Spanish Reconquest in the Chalion Series." Paper at the 43rd Mythopoeic Society Conference (Mythcon 43), University of California, Berkeley, CA, August 5, 2012.

Panel Organizer/Moderator, "East Meets West: The Marco Polo Panel" [Asian Elements in Contemporary Fantasy Literature]. Panel Discussion at the 43rd Mythopoeic Society Conference (Mythcon 43), University of California, Berkeley, CA, August 5, 2012.

Mythopoeic Fantasy and Scholarship Awards Presentation. 42nd Mythopoeic Society Conference (Mythcon 42), Albuquerque, NM, July 17, 2011.

"Magical Historiography: Revisionist Histories and Wainscot Fantasy in J. K. Rowling's Harry Potter Series." Paper at the 42nd Mythopoeic Society Conference (Mythcon 42), Albuquerque, NM, July 16, 2011.

Panel Organizer/Moderator, "He-Monsters vs. She-Monsters: Gender and Monstrosity in Fantasy Fiction." Panel Discussion at the 42nd Mythopoeic Society Conference (Mythcon 42), Albuquerque, NM, July 16, 2011.

"'Out of the Unknown Past into the Unknown Future': Information Technology and Degradation in H. G. Wells's *The Time Machine*." Paper at Upstate Steampunk Conference, Greenville, SC, November 20, 2010. [Paper read in absentia]

Mythopoeic Fantasy and Scholarship Awards Presentation. 41st Mythopoeic Society Conference (Mythcon 41), Dallas, TX, July 11, 2010.

"Appropriating Divinity: Gods and Other Mythological Beings in Fantasy Literature." Panel Discussion at 41st Mythopoeic Society Conference (Mythcon 41), Dallas, TX, July 10, 2010. [Invited]

Mythopoeic Fantasy and Scholarship Awards Presentation. 40th Mythopoeic Society Conference (Mythcon 40), University of California, Los Angeles, CA, July 19, 2009.

Mythopoeic Fantasy and Scholarship Awards Presentation, 39th Mythopoeic Society Conference (Mythcon 39), Central Connecticut State University, New Britain, CT, August 17, 2008.

"Faerië Meets Neverland: J. M. Barrie's Peter Pan in the Worlds of J. R. R. Tolkien." Paper at *Fantasy Matters* Conference, University of Minnesota, Twin Cities, Minneapolis, MN, November 17, 2007.

Panel Presentation on J. R. R. Tolkien at the *Fantasy Matters* Conference, University of Minnesota, Twin Cities, Minneapolis, MN, November 17, 2007.

"A Gandalf Among Hobbits Revisited: The Cosmic Geopolitics of Tolkien's Legendarium." Paper at 37th Mythopoeic Society Conference (Mythcon 37), University of Oklahoma, Norman, OK, August 6, 2006.

"A Brief History of Libraries in Middle-earth: Oral and Manuscript Cultures in Tolkien's Legendarium." Paper at C. S. Lewis and Inklings Society (CSLIS) Conference 2006, John Brown University, Siloam Springs, AR, March 3, 2006.

Moderator for Paper Session, "J. R. R. Tolkien's Fictional Truths" at C. S. Lewis and Inklings Society (CSLIS) Conference, John Brown University, Siloam Springs, AR, March 3, 2006.

"The 'Web of Story': Tolkien's *The Lord of the Rings* and the Origin of Fairy-Stories." Paper at *Past Watchful Dragons: Fantasy and Faith in the Works of C. S. Lewis* Conference, Belmont University, Nashville, TN, November 5, 2005.

"Milton's *Areopagitica* and the Disciplining of Print Culture." Paper at Society for the History of Authorship, Reading, & Publishing Conference, Vancouver, BC, Canada, July 18, 1998.

"Spirit in the Archives: Typography and Transcription in the Papers of James Merrill," Paper at Washington University at St. Louis, St. Louis, MO, March 1997.

"Derrida's *Grammatology* and the Trace," Presentation to Faculty Critical Theory Discussion Group, Texas Tech University, Lubbock, TX, October 1994.

"Phrenology Among the Aborigines: Faces, Heads, and Power in Charlotte Brontë's *The Professor*." Paper at Northwest Conference on British Studies, University of Idaho, Boise, ID, March 1992.

"*Waverley*, Genealogy, History: Scott's Romance of Fathers and Sons." Paper at the Northwest Conference on British Studies, University of Oregon, Eugene, OR, March 1991.

"'I Would Be a Man-Woman': Defoe's *Roxana* and the Legal Representation of Women." Paper at Aphra Behn Society Conference, University of New Mexico, Albuquerque, NM, February 1991.

"James's Purloined Letter: Intersubjective Structures in *The Wings of the Dove*." Paper at the Dickens Project Winter Conference, University of California, Riverside, CA, January 1991.

Regional-Level Library Presentations

"Remembering the Great War: Library Programming for the World War I Centenary at Oklahoma State University." Presentation at Southwest Popular/American Culture Association 36th Annual Conference, Albuquerque, NM, February 10, 2016.

"OkstateShakespeare: Digital Humanities in Undergraduate Student Projects." Presentation at Southwest Popular/American Culture Association 36th Annual Conference, Albuquerque, NM, February 13, 2015.

"From Incunabula to Digital Texts: Teaching the History of Printing to Undergraduates." Presentation at Southwest Popular/American Culture Association 35th Annual Conference, Albuquerque, NM, February 20, 2014.

"Digital Humanities and Popular Culture: An Open Discussion." Presentation and Roundtable Discussion Session at Southwest Popular/American Culture Association 35th Annual Conference, Albuquerque, NM, February 19, 2014.

"What I Did Last Summer...At Library Camp! The Information Matrix Camp 2007–2012 and Beyond." Presentation at Southwest Popular/American Culture Association Conference, Albuquerque, NM, February 14, 2013.

"Words, Words, Words (and Page Images, too!): Using Digital Library and Archival Materials to Teach Renaissance Book History to Students." Presentation with Sarah Coates. Mid-Atlantic Popular/American Culture Conference, Pittsburgh, PA, November 2, 2012.

"Together We're Better: A Little Library Cooperation Goes a Long Way." Presentation with Barbara Miller, et al. Mountain Plains Library Association/Oklahoma Library Association Joint Conference, Oklahoma City, OK, April 21, 2010.

Moderator, "The 24-Hour Library: Increasing Your Database Use." Presentation at the Mountain Plains Library Association/Oklahoma Library Association Joint Conference, Oklahoma City, OK, April 21, 2010.

Moderator, Professional Forum Research Paper Sessions at the Mountain Plains Library Association/Oklahoma Library Association Joint Conference, Oklahoma City, OK, April 20, 2010.

Moderator, "Maintaining Smooth Relationships in the Workplace." Presentation at the Mountain Plains Library Association/ Oklahoma Library Association Joint Conference, Oklahoma City, OK, April 20, 2010.

Moderator, "Crossing Borders: A Cooperative Virtual Reference Project." Presentation at the Mountain Plains Library Association/Oklahoma Library Association Joint Conference, Oklahoma City, OK, April 20, 2010.

"The *Soul of a People* Experience: New Perspectives on the 1930s from Cooperative Library Programming." Presentation with Barbara Miller. Southwest/Texas Popular Culture Association/American Culture Association Conference, Albuquerque, NM, February 10, 2010.

Poster: "Going Virtual: Developing a One Credit-Hour Information Literacy Course at Oklahoma State University." Mountain Plains Library Association/New Mexico Library Association Conference, Albuquerque, NM, March 15, 2007.

Moderator, "Consortial Purchasing: Small Colleges Working Together Can Get a Break." New Mexico Library Association/Mountain Plains Library Association Conference, Albuquerque, NM, March 15, 2007.

Poster: "Keeping Score: The Music Enhancement Program at the Oklahoma State State University Library." Mountain Plains Library Association-North Dakota-South Dakota Library Association Tri-Conference, Fargo, ND, October 4–5, 2002.

Moderator, "Job Search 2001: An Employment Odyssey." Mountain Plains Library Association/ Arizona Library Association Conference, Phoenix, AZ, December 6, 2001.

Regional-Level Literary/Humanities Presentations

Panel Organizer/Moderator: "Digital Humanities: New Media, Literacies, and Pedagogy" and "Teaching Corpus Stylistics with the Tolkien Corpus." Paper/Discussion Sessions at Southwest Popular/American Culture Association 36th Annual Conference, Albuquerque, NM, February 10 & 13, 2016.

Panel Organizer/Moderator, "Quantifying Masculinity in J. R. R. Tolkien's *The Hobbit*," "New Digital Landscapes: Distant Reading, Stylometry, and Virtual Reality," "Digital Humanities in the Classroom and the Archives." Paper Sessions at the Southwest Popular/ American Culture 36th Annual Conference, Albuquerque, NM, Feb. 13, 2015.

Panel Organizer/Moderator, "Digital Humanities in Libraries and Virtual Spaces," "Tolkien Corpus Project," and "Digital Humanities in Art, Society, and Culture." Paper/Discussion Sessions at Southwest Popular/American Culture Association 35th Annual Conference, Albuquerque, NM, February 19, 20, 2014.

Panel Participant, "*The Hobbit*: The Relationships between Tolkien's Book and Jackson's Films." University of New Mexico Honors

College Panel Discussion, Albuquerque, NM, February 11, 2015. [Invited]

Panel Participant, "Tolkien's Legacy: Modern Popular Culture Works in Relation to Tolkien's Texts." University of New Mexico Honors College Panel Discussion, Albuquerque, NM, February 19, 2014. [Invited]

"Rites of (Alien) Encounter: Native and Non-Native Collisions in the Science Fiction of Russell Bates." Paper at Southwest/Texas Popular Culture Association/American Culture Association Conference, Albuquerque, NM, February 8, 2012.

State-Level Library Presentations

"Newell Poems Digital Course Project." Presentation with Andrew Wadoski and Sarah Coates at THATCampOK 2016, OSU Library, Stillwater, OK, May 20, 2016.

"The Embedded Librarian." Presentation at Oklahoma Library Association Annual Conference, Tulsa, OK, March 31, 2016. [Invited]

"Re-thinking the One-Shot: An Integrated Approach to Re-envisioning the Information Literacy Curriculum." Presentation with Cinthya Ippoliti and Steve Locy, Association of College and Research Libraries, Oklahoma Chapter Conference, Tulsa, OK, November 6, 2015.

"What is Digital Humanities?" Presentation for THATCamp OK 2015, University of Oklahoma, Norman, OK, June12, 2015.

"Digital Humanities: An Introduction." Presentation for Community of Oklahoma Instruction Librarians Meeting, OSU, Stillwater, OK, April 23, 2015.

"Guide on the Side: Applied Instruction Side by Side." Panel Presentation at *unCOILed 2014: Teaching with Technology*, Community of Oklahoma Instruction Librarians Summer Workshop, OSU- Tulsa, OK, July 18, 2014.

"Simulations in Library Instruction for International Students." Lightning Round Presentation at Oklahoma Library Association Annual Conference, Tulsa, OK, April 1, 2014.

"Virtual Meetings: From Oklahoma to the Nation and Beyond." Lightning Round Presentation at Oklahoma Library Association Annual Conference, Norman, OK, March 30, 2012.

"A Noteworthy Partnership: Library-Music Department Programming Collaborations at Oklahoma State University." Guest Lecture for LIS 5970, Libraries & Popular Culture, MLIS Course, University of Oklahoma, September 29, 2011. [Repeat of 2011 National PCA presentation; invited]

"Getting Published: Tips and Tricks from Journal Insiders." Panel Presentation at Oklahoma Library Association Annual Conference, Tulsa, OK, March 31, 2011. [Invited]

"From Whiteboard to Discussion Board: The Considerations and Challenges of Teaching a For-Credit Information Literacy Course Online." Presentation with Hui-fen Chang and Helen Clements at *unCOILed: Going the Distance*, Community of Oklahoma Instruction Librarians Summer Workshop, Stillwater, OK, July 30, 2010.

"Wordpress.com and Wordpress.org: Blogs and Web Pages Too!" Presentation at *The Joy of Open Source*, Oklahoma Library Association Information Technology Roundtable Workshop, Norman, OK, March 5, 2010. [Invited]

Poster: "The *Soul of a People* Grant Experience: Expanding Outreach through Cooperative Programming." Presentation with Barbara Miller. Association of College and Research Libraries-Oklahoma Chapter Annual Conference, Tulsa, OK, November 6, 2009.

"OLA Workshops, Step by Step." 2 Presentations at the Oklahoma Library Association Leadership Retreat for Division and Committee Chairs, University of Tulsa, OK, June 11, 2009. [Invited]

Moderator, "Recruiting Minorities in to the Library Profession Panel." Oklahoma Library Association Annual Conference, Midwest City, OK, April 22, 2009.

Moderator, "Scholarship Opportunities for Library Education." Oklahoma Library Association Conference, Midwest City, OK, April 21, 2009.

"Jing and Screencast.com." Presentation at "Creating Online Tutorials" Pre-conference Workshop, Oklahoma Library Association Annual Conference, Midwest City, OK, April 20, 2009. [Invited]

"From Volunteer to Librarian." Presentation at Encyclo-Media 28, Oklahoma City, OK, September 19, 2008. [Presentation on Oklahoma Library Association Information Matrix Camp for School Librarians.]

"Jing and Screencast.com." Presentation at *Tricks of the Tutorial Trade: Exploring Creation Tools* Workshop, Community of Oklahoma Instruction Librarians, Edmond, OK, July 25, 2008. [Invited]

Moderator, "Recruiting Minorities in to the Library Profession Panel." Oklahoma Library Association Annual Conference, Tulsa, OK, April 23, 2008.

"Information Matrix Camp 2007." Oklahoma Library Association Annual Conference, Tulsa, OK, April 23, 2008.

"The Information Literacy Course in the Cyber-Classroom: The Challenges of Online IL Instruction." Presentation at Oklahoma Library Association Annual Conference, Tulsa, OK, April 22, 2008.

Welcome & Moderator for Teen Information/Library Team Inaugural Event, Oklahoma Library Association Career Recruitment and Retention Committee, Midwest City, OK, March 29, 2008.

"Information Literacy Skills for College Freshmen: They're Not in Kansas Anymore!" In-Service Training with Barbara Miller for the Faculty of Hennessey High School, Hennessey, OK, January 21, 2008. [Invited]

Guest Lecture on Careers in Academic Libraries for Academic Librarianship MLIS Course, University of Oklahoma, Tulsa, OK, December 8, 2007. [Invited]

Moderator, "Taming Social Networking Sites: Facebook & MySpace." Oklahoma Library Association University and College Division Workshop, Oklahoma State University, Stillwater, OK, October 19, 2007.

"Unclouding Aquabrowser: Integrating Aquabrowser into OPAC Instruction for a Credit Information Literacy Course." Presentation at *Unconventional Info Lit in Action*, Council for Oklahoma Instructional Librarians Summer Workshop, Broken Arrow, OK, July 27, 2007.

Moderator, "Assessment: The How's and Why's of Self-Study." Oklahoma Library Association Annual Conference, Oklahoma City, OK, April 4, 2007.

Moderator, "Finding and Tracking State Legislation." Oklahoma Library Association Annual Conference, Oklahoma City, OK, April 3, 2007.

Moderator, "Cooperative Learning: Instruction Methods for Reaching Information Literate Students." Oklahoma Library Association Annual Conference, Oklahoma City, OK, April 2, 2007.

"Information Literacy Skills for College Freshmen: They're Not in Kansas Anymore!" In-Service Training Presentation with Barbara Miller and Helen Clements for the Faculty of McAlester High School, McAlester, OK, February 19. 2007. [Invited]

Presentation on Academic Librarianship to University of Oklahoma School of Library and Information Studies Course, LIS 5243 (Academic Library Management), Tulsa, OK, December 8, 2006. [Invited]

"Information Literacy Skills for College Freshmen: They're Not in Kansas Anymore!" 4 In-Service Training Presentations with Barbara Miller and Helen Clements for the Faculty of the Tulsa School for Science and Technology, Tulsa, OK, November 27, 2006. [Invited]

"Information Literacy Skills for the Transition from High School to College." Presentation with Barbara Miller for Encyclo-Media 26, Oklahoma City, OK, August 31, 2006.

Introductory Speaker and Discussion Leader, Council for Oklahoma Instructional Librarians Workshop, Edmond, OK, July 19, 2006.

Moderator, "Buried Treasures in Oklahoma Libraries." Oklahoma Library Association Annual Conference, Tulsa, OK, March 30, 2006.

MPLA Table Talk Discussion Leader. Oklahoma Library Association Annual Conference, Tulsa, OK, March 30, 2006.

"Information Literacy Skills for the Transition from High School to College." In-Service Training For the Faculty of the Perkins-Tyron, OK School District with Helen Clements and Barbara Miller, January 16, 2006.

Guest Lecture on Aggregator/Vendor Library Databases and Database Search Strategies for Graduate Library Science Course, Oklahoma State University, Stillwater, OK, October 2005. [Invited]

"Commonalities of Databases and Search Strategies for Instruction." Presentation at *But Are They Learning?*, Council for Oklahoma Instructional Librarians Workshop, Tulsa, OK, August 23, 2005. [Invited]

"A Librarian's Guide to Middle-earth: Tolkien in Libraryland." Presentation at Oklahoma Library Association Annual Conference, Norman, OK, April 1, 2005.

Moderator for Program on Learning Styles and Information Literacy, Oklahoma Library Association Annual Conference, Norman, OK, April 1, 2005.

Moderator for Paper Presentation Sessions II and III, Oklahoma Library Association Annual Conference, Norman, OK, March 31, April 1, 2005.

Moderator for Breakout Session, "Becoming a Successful Librarian in the 21st Century." Association of College and Research Libraries, Oklahoma Chapter Conference, Norman, OK, November 19, 2004.

Moderator, Council for Oklahoma Information Literacy Workshop/ Bibliographic Instruction Clinic, Tulsa, OK, August 13, 2004.

"Oklahoma Cooperatives." Participant in Panel Discussion at Oklahoma Library Association Annual Conference, Tulsa, OK, April 15, 2004.

Moderator, "Buried Treasures in Oklahoma Libraries." Presentation at Oklahoma Library Association Annual Conference, Tulsa, OK, April 16, 2004.

Moderator, Paper Presentation Sessions II and III, Oklahoma Library Association Annual Conference, Tulsa, OK, April 15–16, 2004.

"Literary Web-Weaving: Finding Literature Sources on the Internet." Presentation at Oklahoma Library Association Annual Conference, Oklahoma City, OK, March 2003.

Co-presenter on Library Science 1011 and Credit Information Literacy Courses, Library Education Division Preconference Program on Information Literacy, Oklahoma Library Association Annual Conference, Oklahoma City, OK, March 2003.

Moderator, Ethics Committee Sessions, *Celebrating the Web* Oklahoma Library Association Summer Conference, Midwest City, OK, July 30–31, 2002.

Panelist, *Help Wanted: Librarians*, Oklahoma Library Association University and College Division Workshop, Tulsa, OK, May 15, 2002.

Poster: "Concept Maps and Keywords: Teaching Critical Thinking Skills in Library Instruction." Oklahoma Library Association Annual Conference, Tulsa, OK, April 18, 2002.

Moderator, Paper Presentation Session I-II, Oklahoma Library Association Annual Conference, Tulsa, OK, April 18, 2002.

Moderator, "On the Frontline: Handling Conflicts with Patrons and Public Groups." Oklahoma Library Association Ethics Committee Workshop, Midwest City, OK, February 5, 2002.

"Teaching Styles for a One Credit-Hour Library Skills Course," Presentation with Helen Clements and Peggy Wolfe, Oklahoma Bibliographic Instruction Council, Stillwater, OK, May 25, 2001.

Moderator, "Are You Being Served?: Distance Learners and Their Libraries," Oklahoma Library Association University and College Division Workshop, Tulsa, OK, May 15, 2001.

"Where's Pete?: Reinventing Bibliographic Instruction After Changing Online Catalogs," Presentation at Oklahoma Library Association Annual Conference, Oklahoma City, OK, April 20, 2001.

Moderator, Paper Presentation Session II, Oklahoma Library Association Annual Conference, Oklahoma City, OK, April 19, 2001.

Moderator, *Can We Agree to Disagree: Conflict Resolution in the Workplace*, Oklahoma Library Association Ethics Committee Workshop, Midwest City, OK, February 9, 2001.

Panel Discussion on Marketing Strategies for Bibliographic Instruction, Oklahoma Bibliographic Instruction Council, Oklahoma City, OK, August 2000.

"Educational Aspects of Electronic Resources: Incorporating Electronic Resources in Teaching and Research," Presentation at *Libraries, 'Lectronic Resources, and the Law*, Oklahoma Library Association University and College Division Workshop, Stillwater, OK, March 9, 2000.

"Job Search 2000," Presentation and Panel Discussion, Oklahoma Library Association Annual Conference, Enid, OK, March 26, 1999.

"Researching, Rethinking, Rebooting: Designing Library Instruction for English Composition." Presentation with Donna Schwarz at Oklahoma Library Association Annual Conference, Enid, OK, March 25, 1999.

Guest Lecture on Reference Sources in the Humanities for Humanities-Social Sciences Reference Sources MLIS course at the University of Oklahoma, Norman, OK, July 1998 [Invited]

Discussion Facilitator, *Surf's Up: Protecting Libraries from Internet Undertow*, Oklahoma Library Association Ethics Committee Workshop, Oklahoma City, OK, October 1, 1998.

State-Level Literary/Humanities Presentations

Scholar's Presentation on Owen Wister, *The Virginian* for *Let's Talk About It, Oklahoma* Book Discussion Series, Pioneer Woman Museum, Ponca City, OK, Sept. 10, 2016. [Invited]

Scholar's Presentation on Mitch Albom, *Tuesdays with Morrie* for *Let's About It, Oklahoma* Book Discussion Series, Perkins Public Library, OK, April 30, 2016. [Invited]

Scholar's Presentation on Parnell Hall, *Cozy* for *Let's About It, Oklahoma* Book Discussion Series, Guthrie Public Library, OK, April 25, 2016. [Invited]

Discussion Leader for F. Scott Fitzgerald, *The Great Gatsby* and Rilla Askew, *Fire in Beulah* for *Two Books One Community* Book Discussion Series, Stillwater Public Library, OK, April 24, 2016.

Discussion Leader for Charles Portis, *True Grit* for *One Book One Community* Book Discussion Series, Stillwater Public Library, OK, April 12, 2015.

Scholar's Presentation on Roger Kahn, *The Boys of Summer* for *Let's Talk About It, Oklahoma* Book Discussion Series, Pioneer Woman Museum, Ponca City, OK, Oct. 10, 2015. [Invited]

Scholar's Presentation on Washington Irving, *Tour on the Prairies* for *Let's About It, Oklahoma* Book Discussion Series, Guthrie Public Library, OK, August 24, 2015. [Invited]

Scholar's Presentation on Bob Avey, *Twisted Perception* for *Let's Talk About It, Oklahoma* Book Discussion Series, El Reno Public Library, OK, April 22, 2015. [Invited]

Discussion Leader for Charles Portis, *True Grit* for *One Book One Community* Book Discussion Series, Stillwater Public Library, OK, April 12, 2015.

Scholar's Presentation on Bram Stoker, *Dracula* and Stephen King, *'Salem's Lot* for *Let's Talk About It, Oklahoma* Book Discussion Series, Guthrie Public Library, OK, March 24, 2015. [Invited]

Scholar's Presentation on Timothy Egan, *The Worst Hard Time* for *Let's Talk About It, Oklahoma* Book Discussion Series, Enid Public Library, OK, February 10, 2015. [Invited]

Scholar's Presentation on Parnell Hall, *Cozy* for *Let's Talk About It, Oklahoma* Book Discussion Series, Enid Public Library, OK, November 13, 2014. [Invited]

Scholar's Presentation on E. B. White, *Charlotte's Web* and Katherine Paterson, *Bridge to Terabithida* for *Let's Talk About It, Oklahoma* Book Discussion Series, Perkins Public Library, OK, October 22, 2014. [Invited]

Scholar's Presentation on Truman Capote, *In Cold Blood* for *Let's Talk About It, Oklahoma* Book Discussion Series, Guthrie Public Library, OK, September 22, 2014. [Invited]

Scholar's Presentation for Jack London, *Call of the Wild* for *Let's Talk About It, Oklahoma* Book Discussion Series, Perkins Public Library, OK, May 7, 2014. [Invited]

Scholar's Presentation on Stephen Crane, *The Red Badge of Courage* for *Let's Talk About It, Oklahoma* Book Discussion Series, Guthrie Public Library, OK, February 24, 2014. [Invited]

Discussion Leader for Thomas King, *Medicine River*, *Let's Talk About It, Oklahoma* Book Discussion Series, Stillwater Public Library, OK, November 5, 2013.

Scholar's Presentation for Carolyn Hart, *Letter from Home* for *Let's Talk About It, Oklahoma* Book Discussion Series, Perkins Public Library, OK, September 25, 2013. [Invited]

Scholar's Presentation on Mario Vargas Llosa, *The Storyteller* for *Let's Talk About It, Oklahoma* Book Discussion Series, Guthrie Public Library, OK, September 23, 2013. [Invited]

Discussion Leader for Woody Guthrie, *Bound for Glory* for *One Book, One Community* Series, Community Discussion, Stillwater, OK, March 26, 2013.

Scholar's Presentation for on Jim Thompson, *Roughneck* for *Let's Talk About It, Oklahoma* Book Discussion Series, Guthrie Public Library, OK, March 4, 2013. [Invited]

Scholar's Presentation on John Steinbeck, *Travels with Charley* for *Let's Talk About It, Oklahoma* Book Discussion Series, Guthrie Public Library, OK, October 22, 2012. [Invited]

Scholar's Presentation on Jack Schaefer, *Shane* for *Let's Talk About It, Oklahoma* Book Discussion Series, Perkins Public Library, OK, October 10, 2012. [Invited]

Scholar's Presentation on Amy Tan, *The Joy Luck Club* for *Let's Talk About It, Oklahoma* Book Discussion Series, Perkins Public Library, OK, October 12, 2011. [Invited]

Scholar's Presentation on Russell Hoban, *Turtle Diary* for *Let's Talk About It, Oklahoma* Book Discussion Series, Newkirk Public Library, OK, May 17, 2011. [Invited]

Scholar's Presentation on William W. Savage, Jr., *Cowboy Life: Reconstructing an American Myth* for *Let's Talk About It, Oklahoma* Book Discussion Series, Perkins Public Library, OK, March 9, 2011. [Invited]

Discussion Facilitator for Rachel Carson, *Silent Spring* for *Let's Talk About It, Oklahoma* Book Discussion Series, Stillwater Public Library, January 24, 2011.

Scholar's Presentation on Carl Hiaasen, *Native Tongue* for *Let's Talk About It, Oklahoma* Book Discussion Series, Guthrie Public Library, OK, November 30, 2010. [Invited]

Scholar's Presentation on Barbara Kingsolver, *Pigs in Heaven* for *Let's Talk About It, Oklahoma* Book Discussion Series, Newkirk Public Library, OK, November 8, 2010. [Invited]

Scholar's Presentation on Kenneth Grahame, *The Wind in the Willows* for *Let's Talk About It, Oklahoma* Book Discussion Series, Tonkawa Public Library, OK, October 24, 2010. [Invited]

Scholar's Presentation on W. E. B. Du Bois, *The Souls of Black Folk* for *Let's Talk About It, Oklahoma* Book Discussion Series, Newkirk Public Library, OK, March 29, 2010. [Invited]

Scholar's Presentation on Richard Harding Davis, "Ranson's Folly" and Russell Bates, "Rite of Encounter" for *Let's Talk About It, Oklahoma* Book Discussion Series, Perkins Public Library, OK, March 10, 2010. [Invited]

Scholar's Presentation on Parnell Hall, *Cozy* for *Let's Talk About It, Oklahoma* Book Discussion Series, Stillwater Public Library, OK, March 9, 2010. [Invited]

Scholar's Presentation on James Cobb, *West on '66: A Mystery* for *Let's Talk About It, Oklahoma* Book Discussion Series, Miami Public Library, OK, November 19, 2009. [Invited]

Introduction to the Screening of *Soul of a People* Documentary, Stillwater Public Library, OK, November 8, 2009. Sixth program in the *Soul of a People: Writing America's Story* Series.

Introduction to *Soul of a People* Series and Moderator for "The Federal Writer's Project: The Oklahoma Connection," Oklahoma State University, Stillwater, OK, October 22, 2009. Fifth Program in the *Soul of a People: Writings America's Story* Series.

Scholar's Presentation on Amanda Cross, *Death in a Tenured Position* for *Let's Talk About It, Oklahoma* Book Discussion Series, Perkins Public Library, OK, October 7, 2009. [Invited]

Introduction to the *Soul of a People* Series & Moderator for Screening of *The Plow That Broke the Plains* and *The River*, Stillwater Public Library, Stillwater, OK, April 24, 2009. Fourth Program in the *Soul of a People: Writing America's Story* Series.

Introduction to the *Soul of a People* Series & Moderator for "Soul of a People: Slave Narratives of the Federal Writers' Project." Oklahoma State University Library, Stillwater, OK, April 24, 2009. Third Program in the *Soul of a People: Writing America's Story* Series.

Scholar's Presentation on Parnell Hall, *Cozy* for *Let's Talk About It, Oklahoma* Book Discussion Series, Perkins Public Library, OK, April 23, 2009. [Invited]

Introduction: "The WPA Federal Writer's Project and Angie Debo & Moderator for "Soul of a People: Angie Debo in the 1930s–1940s." Oklahoma State University Library, Stillwater, OK, April 2, 2009. Second Program in the *Soul of a People: Writing America's Story* Series.

Scholar's Presentation on Michael Karl Witzel, *Route 66 Remembered* for *Let's Talk About It Oklahoma* Book Discussion Series, Newkirk Public Library, OK, March 31, 2009. [Invited]

Introduction to *Soul of a People* Series & Moderator for "Soul of a People: The Federal Writers' Project, WPA, and Stillwater in the 1930s." Sheerar Museum of Stillwater History, Stillwater, OK, March 8, 2009. First Program in the *Soul of a People: Writing America's Story* Series.

Discussion Facilitator for Josephine Johnson, *Now in November* for *Let's Talk About It Oklahoma* Book Discussion Series, Stillwater Public Library, OK, February 17, 2009.

Scholar's Presentation on Jim Thompson, *Roughneck* for *Let's Talk About It, Oklahoma* Book Discussion Series, Okeene Public Library, OK, September 21, 2008. [Invited]

Presentation on Leo Tolstoy, *Death of Ivan Illych* for the "Big Read," Enid Public Library, OK, May 10, 2008. [Invited]

Scholar's Presentation on Judson Jerome, *Flight from Innocence: A Memoir, 1927–1947* for *Let's Talk About It Oklahoma* Book Discussion Series, Okeene Public Library, OK, April 27, 2008. [Invited]

Scholar's Presentation on Carl Hiaasen, *Native Tongue* for *Let's Talk About It, Oklahoma.* Book Discussion Series, Newkirk Public Library, OK, March 4, 2008. [Invited]

Scholar's Presentation on Jim Thompson, *Roughneck* for *Let's Talk About It Oklahoma* Book Discussion Series, Newkirk Public Library, OK, October 23, 2007. [Invited]

Scholar's Presentation on Kenneth Grahame, *The Wind in the Willows* for *Let's Talk About It, Oklahoma* Book Discussion Series, Newkirk Public Library, OK, February 27, 2007. [Invited]

Scholar's Presentation on Judson Jerome, *Flight from Innocence: A Memoir, 1927–1947* for *Let's Talk About It, Oklahoma* Book Discussion Series, Newkirk Public Library, OK, November 7, 2006. [Invited]

OSU Campus Presentations

"Effective Approaches to Archival Research." Presentation on Digital Collections for History, Phi Alpha Theta Colloquium, OSU History Department, Stillwater, OK, March 30, 2016. [Invited]

"*A Christmas Carol* and Victorian Design." Presentation for OSU Theatre Costume Design Studio, Stillwater, OK, October 5, 2015. [Invited]

Discussion Leader for Ray Bradbury, *Fahrenheit 451* for *One Book, One Community* Series, OSU Library, Stillwater, OK, March 11, 2014.

Discussion Leader for Woody Guthrie, *Bound for Glory* for *One Book, One Community* Series, OSU Library, Stillwater, OK, March 29, 2013.

Moderator, "Language, Culture, & Performance—Literary Strategies" Paper Panel, Oklahoma State University Graduate Humanities Conference, Stillwater, OK, March 2, 2013.

Discussion Leader for Betty Rogers, *Will Rogers: His Wife's Story* for *One Book, One Community* Series, OSU Library, Stillwater, OK, April 18, 2012.

Moderator, "Joseph Conrad's *Heart of Darkness*" and "Indigenous American Literature" Paper Panels, Oklahoma State University Graduate Humanities Conference, Stillwater, OK, March 9–10, 2012.

Moderator, "Cult Films" & "Failed Transformations" Paper Panels at *Transforming Words*, Oklahoma State University Graduate Humanities Conference, Stillwater, OK, March 5, 2011.

Discussion Leader for Angie Debo, *Prairie City* for the *One Book, One Community* Series, OSU Library, Stillwater, OK, October 28, 2010.

Panel on Book Discussion Facilitating for Resident Associates in OSU Housing & Residential Life's *Cowboy Book Club*. Presentation with Dan Chaney, Karen Neurohr, Nicole Sump-Crethar, and Lynne Simpson-Scott, OSU, Stillwater, OK, August 10, 2010.

Discussion Leader for Harper Lee's *To Kill a Mockingbird* for the *One Book, One Community* Series, OSU Library, Stillwater, OK, October 27, 2009.

"To Cite or Not to Cite?: Bibliographic Citation Past, Present, and Future." Presentation to OSU Library Faculty, Stillwater, OK, January 21, 1999.

Professional Associations, Committees, & Leadership Positions

National-Level Library Associations

American Library Association (ALA): Member 1998–2002, 2006–Present.

ALA – Association of College and Research Libraries (ACRL): Member 1998–2002, 2006–Present.

Academic/Research Librarian of the Year Award Committee: Chair, 2012–2013; Vice Chair, 2011–2012; Member, 2010–2011. [Appointed]

Friends Fund Disbursement Subcommittee: Member, 2012–2013. [Appointed]

Literatures in English Section (ACRL LES): Member, 2007–Present.

Chair, Virtual Participation Committee, 2011–2013, 2016–2017; Member, 2013–2014; 2014–2016. [Appointed]

Nominating Committee: Member, 2009–2010, 2015–2016. [Appointed]

Planning Committee, Member, 2014–2016.

2015 Conference Program Planning Committee: Member, 2014–2015. [Appointed]

Candidate for LES Chair Elect/Vice Chair, 2014 election.

Chair, 2014 Conference Program Planning Committee, 2013–2014. [Appointed]

Member-at-Large, 2011–2012; Voting member of LES Executive Committee. [Elected]

Chair, 2013 Conference Program Planning Committee, 2012–2013. [Appointed]

Chair, Virtual Participation Task Force, 2010–2011. [Appointed]

Chair, Nominating Committee, 2011–2012. [Appointed]

LES/WESS (ACRL Western European Studies Section) Selection Committee to Appoint ACRL Liaison to the Modern Language Association: Member, 2010. [Appointed]

LES/WESS Task Force to Create Proposal for ACRL/Modern Language Association Liaison: Member, 2009. [Appointed]

Secretary, 2009–210 [Elected]; Voting member of LES Executive Committee.

Chair, Committee for LES Annual Tour, 2008–2009. [Appointed]

Membership Committee: Member, 2008–2010; 2010–2012. [Appointed]

Mentor Program, 2006–Present.

Instruction Section (ACRL IS): Member, 2007–Present.

Chair, 2017 Conference Program Committee, 2016–2017. [Appointed]

Chair, 2016 Preconference Conference Committee, 2014–2016. [Appointed]

Chair, Research and Scholarship Committee, 2014–2015; Member, 2012–2014. [Appointed]; Member of IS Advisory Council.

Awards Committee: Member, 2008–2010; 2010–2012. [Appointed]

Mentor Program, 2008–Present.

Western European Studies Section (ACRL WESS): Member, 2010–Present.

Awards Committee: Member, 2016–2017. [Appointed]

Chair, Research and Planning Committee, 2014–2015; 2015–2016. [Appointed]

2016 Conference Program Planning Committee: Member, 2015–2016. [Appointed]

Fundraising Committee: Member, 2013–2015. [Appointed]

2014 Conference Program Planning Committee: Member, 2013–2014. [Appointed]

2013 Conference Program Planning Committee: Member, 2012–2013. [Appointed]

Nominating Committee: Member, 2011. [Appointed]

ALA – Reference and User Services Association (RUSA): Member, 2007–2011.

Access to Information Committee: Member, 2010–2012. [Appointed]

Collection Development Section (RUSA CODES): Member, 2007–2011.

Reference Publishing Advisory Committee, Member, 2008–2010. [Appointed]

National-Level Literature/Humanities Associations

Modern Language Association of America (MLA): Member, 1991–1997, 2008–Present.

Advisory Committee on the *MLA International Bibliography*: Chair, 2016–2017; Member, 2014–2017. [Appointed]

Libraries and Research in Languages and Literatures Discussion Group

Paper Panel Organizer, "Libraries, Archives, and Public Memory," for 2015 Modern Language Association Convention, Vancouver, BC, Canada. [Appointed]

Executive Committee: Member, 2011–2014 [Elected]: Past Chair, 2013–2014; Chair, 2012–2013; Secretary, 2011–2012.

Mythopoeic Society: Member, 2004–Present.

Papers and Panels Coordinator, 2014 Mythopoeic Society Conference (Mythcon 45), Wheaton College, Norton MA, August 8–11, 2014.

Administrator of the Mythopoeic Scholarship Award and Mythopoeic Fantasy Awards, 2007–Present. [Elected]

Council of Stewards (governing board), Chair and President of the Mythopoeic Society, 2012; Vice Chair, 2006; Member, 2006–Present. [Elected]

Secretary of the Mythopoeic Press, 2006–2010. [Elected]; Member, Mythopoeic Press Advisory Board, 2011–Present. [Appointed]

Judge for Alexei Kondratiev Memorial Student Paper Award, 2010–2013.

Popular Culture Association: Member, 2010–Present.

Society for the History of Authorship, Printing, and Reading (SHARP): Member, 1998–2008.

Regional-Level Library Associations

Mountain Plains Library Association (MPLA): Member, 1998–Present.

Awards Committee: Member, 2012–2014.

Membership Committee: Member, 2010–2011.

Candidate for President/President Elect, 2007, 2008, 2010 elections.

Communications Committee: Chair, 2007–2008. [Appointed]

Chair, Electronic Communities Restructuring Task Force, 2007 [Appointed]; Chair of Community Portal Implementation Task Force, 2007. [Appointed]

Moderator, Collection Development Electronic Discussion Community, 2006–2007. [Appointed]

Interim MPLA Representative for Oklahoma, October 2005–June 2006.

Recording Secretary, 2002–2003 [Elected]; Member of Finance and Management Committee (senior MPLA officers).

Chair, New Members Roundtable, Member of MPLA Board of Directors, 1999–2000, 2000–2001, 2002–2003. [Elected]

Chair, Nominating Committee, 2004–2005, 2005–2006. [Appointed]

Nominating Committee: Member, 1999–2000, 2008–2009, 2009–2010.

Continuing Education Committee: Member, 2002–2003.

Finance Committee: Member, 1999–2000, 2002–2003.

Regional-Level Humanities Association

Southwest Popular/American Culture Association [formerly *Southwest/Texas Popular Culture Association*]

Subject Area Chair, Digital Humanities, 2013–Present.

State-Level Library Associations

ACRL – Oklahoma Chapter (OK-ACRL): Member, 1998–Present.

Archivist, 2006–Present. [Appointed]

President, 2007; Vice President, 2006. [Elected]

Secretary, 2005. [Elected]

Chair, Council for Oklahoma Instructional Librarians (COIL), 2004, 2005. [Elected]

Secretary, Oklahoma Bibliographic Instruction Council (OBIC), 2001–2002. [Elected]

Oklahoma Library Association (OLA): Member, 1998–Present.

Chair, Resolutions Committee: 2006–2007, 2010–2011, 2011–2012, 2012–2013, 2013–2014, 2014–2015. [Appointed]

OLA Leadership Institute Committee: Member, 2013–2014.

Co-Chair, Continuing Education Committee, 2009–2010, 2010–2011, 2011–2012. [Appointed]

Co-Chair, Career Recruitment & Retention Committee, 2007–2008, 2008–2009. [Appointed]

Chair, Interlibrary Co-operation Committee, 2006–2007. [Appointed]

Nomination Task Force for Oklahoma Poet Laureate: Member, 2006. [Appointed]

Chair, Nominating Committee, 2005–2006 [Appointed]; Member, 2004–2005, 2006–2007.

Chair, Ethics Committee, 2000–2001, 2001–2002, 2002–2003. [Appointed]

Program Committee: Member, 2000–2012.

OLA University and College Division: Member, 1998–Present.

Chair, 2003–2004; Chair Elect/Vice Chair, 2015–2016, 2002–2003. [Elected]

Secretary, 2001–2002. [Elected]

Conference Committee: Member, 1998–1999.

Chair, Poster and Paper Presentations Committee, 1999–2000, 2001–2002. [Appointed]

> Workshop Planning Committee: Member, 1999–2000, 2001–2002.
>
> *Library Education Division*: Member 1999–2010.

Grants, Grant-Funded Projects, & Funded Programming Series Organized

The Great War and its Legacy, 1914–1918, a 4-year programming series commemorating the centenary of World War I co-sponsored by OSU Library and OSU Department of History with partial funding provided by the W. P. Wood Professorship, 2014–Present.

Soul of a People Public Programming Series Grant on Federal Writers' Project, ALA /National Endowment for the Humanities, Project Director/Principal Investigator, 2009.

Information Matrix Camp Grant from Institute of Museum and Library Services, Co-Chair of OLA Career Recruitment and Retention [Sponsoring] Committee, 2007–2010.

Honors & Awards

OSU Library Faculty Award for Noteworthy Achievement, 2015; Honorable Mention, 2014, 2008.

Named W. P. Wood [Endowed] Professor of Library Service, OSU, 2013.

ACRL – Oklahoma Chapter (OK-ACRL) Outstanding Service Award, 2012.

Oklahoma Library Association Special Project Award for the Information Matrix Camp, 2008.

Outstanding Review Award, *Electronic Resources Reviews* for "The Pompeii Forum Project," 1998.

Phi Beta Mu-Pi Chapter, University of Pittsburgh, Initiated 1997.

H. W. Wilson Foundation Scholarship, University of Pittsburgh, 1996.

Humanities Research Grant, University of California, Irvine, for dissertation research at the British Library and the Wellcome Institute for the History of Medicine, 1992.

University of California Intercampus Research Grant, 1991.

Dissertation Fellowship, University of California, Irvine, 1991.

Outstanding Teaching Assistant Award, University of California, Irvine, 1990.

Regents' Irvine Intern Fellowship, University of California, Irvine, 1987.

William C. Willoughby Scholarship, Rice University, 1985.

Consultation & Other Professional Service

External reviewer of faculty tenure/promotion dossiers:

> Texas Tech University Libraries (promotion from Associate Librarian to Librarian), 2016.
>
> University of Colorado Libraries (promotion to Professor), 2016.
>
> University of Nebraska, Lincoln Library (promotion to Associate Professor), 2015.

University of Colorado Libraries (promotion to Professor), 2014.

Texas Tech University Libraries (tenure & promotion to Associate Librarian [Associate Professor]), 2014.

Mississippi State University (tenure & promotion to Associate Professor), 2013.

Texas Tech University Libraries (promotion to Full Librarian [Professor]), 2013.

University of Evansville Libraries (tenure & promotion to Associate Professor), 2013.

University of Oklahoma Libraries (tenure & promotion to Associate Professor), 2012.

University of New Mexico Libraries (promotion to Professor), 2011.

University of Evansville Libraries (promotion to Professor), 2010.

University of Idaho Library (tenure & promotion to Associate Professor), 2010.

Montana State University Library (tenure & promotion to Associate Professor), 2006.

University of Nebraska, Lincoln Library (tenure & promotion to Associate Professor), 2002.

External examiner of Ph.D. dissertation for candidate at Indian Institute of Technology, Bhubaneswar, India (English Dept.; Indian and Native American postcolonial literature), 2014.

Peer reviewer for British Literature section of core collection bibliography for *Resources for College Libraries (RCLweb)* from ACRL/*Choice*, 2011.

External member of MLIS Portfolio Committee for School of Library and Information Studies, University of Oklahoma:
Sarah Coates, 2012.
Caleb Puckett, 2009.

Mentor, Oklahoma Library Association "OLA Gold" Library Leadership Institute, Ardmore OK, 2010. [Invited]

Judge for Oklahoma National History Day, Oklahoma Historical Center, Oklahoma City, OK, 2010, 2011.

Developed (with Barbara Miller) "The Worst Hard Time Revisited: Oklahoma in the Dust Bowl Years" book discussion series for the *Let's Talk About It, Oklahoma* program, Oklahoma Humanities Council, 2008.

Rice University, Rice Alumni Volunteers for Admission (RAVA) coordinator of alumni admissions interviews for applicants in Oklahoma and Arkansas, 2007–2010.

Professional Conferences/Workshops Organized & Planning Committee Service

Organizer for "Teaching Data Information Literacy" Preconference, ALA Annual Conference, Orlando, FL, June 24, 2016.

Registrar, 2016 Mythopoeic Society Conference (Mythcon 47), San Antonio, TX, August 3–8, 2016.

THATCampOK 2016. Served as co-director with Nicole Sump-Crethar for the Second OSU/OU- sponsored digital humanities workshop/unconference at the OSU Libraries. Made arrangements for plenary speakers from Texas A&M-Commerce, coordinated breakouts, logistics, and other aspects of the event.

Papers Coordinator, 2014 Mythopoeic Society Conference (Mythcon 44), Wheaton College, Norton, MA, July 31–August 3, 2014. Issued call for papers and vetted proposals from faculty, graduate students, and independent scholars from six countries; selected papers and set schedule; handled AV and other issues on-site.

THATCamp OK 2015. Served as one of the OSU representatives on the OU/OSU planning committee for the first digital humanities workshop/unconference offered in the state. Publicized with OSU faculty and graduate students, and with other institutions.

OLA Leadership Institute Committee Preconference: "Finding Your Inner Leader," OLA Annual Conference, Midwest City, OK, April 29, 2015. Handled all aspects of planning including work with the business consultant speaker, publicity, and on-site logistics.

MLA Paper Session, "Libraries, Archives, and Public Memory," MLA Convention, Vancouver, BC, Canada, January 2015. Created call for papers, reviewed 20+ proposals from 5 countries, selected 3 papers for presentation (from United Kingdom and Canada), organized publicity with sponsoring Libraries and Research in Languages and Literatures Discussion Group, presided and served as respondent at session.

ACRL LES/WESS/Slavic and Eastern European Studies Program, "'Embedded' Ethnic Communities: New Challenges for Librarians," ALA Annual Conference, Las Vegas, NV, June 2014. Chaired planning committee for LES.

Organized author book reading and signing for OSU Professor Emerita Linda Leavell's *Holding on Upside Down: the Life and Work of Marianne Moore*, Stillwater, OK, November 21, 2013.

ACRL LES/WESS/Slavic and Eastern European Studies Program, "Literary Texts and the Library in the Digital Age: New Collaborations in European and American Studies," ALA Annual Conference, Chicago, IL, June 29, 2013. Chaired planning committee for LES.

MLA Convention Program for Libraries and Research in Languages an Literatures Discussion Group, "How Many Copies is Enough? Too Many? Libraries and Shared Monograph Archives," MLA Convention, Boston, MA, January 4, 2013. Chaired planning committee.

Continuing Education Consultant for various OLA divisions and committee organizing workshops, 2009–Present.

Registrar, 2011 Mythopoeic Society Conference (Mythcon 42), Albuquerque, NM, July 2011. Conference committee member.

unCOILed: Going the Distance, COIL Summer Workshop, Stillwater, OK, July 30, 2010. Coordinated local site arrangements.

Registrar, 2010 Mythopoeic Society Conference (Mythcon 41), Dallas, TX, July 2010. Conference Committee Member.

unCOILed: Participatory Learning in the Age of the Unengaged, COIL Summer Workshop, Muskogee, OK, July 17, 2009. Served on planning committee.

ACRL-LES Tour of the University of Chicago Special Collections Research Center, ALA Annual Conference, Chicago, IL, July 13, 2009. Coordinated tour.

Creating Online Tutorials, Pre-Conference Workshop for the OLA Annual Conference, Midwest City, OK, April 20, 2009. Served on planning committee.

Chaired planning group for a proposed workshop for the OLA Career Recruitment and Retention Committee/Rose State College on diversity in libraries.

Teen Information/Library Team (OLA Teen Library Association) Inaugural Event, Oklahoma Library Association Career Recruitment and Retention Committee, Midwest City, OK, March 2008. Organized first event for a proposed Teen Library Association.

ACRL-Oklahoma Chapter Annual Conference, November 2007. As President led planning for fall conference with Dr. David Silver (University of San Francisco) and Lynn Connaway (OCLC).

ACRL-Oklahoma Chapter Annual Conference. Assisted with conference planning as member and ex-officio member of the OK-ACRL Board, 2003–2006; 2008–2010.

Regional Meetings for the Oklahoma Library Association Career Recruitment and Retention Committee (Muskogee, OK; McAlester, OK; Weatherford, OK; and Alva, OK), 2007–2008. Organized informational/recruitment meetings for OLA.

OLA University and College Division Web 2.0 and Social Networking Applications Workshops: Taming Social Networking Sites (OSU, October 19, 2007; Taming IM and Wikis, OSU-Tulsa, February 29, 2008; Free Web Resources, April 21, 2008. Served on planning committee.

Co-coordinated OLA Information Matrix Camp to introduce middle-school students to the library profession, 2007–2009.

Registrar, 2006 Mythopoeic Society Conference (Mythcon 37), August 2006. Conference Committee Member.

But Are They Learning? COIL Summer Workshop, Tulsa, OK, August 2005. Served on the planning committee.

ILL for All Libraries, Oklahoma Library Association University and College Division Workshop, Midwest City, OK, January 28, 2005. Chaired planning committee.

COIL Summer Workshop on Information Literacy Instruction, Tulsa, OK, August 13, 2004. Chaired planning committee for first COIL summer workshop on library instruction.

Copyright Law in the Digital Age, Oklahoma Library Association University and College Division workshop, Norman, Stillwater, Midwest City, OK, December 8–10, 2003. Organized 3 workshop series on copyright issues with Laura Gasaway (University of North Carolina, Chapel Hill).

Celebrating the Web, Oklahoma Library Association Summer Conference, Midwest City, OK, July 30–31, 2002. Organized 3 programs in Ethics Committee track.

On the Frontline: Handling Conflicts with Patrons and Public Groups. Oklahoma Library Association Ethics Committee Workshop, Midwest City, OK, February 5, 2002. Chaired planning committee.

Can We Agree to Disagree: Conflict Resolution in the Workplace, Oklahoma Library Association Ethics Committee Workshop, Midwest City, OK, February 9, 2001. Chaired planning committee.

Libraries, 'Lectronic Resources, and the Law, Oklahoma Library Association University and College Division Workshop, Stillwater, OK, March 9, 2000. Served on planning committee.

Coordinated Poster/Contributed Paper Sessions at Oklahoma Library Association Annual Conference for University and College Division, 2000–2002, 2004–2005.

OSU University Committees

Faculty Council, Library Representative, 2015–2017. [Elected]

Chair, Academic Standards and Policies Committee, 2016–2017. [Appointed]

Faculty Committee, 2015–2016, 2016–2017. [Appointed]

Long-Range Planning and Information Technology Committee, 2015–2016. [Appointed]

Allied Arts and Campus Entertainment Committee, 2007–2010; 2011–2014; 2014–2017. [Appointed]

Grade Appeals Board, 2009–2011, 2012–2014; 2014–2016. [Appointed]

Book Collecting Essay Judging Panel (Scholar Development & Undergraduate Research Scholarship Prize), 2013. [Appointed]

Allied Arts Coordinator Search Committee, 2011.

Traffic Appeals Board, 2004–2006. [Appointed]

Student Activity Fee Allocation Committee, 2000–2001. [Appointed]

Other OSU University Service

Faculty Mentor, First2Go Program (First-Generation College Students), 2014.

Faculty Mentor, Leaders Advising, Mentoring, and Building Diversity Allies Program, 2012.

Faculty Mentor, Native American Resiliency Through Education and Leadership Program, 2010.

Faculty Judge for OSU Research Symposium, 2004–2015.

OSU Library Committees, Task Forces, & Other Service

Review Committee for Doris Neustadt Professorship, 2016.

Library Faculty Affairs Committee, 2016–Present.

Chair, College-Level Review Committee [Elected], 2014–2015; Member, 2015–2016,

Undergraduate Library Research Award Committee, 2014–Present.

Chair, LibGuides Template Committee, 2014.

Reappointment, Tenure, and Promotion Committee [Elected]: Chair, 2012–2013; Member, 2002–2003, 2003–2004, 2008–2009, 2013–2014.

Chair, Noon Concert Series at the Library Committee and Co-Director of Series, 2009–Present.

Room 206 (Library Computer Training Room) Improvements Task Force, 2012–Present.

Greenberg/Howland Personnel Development Award Selection Committee, 2012.

LibGuides Review Committee, 2011.

ProQuest Test Phase II Group, 2010.

SerialsSolutions Summon Beta Testing Group, 2009–2010.

Library Administrative Planning Retreat Participant, 2004–2007.

Multimedia Acquisitions Task Force, 2007–2008. [Appointed]

Library Faculty Search Committees [Appointed]:
> Digital Archivist, 2015.
> Digital Library Services Librarian, 2010.
> Humanities-Social Sciences Instruction Librarian, 2008.
> Associate Dean for Research, Instruction, and Collections, 2005.
> Digital Library Services Librarian, 2001.
> Humanities-Social Sciences Instruction Librarian, 2000.
> Science-Engineering Librarian (2 Committees), 2000.
> Patent & Trademark/Digitization Librarian, 1999.

Curriculum Materials Library 50th Anniversary Planning Committee, 2007.

OPAC Redesign Task Force, 2005. [Appointed]

Developed and maintained the Quick Guides to MLA and APA Style and the informational page on Peer-Reviewed Journals for the OSU Library Website, 2004–Present.

Assisted with New Student Orientation programming for new freshmen for the OSU Library, Various years.

External Events Committee 2002–2003. [Appointed]

Digitization Task Force, 1999. [Appointed]

User Survey Task Force, 1998–1999. [Appointed]

Coordinated the vendor demonstrations of new classroom control system for OSU Library computer training room, 1998. [Appointed]

Credit Courses Taught

OSU: "Library and Internet Information Competencies," 6–8 week face-to-face and online via Desire2Learn Course Management System (undergraduate).

Texas Tech University: "Studies in British Fiction" [Victorian Novel] (graduate); "Studies in Nineteenth-Century British Literature" (graduate & undergraduate); "Studies in Fiction" (3000-level and honors undergraduate); "Introduction to Literature I & II" (2000-level undergraduate).

National-Level Workshops & Institutes Attended (Selected List)

Digital Humanities Summer Institute, University of Victoria, Victoria, BC, Canada, June 1–6, 2014. Course: *The Pre-Digital Book.*

ALA/NEH *Soul of a People: Writing America's Story* Project Planning Workshop, Washington, DC, February 19–20, 2009.

MPLA Leadership Institute, Ghost Ranch, NM, 2002. [Selected as a participant]

LOEX Conference on Bibliographic Instruction, Ypsilanti, MI, 2000, 2001.

School for Scanning: Issues of Preservation and Access for Paper-Based Collections, Northeast Document Conservation Center, New Orleans, LA, Dec. 7–9, 1998.

Rare Book School, University of Virginia, Charlottesville, Virginia, July 20–25, 1997. Course: *Introduction to Rare Book Librarianship.*

Dickens Project Summer Workshop, University of California, Santa Cruz, August 20–27, 1992; August 19–26, 1991.

Other Workshops & Professional Development (Selected List)

Software Carpentry Instructor Training, OSU Library, January 5–6, 2016.

Software Carpentry Workshop, OSU Library, December 10–11, 2015. [UNIX Shell, Python, Git/GitHub, Beautiful Soup for data analysis, web scraping, etc.]

Languages

French (fluent), Spanish (fluent), German (reading), Italian (reading), Portuguese (reading).

About the Contributors

SUSAN ADAMS-JOHNSON is the leading expert in fine arts student recruitment, having earned her Ph.D. in Music and Adult Education Administration from the University of Oklahoma in 2015 with that as her topic. She has performed and taught voice for nearly 30 years; her Master of Music is in Vocal Performance/Opera. She currently teaches at the University of Science and Arts of Oklahoma and works with Phillips Theological Seminary on deeper understanding and use of hymnody. Susan is the founding co-executive director of Scissortail Productions, which produces free music events for underserved communities. She continues to conduct research and publish in arts, higher education administration, and information processing.

CAMI AGAN is Professor of English at Oklahoma Christian University, where she teaches British Literature, World Literature, and in the Honors Program. She is currently working on the collection *Cities and Strongholds of Middle-earth; Essays on the Habitations of Tolkien's Legendarium* for Mythopoeic Press. She has published in *Mythlore*, *The Journal of the Fantastic in the Arts*, and has essays in *Approaches to Teaching J. R. R. Tolkien* and *Perilous and Fair*. Her essay on Christopher Tolkien appears in the *Proceedings of the Tolkien Society* from 2020. Agan's research focuses primarily on the First Age materials of *The Silmarillion* and *History of Middle-earth*, with an interest in the elegiac resonances of the tales of the lost Beleriand.

NICHOLAS BIRNS teaches at the New School; his books include *Understanding Anthony Powell* (U South Carolina P, 2004), *Theory After Theory: An Intellectual History of Literary Theory Since 1950* (Broadview, 2010), *Barbarian Memory: The Legacy of Early Medieval History in Early Modern Literature* (Palgrave, 2013), *Contemporary Australian Literature: A World Not Yet Dead* (U of Sydney P, 2015), and *The Hyperlocal in Eighteenth and Nineteenth Century Literary Space* (Lexington, 2019).

JANET BRENNAN CROFT (ORCID 0001-0001-2691-3586) is an Associate University Librarian at the University of Northern Iowa. She is the author of *War in the Works of J. R. R. Tolkien* (Praeger, 2004; winner, Mythopoeic Society Award for Inklings Studies). She has also written on the Peter Jackson Middle-earth films, the Whedonverse, *Orphan Black*, J. K. Rowling, Terry Pratchett, Lois McMaster Bujold, *The Devil*

Wears Prada, and other authors, TV shows, and movies. She is also editor or co-editor of many collections of literary essays, the most recent (before this one) being *'Something Has Gone Crack': New Perspectives on Tolkien in the Great War* (Walking Tree, 2019) with Anna Röttinger. She edits the refereed scholarly journal *Mythlore* and is archivist and assistant editor of *Slayage: The International Journal of Buffy+*. You can follow her work on Academia.edu.

DAVID L. EMERSON is an independent scholar living in Iowa. As a generalist, he is fond of making connections between disparate areas of fantasy, science fiction, graphic novels, and even music. He has made presentations at Tolkien conferences in years past on Michael Moorcock, Neil Gaiman, Alan Moore, Jasper Fforde, Miyazaki's *Spirited Away,* and on Donald Swann's setting of "Errantry." He has been known to collaborate with Professor Mike Foster in setting Tolkien-themed lyrics to Beatles and Bob Dylan songs. He is currently investigating the mythopoeic dimensions of the Grateful Dead.

JASON FISHER is the editor of *Tolkien and the Study of His Sources* (McFarland, 2011), which won the 2014 Mythopoeic Scholarship Award in Inklings Studies. With Salwa Khoddam and Mark R. Hall, he co-edited *C. S. Lewis and the Inklings: Faith, Imagination, and Modern Technology* and *C. S. Lewis and the Inklings: Discovering Hidden Truth* (Cambridge Scholars, 2012 and 2015). Fisher's work has appeared in *Tolkien Studies, Mythlore, Beyond Bree, The Journal of Inklings Studies, Sehnsucht,* and other journals, books, and encyclopedias. He can be reached through his occasional blog, "Lingwë—Musings of a Fish" *lingwe.blogspot.com.*

PHILLIP FITZSIMMONS is the Reference and Digitization Librarian at Southwestern Oklahoma State University in Weatherford, Oklahoma. He is the Archivist for the Mythopoeic Society and administrator of the SWOSU Digital Commons, where digital versions of the Mythopoeic Society publications may be read for free at dc.swosu.edu/mythsoc. His research interests include the works of J. R. R. Tolkien, Owen Barfield, the Inklings, Joseph Campbell, digital services for academic libraries with an emphasis on institutional repository administration, and library reference services. He is an official adviser to the Owen Barfield Literary Estate.

VICTORIA GAYDOSIK completed a Ph.D. in literature at the University of Rochester and retired in 2021 from the Language and Literature Department at Southwestern Oklahoma State University after teaching in higher education for 32 years. She is the author of *The Facts on File Companion to the British Novel, Volume 2: The Twentieth Century*; all the articles on George Eliot/Mary Ann Evans and her works in volume 1 of the same book; and several other articles. Since 2020, Victoria has been the editor of *The Mythic Circle*, the creative writing journal of the Mythopoeic Society, and is currently a co-sponsor of the Mythopoeic Society's first annual Online Midwinter Seminar in 2022.

LIORAH GOLOMB is Associate Professor and Humanities Librarian at the University of Oklahoma. She has written on a variety of topics both library and non-library related. Her previous work on *Supernatural* includes "'Let's Go Gank Ourselves a Paris Hilton': A Textual Analysis of the Dialogue of *Supernatural* (the First 10 Years)". Liorah identifies as a Sam Girl/Dean Curious.

ANNA HOLLOWAY holds two bachelor's degrees and two terminal master's degrees; she refuses to get a doctorate because she doesn't have time for two. She has taught writing skills at the University of Oklahoma in Human Relations and composition, introduction to literature, western humanities, and philosophy at Langston University in English and in Social Sciences. She was the program director of interreligious understanding at Phillips Theological Seminary. She currently works as a freelance editor. Her published writing includes several academic articles, a decade of work as a theatre critic, and some short fiction. Her published sermons (she is ordained) fall into one or more of the above categories.

CONNER KIRK is a 2019 graduate of Southwestern Oklahoma State University, where he completed a B.A. in English: Literature. He is currently working on a Master's of Library and Information Studies degree at the University of Oklahoma, which he will complete in May, 2022. Additionally, he has worked in many roles for the Western Plains Library System since 2016. He has a deep passion for intellectual freedom, and he holds libraries, along with their many tomes of literature, close to his heart.

KRISTINE LARSEN is an Astronomy Professor at Central Connecticut State University. She is the author of *Cosmology 101, Stephen Hawking: A Biography, Particle Panic,* and co-editor of *The Mythological Dimensions of Doctor Who* and *The Mythological Dimensions of Neil Gaiman.* Her Tolkien scholarship has been published in a variety of books, as well as the journals *Tolkien Studies, Mallorn, Silver Leaves,* and *Amon Hen,* and posted in *Lembas* and *Journal of Tolkien Research.*

NANCY MARTSCH is the editor of *Beyond Bree,* newsletter of the J. R. R. Tolkien Special Interest Group of American Mensa, now in its 40th year. A long-time Tolkien enthusiast, she has given talks and published articles on *Tolkien, and co-edited Tolkien in the New Century: Essays in Honor of Tom Shippey.*

ELISE CAEMASACHE MCKENNA is a Course Director in the Creative Writing Department at Full Sail University and teaches story development. She has been studying Tolkien for over thirty years and has presented and guest lectured on the Professor and his Legendarium, Harry Potter, and H. P. Lovecraft at conferences all over the United States, England, Australia, and New Zealand. Her articles appear in *How We Became Middle-earth, LEMBAS EXTRA, Mythlore,* Luna Press, and Conference Proceedings for the Tolkien Society. Aside from Tolkien, her interests include making small furry animals from wool roving, living with small furry animals, and rescuing small furry animals. She loves traveling and plans to live in New Zealand when she grows up.

DAVID D. OBERHELMAN was a Professor in the Humanities-Social Sciences Division of the Oklahoma State University Library. He held a Ph.D. in English with an Emphasis in Critical Theory from the University of California, Irvine, and a Master's in Library and Information Science from the University of Pittsburgh. He specialized in Victorian British fiction and Anglo-American fantasy literature of the nineteenth and twentieth centuries. Oberhelman was the editor (with Amy H. Sturgis) of *The Intersection of Fantasy and Native America* (Mythopoeic Press, 2009) and author of *Dickens in Bedlam* (York Press, 1995), a study of madness in the novels of Dickens and his contemporaries. He published articles, book chapters, and encyclopedia entries on Tolkien and other fantasists. In the field of Library Science, he presented and published on topics ranging from digital humanities and scholarly communication to the history of the book. For the Mythopoeic

Society, he was Administrator of the Mythopoeic Fantasy and Scholarship Awards and served on the Council of Stewards.

MICHELE SEIKEL is a tenured professor on the library faculty at Oklahoma State University. She has held positions at Norman Public Library, the University of Oklahoma, and Stanford University, and served as a professional librarian at Oklahoma Panhandle State University and at Oklahoma State University. Michele's primary professional focus is in cataloging, and she has published several research papers in peer-reviewed technical services journals and co-edited a monograph entitled *Linked Data for Cultural Heritage*. In ALA, she has co-chaired the Cataloging Norms Interest Group and the Cataloging and Metadata Management Section's Policy and Planning Committee. She also chaired the ALCTS Planning Committee for two terms in 2015/2016 and 2016/2017, and most recently chaired the Bibliographic Conceptual Models Interest Group.

INDEX

This index concentrates on topics and persons related to the overall themes of the book, such as librarianship, history of the book, and organization and research methods. It does not include real-world persons playing a role in alternate history or historical novels, or real-world places unless significant to the topics covered or to David Dean Oberhelman's biography. It does not include every named fictional character unless significant to the book's themes; look more generally under the author, or under the title for media works. This book's contents are also indexed in the *Mythlore Index Plus*, available for free download at https://www.mythsoc.org/press/mythlore-index-plus.htm.